America Online® For Dummies
4th Edition

S0-BAY-497

Cheat Sheet

Top Emoticons and Abbreviations for Chatting

When you use America Online's chat rooms to communicate with other members, you may wish to express yourself in ways that mere words can't accomplish. Use emoticons to convey the facial expressions and body language that accompany spoken conversation, but are a little hard to type. Abbreviations allow you to use familiar phrases without typing out the entire phrase. (You can find more on emoticons and abbreviations in Chapter 31.)

:-)	Smile, you're on America Online.	LOL	Laughing out loud
:-D	Big smile. The sun is shining on you today.	ROFL	Rolling on the floor laughing
;-)	Wink, wink. Nudge, nudge. Just kidding.	AFK	Away from the keyboard
:-(	Frown. Just got the phone bill, eh?	BAK	Back at the keyboard
:-o	Mr. Bill. Oh, no!	BTW	By the way

Macintosh and Windows Shortcut Keys

Group	Function	Macintosh	Windows
Editing	Cut	⌘+X	Ctrl+X
	Copy	⌘+C	Ctrl+C
	Paste	⌘+V	Ctrl+V
	Undo	⌘+Z	Ctrl+Z
Mail	Compose new mail	⌘+M	Ctrl+M
	Read new messages	⌘+R	Ctrl+R
People-related	Locate AOL member online	⌘+L	Ctrl+L
	Get info (user profile)	⌘+G	Ctrl+G
	Send an Instant Message	⌘+I	Ctrl+I
Navigation	Go to a keyword	⌘+K	Ctrl+K
	Make current window a Favorite Place	none	Ctrl++ (plus sign)
	Custom Favorites⇨My Shortcuts items	⌘+1 to ⌘+0	Ctrl+1 to Ctrl+0
Documents	Stop incoming text	⌘+. (period)	Esc
	Save a document	⌘+S	Ctrl+S
	Print a document	Ô+P	Ctrl+P

Copyright © 1998 IDG Books Worldwide, Inc. All rights reserved.

Cheat Sheet $2.95 value. Item 0192-5.

For more information about IDG Books, call 1-800-762-2974.

...For Dummies: #1 Computer Book Series for Beginners

America Online® For Dummies, 4th Edition

Cheat Sheet

Local America Online Access Numbers

Fill in the blanks and use this as a handy reference guide for your AOL access numbers at home and on the road. (Turn to Chapter 26 for information on using America Online away from home.)

Location	Phone Number	Modem Speed	Network
Main local access			
Alternate local #1			
Alternate local #2			
Alternate local #3			

A Few Favorite Places

Record your Favorite Places to go in America Online. Each line has room for the keyword that takes you there and a short description of the area. (Refer to Chapter 24 for details on how to modify your personal My Shortcuts menu in the Favorites toolbar button.)

Favorite Place	Keyword	Brief Description

Screen Names and Passwords

Use this space to record your America Online screen names and passwords. An AOL account can have up to five screen names. (If you fill in the Password area, be sure to keep this card in a safe place!)

Screen Name	Password
Primary	

...For Dummies: #1 Computer Book Series for Beginners

References for the Rest of Us!®

COMPUTER BOOK SERIES FROM IDG

Are you intimidated and confused by computers? Do you find that traditional manuals are overloaded with technical details you'll never use? Do your friends and family always call you to fix simple problems on their PCs? Then the ...*For Dummies*® computer book series from IDG Books Worldwide is for you.

...*For Dummies* books are written for those frustrated computer users who know they aren't really dumb but find that PC hardware, software, and indeed the unique vocabulary of computing make them feel helpless. ...*For Dummies* books use a lighthearted approach, a down-to-earth style, and even cartoons and humorous icons to diffuse computer novices' fears and build their confidence. Lighthearted but not lightweight, these books are a perfect survival guide for anyone forced to use a computer.

"I like my copy so much I told friends; now they bought copies."

Irene C., Orwell, Ohio

"Quick, concise, nontechnical, and humorous."

Jay A., Elburn, Illinois

"Thanks, I needed this book. Now I can sleep at night."

Robin F., British Columbia, Canada

Already, millions of satisfied readers agree. They have made ...*For Dummies* books the #1 introductory level computer book series and have written asking for more. So, if you're looking for the most fun and easy way to learn about computers, look to ...*For Dummies* books to give you a helping hand.

IDG BOOKS WORLDWIDE

5/97

AMERICA ONLINE®
FOR
DUMMIES®
4TH EDITION

AMERICA ONLINE® FOR DUMMIES®
4TH EDITION

by John Kaufeld

Foreword by Steve Case

IDG BOOKS WORLDWIDE

IDG Books Worldwide, Inc.
An International Data Group Company

Foster City, CA ♦ Chicago, IL ♦ Indianapolis, IN ♦ Southlake, TX

America Online® For Dummies,® 4th Edition

Published by
IDG Books Worldwide, Inc.
An International Data Group Company
919 E. Hillsdale Blvd.
Suite 400
Foster City, CA 94404
www.idgbooks.com (IDG Books Worldwide Web site)
www.dummies.com (Dummies Press Web site)

Copyright © 1998 IDG Books Worldwide, Inc. All rights reserved. No part of this book, including interior design, cover design, and icons, may be reproduced or transmitted in any form, by any means (electronic, photocopying, recording, or otherwise) without the prior written permission of the publisher.

Library of Congress Catalog Card No.: 97-81236

ISBN: 0-7645-0192-5

Printed in the United States of America

10 9 8 7 6 5 4

40/SX/QR/ZY/IN

Distributed in the United States by IDG Books Worldwide, Inc.

Distributed by Macmillan Canada for Canada; by Transworld Publishers Limited in the United Kingdom; by IDG Norge Books for Norway; by IDG Sweden Books for Sweden; by Woodslane Pty. Ltd. for Australia; by Woodslane Enterprises Ltd. for New Zealand; by Longman Singapore Publishers Ltd. for Singapore, Malaysia, Thailand, and Indonesia; by Simron Pty. Ltd. for South Africa; by Toppan Company Ltd. for Japan; by Distribuidora Cuspide for Argentina; by Livraria Cultura for Brazil; by Ediciencia S.A. for Ecuador; by Addison-Wesley Publishing Company for Korea; by Ediciones ZETA S.C.R. Ltda. for Peru; by WS Computer Publishing Corporation, Inc., for the Philippines; by Unalis Corporation for Taiwan; by Contemporanea de Ediciones for Venezuela; by Computer Book & Magazine Store for Puerto Rico; by Express Computer Distributors for the Caribbean and West Indies. Authorized Sales Agent: Anthony Rudkin Associates for the Middle East and North Africa.

For general information on IDG Books Worldwide's books in the U.S., please call our Consumer Customer Service department at 800-762-2974. For reseller information, including discounts and premium sales, please call our Reseller Customer Service department at 800-434-3422.

For information on where to purchase IDG Books Worldwide's books outside the U.S., please contact our International Sales department at 650-655-3200 or fax 650-655-3295.

For information on foreign language translations, please contact our Foreign & Subsidiary Rights department at 650-655-3021 or fax 650-655-3281.

For sales inquiries and special prices for bulk quantities, please contact our Sales department at 650-655-3200 or write to the address above.

For information on using IDG Books Worldwide's books in the classroom or for ordering examination copies, please contact our Educational Sales department at 800-434-2086 or fax 817-251-8174.

For press review copies, author interviews, or other publicity information, please contact our Public Relations department at 650-655-3000 or fax 650-655-3299.

For authorization to photocopy items for corporate, personal, or educational use, please contact Copyright Clearance Center, 222 Rosewood Drive, Danvers, MA 01923, or fax 978-750-4470.

LIMIT OF LIABILITY/DISCLAIMER OF WARRANTY: AUTHOR AND PUBLISHER HAVE USED THEIR BEST EFFORTS IN PREPARING THIS BOOK. IDG BOOKS WORLDWIDE, INC., AND AUTHOR MAKE NO REPRESENTATIONS OR WARRANTIES WITH RESPECT TO THE ACCURACY OR COMPLETENESS OF THE CONTENTS OF THIS BOOK AND SPECIFICALLY DISCLAIM ANY IMPLIED WARRANTIES OF MERCHANTABILITY OR FITNESS FOR A PARTICULAR PURPOSE. THERE ARE NO WARRANTIES WHICH EXTEND BEYOND THE DESCRIPTIONS CONTAINED IN THIS PARAGRAPH. NO WARRANTY MAY BE CREATED OR EXTENDED BY SALES REPRESENTATIVES OR WRITTEN SALES MATERIALS. THE ACCURACY AND COMPLETENESS OF THE INFORMATION PROVIDED HEREIN AND THE OPINIONS STATED HEREIN ARE NOT GUARANTEED OR WARRANTED TO PRODUCE ANY PARTICULAR RESULTS, AND THE ADVICE AND STRATEGIES CONTAINED HEREIN MAY NOT BE SUITABLE FOR EVERY INDIVIDUAL. NEITHER IDG BOOKS WORLDWIDE, INC., NOR AUTHOR SHALL BE LIABLE FOR ANY LOSS OF PROFIT OR ANY OTHER COMMERCIAL DAMAGES, INCLUDING BUT NOT LIMITED TO SPECIAL, INCIDENTAL, CONSEQUENTIAL, OR OTHER DAMAGES.

Trademarks: All brand names and product names used in this book are trade names, service marks, trademarks, or registered trademarks of their respective owners. IDG Books Worldwide is not associated with any product or vendor mentioned in this book.

is a trademark under exclusive license to IDG Books Worldwide, Inc., from International Data Group, Inc.

About the Author

John Kaufeld got hooked on computers a long time ago. Somewhere along the way, he discovered that he *enjoyed* helping people understand how computers worked (a trait his computer science friends generally considered a character flaw but that everyone else seemed to appreciate). John finally graduated with a B.S. degree in Management Information Systems from Ball State University and became the first PC support technician for what was then Westinghouse, outside Cincinnati, Ohio. He learned about online services in the Dark Ages of Telecommunication (the 1980s) by guessing, failing, and often doing unmentionable things to his modem.

Since then, John has logged over a decade of experience working with normal people who, for one reason or another, were stuck using a "friendly" personal computer. Today, he is the president of Access Systems, a computer consulting firm. He still does troubleshooting, conducts technical and interpersonal skills seminars for up-and-coming computer gurus, and writes in his free moments.

John's other IDG Books titles include *Internet Games For Dummies, Access 97 For Dummies, Access For Windows 95 For Dummies, FoxPro 2.6 For Windows For Dummies,* and *Paradox 5 For Windows For Dummies.* He regularly uses America Online (where he's known as `JKaufeld`) and other online services. He loves to get e-mail and valiantly attempts to answer every message he gets.

John lives with his wife, two children, one lovable American Eskimo dog, and (most delightfully) *no* canary in Indianapolis, Indiana.

Dedication

To Jenny, for last-minute help above and beyond the limits of sanity.

To J.B. and the Pooz, for being incredibly patient *again*. Chuck E. Cheese, anyone?

To my friends and compatriots at IDG Books Worldwide Inc., for the opportunity of a lifetime.

Thank you, one and all.

ABOUT IDG BOOKS WORLDWIDE

Welcome to the world of IDG Books Worldwide.

IDG Books Worldwide, Inc., is a subsidiary of International Data Group, the world's largest publisher of computer-related information and the leading global provider of information services on information technology. IDG was founded more than 25 years ago and now employs more than 8,500 people worldwide. IDG publishes more than 275 computer publications in over 75 countries (see listing below). More than 60 million people read one or more IDG publications each month.

Launched in 1990, IDG Books Worldwide is today the #1 publisher of best-selling computer books in the United States. We are proud to have received eight awards from the Computer Press Association in recognition of editorial excellence and three from *Computer Currents*' First Annual Readers' Choice Awards. Our best-selling *...For Dummies*® series has more than 30 million copies in print with translations in 30 languages. IDG Books Worldwide, through a joint venture with IDG's Hi-Tech Beijing, became the first U.S. publisher to publish a computer book in the People's Republic of China. In record time, IDG Books Worldwide has become the first choice for millions of readers around the world who want to learn how to better manage their businesses.

Our mission is simple: Every one of our books is designed to bring extra value and skill-building instructions to the reader. Our books are written by experts who understand and care about our readers. The knowledge base of our editorial staff comes from years of experience in publishing, education, and journalism — experience we use to produce books for the '90s. In short, we care about books, so we attract the best people. We devote special attention to details such as audience, interior design, use of icons, and illustrations. And because we use an efficient process of authoring, editing, and desktop publishing our books electronically, we can spend more time ensuring superior content and spend less time on the technicalities of making books.

You can count on our commitment to deliver high-quality books at competitive prices on topics you want to read about. At IDG Books Worldwide, we continue in the IDG tradition of delivering quality for more than 25 years. You'll find no better book on a subject than one from IDG Books Worldwide.

John Kilcullen
John Kilcullen
CEO
IDG Books Worldwide, Inc.

Steven Berkowitz
Steven Berkowitz
President and Publisher
IDG Books Worldwide, Inc.

VIII WINNER
Eighth Annual Computer Press Awards ≥ 1992

IX WINNER
Ninth Annual Computer Press Awards ≥ 1993

X WINNER
Tenth Annual Computer Press Awards ≥ 1994

XI WINNER
Eleventh Annual Computer Press Awards ≥ 1995

IDG Books Worldwide, Inc., is a subsidiary of International Data Group, the world's largest publisher of computer-related information and the leading global provider of information services on information technology. International Data Group publishes over 275 computer publications in over 75 countries. Sixty million people read one or more International Data Group publications each month. International Data Group's publications include: **ARGENTINA:** Buyer's Guide, Computerworld Argentina, PC World Argentina; **AUSTRALIA:** Australian Macworld, Australian PC World, Australian Reseller News, Computerworld, IT Casebook, Network World, Publish, Webmaster; **AUSTRIA:** Computerwelt Osterreich, Networks Austria, PC Tip Austria; **BANGLADESH:** PC World Bangladesh; **BELARUS:** PC World Belarus; **BELGIUM:** Data News; **BRAZIL:** Annuário de Informática, Computerworld, Connections, Macworld, PC Player, PC World, Publish, Reseller News, Supergamepower; **BULGARIA:** Computerworld Bulgaria, Network World Bulgaria, PC & MacWorld Bulgaria; **CANADA:** CIO Canada, Client/Server World, ComputerWorld Canada, InfoWorld Canada, NetworkWorld Canada, WebWorld; **CHILE:** Computerworld Chile, PC World Chile; **COLOMBIA:** Computerworld Colombia, PC World Colombia; **COSTA RICA:** PC World Centro America; **THE CZECH AND SLOVAK REPUBLICS:** Computerworld Czechoslovakia, Macworld Czech Republic, PC World Czechoslovakia; **DENMARK:** Communications World Danmark, Computerworld Danmark, Macworld Danmark, PC World Danmark, Techworld Denmark; **DOMINICAN REPUBLIC:** PC World Republica Dominicana; **ECUADOR:** PC World Ecuador; **EGYPT:** Computerworld Middle East, PC World Middle East; **EL SALVADOR:** PC World Centro America; **FINLAND:** MikroPC, Tietoverkko, Tietoviikko; **FRANCE:** Distributique, Hebdo, Info PC, Le Monde Informatique, Macworld, Reseaux & Telecoms, WebMaster France; **GERMANY:** Computer Partner, Computerwoche, Computerwoche Extra, Computerwoche FOCUS, Global Online, Macwelt, PC Welt; **GREECE:** Amiga Computing, GamePro Greece, Multimedia World; **GUATEMALA:** PC World Centro America; **HONDURAS:** PC World Centro America; **HONG KONG:** Computerworld Hong Kong, PC World Hong Kong, Publish in Asia; **HUNGARY:** ABCD CD-ROM, Computerworld Szamitastechnika, Internetto online Magazine, PC World Hungary, PC-X Magazin Hungary; **ICELAND:** Tolvuheimur PC World Island; **INDIA:** Information Communications World, Information Systems Computerworld, PC World India, Publish in Asia; **INDONESIA:** InfoKomputer PC World, Komputek Computerworld, Publish in Asia; **IRELAND:** ComputerScope, PC Live!; **ISRAEL:** Macworld Israel, People & Computers/Computerworld; **ITALY:** Computerworld Italia, Macworld Italia, Networking Italia, PC World Italia; **JAPAN:** DTP World, Macworld Japan, Nikkei Personal Computing, OS/2 World Japan, SunWorld Japan, Windows NT World, Windows World Japan; **KENYA:** PC World East African; **KOREA:** Hi-Tech Information, Macworld Korea, PC World Korea; **MACEDONIA:** PC World Macedonia; **MALAYSIA:** Computerworld Malaysia, PC World Malaysia, Publish in Asia; **MALTA:** PC World Malta; **MEXICO:** Computerworld Mexico, PC World Mexico; **MYANMAR:** PC World Myanmar; **NETHERLANDS:** Computer! Totaal, LAN Internetworking Magazine, LAN World Buyers Guide, Macworld Netherlands, Net, WebWereld; **NEW ZEALAND:** Absolute Beginners Guide and Plain & Simple Series, Computer Buyer, Computer Industry Directory, Computerworld New Zealand, MTB, Network World, PC World New Zealand; **NICARAGUA:** PC World Centro America; **NORWAY:** Computerworld Norge, CW Rapport, Datamagasinet, Financial Rapport, Kursguide Norge, Macworld Norge, Multimediaworld Norge, PC World Ekspress Norge, PC World Nettverk, PC World Norge, PC World ProduktGuide Norge; **PAKISTAN:** Computerworld Pakistan; **PANAMA:** PC World Panama; **PEOPLE'S REPUBLIC OF CHINA:** China Computer Users, China Computerworld, China InfoWorld, China Telecom World Weekly, Computer & Communication, Electronic Design China, Electronics Today, Electronics Weekly, Game Software, PC World China, Popular Computer Week, Software Weekly, Software World, Telecom World; **PERU:** Computerworld Peru, PC World Profesional Peru, PC World SoHo Peru; **PHILIPPINES:** Click!, Computerworld Philippines, PC World Philippines, Publish in Asia; **POLAND:** Computerworld Poland, Computerworld Special Report Poland, Cyber, Macworld Poland, Networld Poland, PC World Komputer; **PORTUGAL:** Cerebro/PC World, Computerworld/Correio Informático, Dealer World Portugal, Mac*In/PC*In Portugal, Multimedia World; **PUERTO RICO:** PC World Puerto Rico; **ROMANIA:** Computerworld Romania, PC World Romania, Telecom Romania; **RUSSIA:** Computerworld Russia, Mir PK, Publish, Seti; **SINGAPORE:** Computerworld Singapore, PC World Singapore, Publish in Asia; **SLOVENIA:** Monitor; **SOUTH AFRICA:** Computing SA, Network World SA, Software World SA; **SPAIN:** Communicaciones World España, Computerworld España, Dealer World España, Macworld España, PC World España; **SRI LANKA:** Infolink PC World; **SWEDEN:** CAP&Design, Computer Sweden, Corporate Computing Sweden, Internetworld Sweden, it.branschen, Macworld Sweden, MaxiData Sweden, MikroDatorn, Nätverk & Kommunikation, PC World Sweden, PCaktiv, Windows World Sweden; **SWITZERLAND:** Computerworld Schweiz, Macworld Schweiz, PCtip; **TAIWAN:** Computerworld Taiwan, Macworld Taiwan, NEW ViSiON/Publish, PC World Taiwan, Windows World Taiwan; **THAILAND:** Publish in Asia, Thai Computerworld; **TURKEY:** Computerworld Turkiye, Macworld Turkiye, Network World Turkiye, PC World Turkiye; **UKRAINE:** Computerworld Kiev, Multimedia World Ukraine, PC World Ukraine; **UNITED KINGDOM:** Acorn User UK, Amiga Action UK, Amiga Computing UK, Apple Talk UK, Computing, Macworld, Parents and Computers UK, PC Advisor, PC Home, PSX Pro, The WEB, United States: Cable in the Classroom, CIO Magazine, Computerworld, DOS World, Federal Computer Week, GamePro Magazine, InfoWorld, I-Way, Macworld, Network World, PC Games, PC World, Publish, Video Event, THE WEB Magazine, and WebMaster; online webzines: JavaWorld, NetscapeWorld, and SunWorld Online; **URUGUAY:** InfoWorld Uruguay; **VENEZUELA:** Computerworld Venezuela, PC World Venezuela; and **VIETNAM:** PC World Vietnam.   3/24/97

Author's Acknowledgments

I think I finally figured out why book acknowledgments are always kind of philosophical. It's because the author has just spent most of the last two weeks (and particularly the preceding 72 hours) on a constant caffeine high and is currently devoting a large portion of his time to preventing his brain from floating off into space.

Luckily, that's not going to happen to me. I've got a hat on.

First, I want to thank my project editor, Tere Drenth, without whom this book simply wouldn't be! Thanks to her extraordinary leadership, management, and organization skills (it's both illegal and immoral in some states to be as organized as she is), this book is in your hands.

Extraordinary thanks also to my technical reviewer, Matt Converse, who made extra-special-sure the book was actually correct. Without Matt's help, I *never* could have kept up with the myriad updates from America Online's *Let's Move the Menu Items* department.

Incredibly special thanks (and more than a few imported chocolates) go to my researcher, Michele Phillips. Thanks to her dedication and tireless efforts, my work on the channels went far faster than it ever could have without her. You're one in a million, Michele!

Further up the Editorial Food Chain, thanks to Diane Steele and Milissa Koloski for being the best folks to work with on the planet. Way out at the other end of the known world, thanks to Mike Kelly (who runs my particular corner of the Dummies Press Acquisitions Department).

At America Online, thanks go to Marshall Rens, Pam McGraw, Kelly Richmond, and Brad Schepp. Extra-special "You're the greatest" thanks to Adam Bart, Jon Brendsel, Reggie Fairchild, who rank just below Ben & Jerry's Chocolate Chip Cookie Dough Ice Cream in my world. And a special tip of the hat to Steve Case for the original vision that spawned AOL.

Finally, my sincere thanks to (in alphabetical order) Art, Barb, Cap, Jen, Lau, Leah, Melissa, Nick, Ro, Rodney, and all the other online friends and acquaintances who helped me maintain a few shreds of sanity while writing this book. Jen gets an extra virtual cookie for being an accountant (after all, *somebody* has to do it) and because she let me use the profile of a certain reindeer as an example in this book. Let's JKPARTY, y'all!

Publisher's Acknowledgments

We're proud of this book; please register your comments through our IDG Books Worldwide Online Registration Form located at http://my2cents.dummies.com.

Some of the people who helped bring this book to market include the following:

Acquisitions, Development, and Editorial

Project Editor: Tere Drenth

Acquisitions Editor: Michael Kelly

Media Development Manager: Joyce Pepple

Permissions Editor: Heather H. Dismore

Copy Editor: Felicity O' Meara

Technical Reviewer: Matt Converse

Editorial Manager: Elaine Brush

Editorial Assistant: Paul Kuzmic

Production

Project Coordinator: Regina Snyder

Layout and Graphics: Lou Boudreau, Angela F. Hunckler, Todd Klemme, Brent Savage, Janet Seib, Michael A. Sullivan

Proofreaders: Christine Sabooni, Christine Berman, Nancy Price, Janet M. Withers

Indexer: Sharon Hilgenberg

Special Help

Ted Cains, Copy Editor; Stephanie Koutek, Proof Editor; Michele Phillips, Researcher; Joell Smith, Associate Technical Editor; Linda S. Stark, Copy Editor

General and Administrative

IDG Books Worldwide, Inc.: John Kilcullen, CEO; Steven Berkowitz, President and Publisher

IDG Books Technology Publishing: Brenda McLaughlin, Senior Vice President and Group Publisher

Dummies Technology Press and Dummies Editorial: Diane Graves Steele, Vice President and Associate Publisher; Mary Bednarek, Acquisitions and Product Development Director; Kristin A. Cocks, Editorial Director

Dummies Trade Press: Kathleen A. Welton, Vice President and Publisher; Kevin Thornton, Acquisitions Manager

IDG Books Production for Dummies Press: Beth Jenkins Roberts, Production Director; Cindy L. Phipps, Manager of Project Coordination, Production Proofreading, and Indexing; Kathie S. Schutte, Supervisor of Page Layout; Shelley Lea, Supervisor of Graphics and Design; Debbie J. Gates, Production Systems Specialist; Robert Springer, Supervisor of Proofreading; Debbie Stailey, Special Projects Coordinator; Tony Augsburger, Supervisor of Reprints and Bluelines; Leslie Popplewell, Media Archive Coordinator

Dummies Packaging and Book Design: Patti Crane, Packaging Specialist; Kavish + Kavish, Cover Design

♦

The publisher would like to give special thanks to Patrick J. McGovern, without whom this book would not have been possible.

♦

Contents at a Glance

Cartoons at a Glance

By Rich Tennant

page 75

page 255

page 239

page 141

page 7

page 205

Fax: 978-546-7747 • E-mail: the5wave@tiac.net

Table of Contents

Part II: The Basics of Online Life *75*

Foreword

Several years ago, we founded America Online, Inc., with a simple objective: to make on-line services more accessible, more affordable, more useful, and more fun for people from all walks of life. And that formula appears to be working. America Online is now the largest consumer on-line service in the nation.

That success has been driven in large part by remaining faithful to our original charter: making online services accessible to everyone. In designing the service, we wanted to make it as intuitive as possible, meaning everybody from Fortune 500 executives to elementary school students could surf throughout our many departments. We wanted to make the software easy to install and use, and as a result, new America Online customers are usually up and running in less than 15 minutes. Try doing this with your VCR.

We've also worked hard to continually add new services through strategic partnerships with content providers. If it seems as if America Online is in the business sections of major newspapers on an almost daily basis, it's because we are; we are adding new content to our service at an incredibly rapid pace and have no plans to slow down.

And still there's more: With increased interest in the Internet and the World Wide Web, we are upgrading our Internet gateway to permit AOL subscribers full access to this network of networks and all it has to offer. And it's all there at a simple, affordable price.

But as good as we've been at making the service simple to operate, the sheer volume of information available has made the on-line world akin to trying to tour the Smithsonian in one day. That's where this book, *America Online For Dummies,* 4th Edition, comes in. Although we think American Online is already "dummy-proof," John's book makes AOL just that much easier to enjoy. And enjoy you will as we continue to add unique new services, sign on more content providers, and expand AOL subscribers' access to the Internet.

As you'll discover, America Online is a living, breathing, electronic community that bridges the lives of all our members in an engaging, interactive format. Every day, tens of thousands of AOL subscribers go online and scan their stock portfolios, talk to friends, make airline reservations, read their favorite magazines and newspapers, and actively participate in discussions about hundreds of different topics. We provide the framework; beyond that, America Online is shaped by the collective imagination of its participants.

How often do you get take part in a revolution? A new interactive communications medium is emerging, and it will change the way we live, work, and play. America Online is at the forefront of this revolution, and we invite you to join us in shaping this new medium.

Steve Case, President and CEO
America Online, Inc.

Introduction

. . . .

*"H*i — welcome to the neighborhood!"

That probably wasn't the first thing you expected to hear when you joined America Online, but it's just the first of many surprises awaiting you. America Online is quite different from those *other* online services. Luckily for you, *America Online For Dummies,* 4th Edition, is equally unique.

This book is your friendly tour guide and road map to an intriguing corner of the digital world. In here is everything you need to get started with (and get the most from) the friendliest and fastest growing online service in the country: America Online. The best part is that you don't need to be some normalcy-challenged computer technoid to make sense of it all. *America Online For Dummies,* 4th Edition, is written in plain language — the way everyone talked back when *computers* interfaced and *people* had conversations. The book is designed to give you the information you need quickly so that you can get back to the fun stuff at hand.

But don't just take my word for it — jump on in and discover what's here for you. I think you'll be pleasantly surprised.

Who I Think You Are

To know you is to understand you, and goodness knows, if I can't understand you, I can't help you. With that statement in mind (a challenge in itself), here's what I know about you:

- ✔ You're either interested in America Online or are currently using it (and are feeling the effects).
- ✔ You use an IBM-compatible or a Macintosh computer.
- ✔ You have a modem attached to your computer.
- ✔ You care more about dinner than about modems and computers *combined.*
- ✔ Terms such as *BPS, download,* and *Internet* nip at your heels like a pack of disturbed Chihuahuas.

If these statements sound familiar, this book is for you.

Although the book's instructions are primarily geared toward the Wonderful World of Windows (the new Macintosh software wasn't ready while I wrote), Macintosh users still benefit from the *AOL Channels For Dummies* book-within-a-book, plus all of the content information in Parts III, IV, and V. After the America Online 4.0 software comes out for the Macintosh, the instructions in Parts I and II should help, too.

It's All English — Except for Parts in "Geek"

When you're working with America Online, it's kind of like being in a two-way conversation: You give commands to the system, and the system displays messages back at you (so be careful what you say!). This book contains stuff about both sides of the conversation, so keep in mind the following ways to help you figure out who's talking to whom:

```
If the text looks like this, America Online is saying some-
thing clever on-screen that you don't want to miss. World
Wide Web sites and other Internet addresses also look like
this. It's the computer book version of the high-tech com-
puter look.
```

If the text looks like this, it's something you need to tell America Online by typing it somewhere on-screen. (Remember to be nice — no yelling.) If you need to choose something from a menu or from one of the funky drop-down menus that pop out from underneath some of the Toolbar buttons, the text shows some options separated by an arrow — for example, Mail Center⇨Write Mail. That means you should choose the menu or Toolbar button marked Mail Center and then click the Write Mail option. None of the menu items and Toolbar buttons share the same name, so don't fret about clicking the wrong thing.

Because you're using America Online in a Microsoft Windows environment, you also must deal with the mouse. In this book, I assume that you know the following basic mouse maneuvers:

Click	Position the mouse pointer and then quickly press and release the mouse button (specifically, the *left* button, if your mouse has two to choose from).
Double-click	Position the mouse pointer and then click twice — basically, two regular clicks. (Remember, the people who designed this stuff weren't hired to be clever.)

Click and drag	Position the mouse pointer and then press *and hold* the mouse button as you move the mouse across the screen. As before, use the left button if you have more than one button. After the mouse pointer gets to wherever it's going, release the button.
Right-click	Click the right mouse button. The most popular place to use the right mouse button with America Online is in an e-mail message or Instant Message. Right-click in the area where you write the message to see a pop-up menu of cool options (see Chapter 6 for more about that).

If all this mouse stuff is news to you, I wholeheartedly recommend picking up a copy of *Windows 3.11 For Dummies,* 4th Edition, *Windows 95 For Dummies,* 2nd Edition (both by Andy Rathbone), or *Macs For Dummies,* 5th Edition, by David Pogue (all from IDG Books Worldwide, Inc.).

Frolicking (Briefly) through the Book

This book is organized into six distinct parts and a special minibook. To whet your appetite, here's a peek at what each section contains. Pay special attention to the *AOL Channels for Dummies* minibook. It's your roadmap to the best content on America Online.

Part I: Driver's Ed for the Digital Traveler

This answers the stirring question, "Just what the heck *is* America Online and why do I care?" Part I gives you a broad overview of what the whole service is about. It explains what you need to know about online services in general, walks you through an average America Online day, points out the features and highlights of the America Online access software, and gives you some pointers for making the place a little more like home. In short, it's kinda like digital driver's education.

Part II: The Basics of Online Life

As part of their quest to join society, people learn a lot of basic skills — things like walking, talking, ordering in a restaurant, balancing a checkbook, and julienning a potato into french fries (although I somehow skipped that particular session in the school of life).

Likewise, to take your place in the online world, you need to know how to handle the basic tools of this new realm — and that's what Part II is all about. It starts with ways to navigate through the digital world and remember your favorite online hot spots, and then continues through the rest of the basic tools, like e-mail, chat rooms, Instant Messages, and discussion boards.

Part III: Diving into the Fun Stuff

The questions I hear most often from both new and existing America Online members are straightforward: Where's the way-cool online information? Where are the best chats? I'm getting hungry — where's the kitchen? The chapters in Part III deliver the goods by focusing on the *what's out there* side of online life. You uncover and explore America Online's lively, topical, and up-to-date content areas; hack, slash, and blast your way through the games; take a trip on the Internet; and fill your computer with new software (courtesy of America Online's voluminous file libraries).

Part IV: Going Your Own Way

This part is especially for you — well, for you, your kids, your neighbors, and various broad strata of the country's entire populace. You see, this part has a chapter for just about everyone. That's the whole point of Part IV: to give you a view of America Online from whatever unique perspective you may have, whether as a parent, a student, a small-business person . . . or something else. Instead of describing the broad scope of America Online, Part IV turns the telescope around and pinpoints places to go depending on *your* particular interests.

Part V: Secret Tricks of the AOL Gurus

Shhh. We don't want *everyone* to hear about this part. Well, at least we don't want *them* to hear about it just yet (you know how spurned techno-weenies behave sometimes). Part V contains the collected wisdom of many America Online experts. It's filled with tips and goodies for making your America Online connection truly come alive. Customizing your member profile with new categories and tweaking the Toolbar until it's uniquely yours are just two of the cool techno-tricks documented in this part. Enjoy!

Part VI: The Part of Tens

It just wouldn't be a ...*For Dummies* book without a Part of Tens. Here you find tips for getting the most out of your America Online experience, code charts that decipher the sometimes peculiar comments in the chat areas, ways to find help when your connection doesn't work, and places to visit when the urge to explore takes hold of your mind. It's a potpourri of things to brighten your digital day.

AOL Channels For Dummies

In yet another attempt to keep you from completely shorting out when faced with all the stuff America Online has to offer, the helpful folks at America Online organize all of the content areas into a series of channels. *AOL Channels For Dummies* — a unique book-within-a-book — takes you for a trot through all of the channels, introducing you to the goodies within each one. You find out what's available in each channel and each channel's departments (subsections of a channel, just like departments within a large store). Plus, you uncover tips for making the most of each channel's special features or content.

Because it's a minibook, *AOL Channels For Dummies* contains all the things you expect of a good reference book, like a Table of Contents and chapter numbers that start over from scratch. The book's pages even carry a gray bar along the side, making the minibook easy to find (the marketing department nixed my idea of including a personal attendant with each book — they said that packaging would be an issue).

Don't pay extra for software!

Don't waste your money on AOL software, because, as a bonafide ...*For Dummies* reader, you can get it for free! Call America Online at 800-827-6364 to try AOL for 50 hours free, after which regular connection charges apply. Be sure to tell them that your registration code is 76540, when calling. (Use of America Online requires a major credit card or direct debit from a checking account.)

Icons, Icons Everywhere

To make finding the important stuff in the book a little easier (and to help you steer clear of the technical hogwash), this book has a bunch of icons scattered throughout. Each icon marks something in the text that's particularly vital to your online existence. Here's a brief guide to what these little road signs mean:

If you see a Remember icon, get out your highlighter, because the text is definitely worth bearing in mind, both now and in the future.

You can benefit from my experience (both good and bad) whenever you spy a Tip icon. Whether it marks a trap to avoid or a trick to make your life easier, you can't go wrong heeding a Tip.

Like it or not, I have to include some truly technical twaddle. To shield you from it as much as possible, I mark the techie stuff with this icon. If you see this turkey, flip — don't lazily turn — to the next page. Really, it's better for everyone this way.

If you need to do something that's just the tiniest bit dangerous (such as walking the trail into the Grand Canyon while blindfolded and on laughing gas), this icon tells you to proceed with caution. Pay close attention to these warnings; they mark the most dire of pitfalls. (Don't worry, though; they aren't too frequent in America Online.)

It's Time to Get Started!

The beauty of a *...For Dummies* book — apart from the friendly yellow cover and the cute little Dummies guy — is how it presents information. Unlike a lot of books on the market, you don't need to read *America Online For Dummies,* 4th Edition, in chapter-by-chapter order. Sure, you *can* do it that way (after all, it is your book), but the information in here comes out just as easily whether you march sequentially through the chapters or bound and romp from topic to topic. The choice is yours, driven by the needs of your quest for knowledge.

Either way, go on out there and have some fun — and keep this book handy, just in case you need a little help now and then.

Part I
Driver's Ed for the Digital Traveler

The 5th Wave   By Rich Tennant

"You know, I liked you a whole lot more on AOL."

In this part . . .

Driver's Education class is the only thing holding this country together. It's a massively shared experience. Everyone, at one time or another, learns how to drive. And we all do it with white knuckles the first time, thinking that 20 miles per hour is kinda fast and that maybe we ought to ease it down to a nice, pedestrian 10 miles per hour for a while.

The first time you face the vast plains of the online world, that old memory may rise up. Gripping the disks with white knuckles, wondering if maybe 28,800 bps isn't just a little fast and that perhaps you should just run the modem at 9,600 bps until you get the hang of it.

Hey — it's going to be okay. The truth is that you can surf the Internet, hold an interactive conversation with people all over the country, and receive files from a computer that's 7,000 miles away without knowing (or caring to know) the details of how it all works.

This part gives you an overview of what this crazy America Online thing is all about and what it can do. It also offers some tips for getting comfortable in your new digital habitat and a note or two about working and playing well with others online.

Get ready for the ride of your life. Now, where did I put those car keys?

Chapter 1

What You've Gotten Yourself Into (And What You Need to Get Out)

In This Chapter

▶ Discovering what this *online* thing is all about

▶ Scoping out the stuff you need to make it work

▶ Getting down to details about hardware, software, modems, and more

*P*erhaps you just bought a new computer and happened across a stray icon labeled *America Online*. Or maybe your parent, child, or significant other decided that it was time for you to join the online revolution and endowed you with all the goodies this revolution requires. Or perhaps you don't quite know what to make of all this talk about the Information Super-highway and worry that you're getting left behind at the rest stop.

If you want to get an idea of what *online* means and understand what it takes to get there with America Online, this is the place to start. This chapter explains all the introductory stuff to prepare you for the real meat of the issue: Actually going online. (Don't panic — that happens in the next chapter.) For now, kick back and get ready to understand what your parent, child, or significant other has been talking about all this time.

What Online Really Means

What is this "online service" stuff, anyway? And does it have something to do with the Information Superhighway? Do you even care? Why or why not? Please write a detailed answer on the inside cover of a matchbook and then set the whole thing on fire, watching with pleasure as it burns to a crisp. Don't you feel better now?

If you do, you're not alone. Many people feel apprehensive about this mysterious electronic world that you're entering. Take heart, though, because online services used to be much more mysterious than they are today. Don't worry if the whole concept seems more than a bit bizarre to you right now. That's okay; the reaction is normal. Mainly, those feelings prove that you're not a nerd. Congratulations on passing the test!

But back to the question at hand: What is an online service? Conceptually, it's a lot like cable TV. With cable TV, you buy a subscription from your local cable company and hook your television into its network with a funny-looking box that freaks out sometimes. A special wire connects the box to a wall socket. If everything does what it's supposed to, you turn on the TV and choose among a wide variety of programming, depending on your interests. When it doesn't work, the problem may be in your TV, with the brain-dead little box, or somewhere from the wall jack to the cable company itself. At the end of the month, you get a bill that you grudgingly pay, all the while wondering if cable TV is really worth all the money you spend on it.

With a few clever substitutions, that describes America Online (and those other online services as well). You hook your computer to a funny-looking box called a modem (which, like its cable TV counterpart, sometimes freaks out), and plug a plain phone cord from the modem to the phone jack on the wall. With some special software, you sign up for an America Online account. If everything does what it's supposed to do, you dial a local number and contact America Online's computers in Virginia. After connecting, you choose among a wide variety of services, depending on your interests. When things don't work, the problem may be with your computer, the software, the modem (stupid modems . . .), or somewhere from the wall jack to America Online itself. At the end of the month, you get a bill that you gleefully pay, flush with the happy memory of everything you did online.

By the way, the term *online* means "connected." If you're online with America Online, a link is actually set up through the phone between your computer and America Online's computers. When you get right down to it, the computers are having this swell digital conversation behind the scenes, while you're busy reading the news, sending electronic mail, or doing whatever else you do on America Online. The entire process looks much like Figure 1-1. Your computer, running America Online's special software, tells the modem to call a particular phone number. The modem dials the number and waits to hear from another modem. The two modems whistle and beep at each other for a while (the technical term for this is *feature negotiation,* although I always thought of it as some kind of electronic flirting). After the modems settle down, they get to work completing your connection to America Online's computer system.

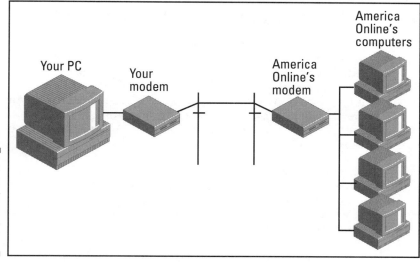

Figure 1-1:
Going online
usually
means
"going on-
phone-line."

And now for the great part: That's *all* you need to know about the technology behind America Online. Really — I wouldn't kid you about something like this. All the cool things you can do, all the fun tricks, all the stuff that makes America Online a really wild and woolly place — all these do require a lot of technology, but *it doesn't matter to you*. You don't have to know any of this to use America Online!

All It Takes Is a Bunch of Stuff

Now that you have a conceptual picture of how all this online business happens, you're ready to dig a little deeper and get into some specifics. You need four parts to make the online thing a reality: the America Online software, a computer, a modem, and a phone line. The following sections explore each element just enough to give you a good understanding of what you need without turning you into a computer nerd (ewww — the very thought gives me the shivers).

If you're starting from scratch and need to get *everything*, I recommend finding a computer guru to give you a hand. Depending on where you find your guru, this help may cost anywhere from a few dozen brownies to a few dozen greenbacks. If you do seek expert help, make sure that your expert understands online services (preferably America Online) and gives sound, unbiased advice. Don't get help from someone you just met whose primary experience comes from working at a computer store. Check with your friends for the name of a trusted and handy computer guru you can borrow for a while.

First, you need the right software

America Online is a pretty special place, not only because of its content and services but also for the look-and-feel of its interface (the buttons, menus, and windows that are on-screen). America Online's programmers decided to do things the *right* way from the start. This decision meant a break with tradition, because people would need special software to join America Online; they couldn't use the good ol' modem program they knew and loved with other online services. It was a risk, but it paid off handsomely in better features, ease of use, and consistency.

To sign on to America Online, you need the official America Online access software — accept no substitutes. You can't use PROCOMM PLUS, MicroPhone, or any other plain-vanilla modem program. Nope, they just won't work with America Online. But don't let that worry you, because the access software is (lean in closer, I don't want everybody to hear this) *free*.

That's right: By purchasing this book, you can try America Online for 50 hours, all within a 30-day period (after which regular charges apply). Just call 800-827-6364 and tell the friendly folks at AOL that your access code is 76540. (Use of America Online requires a major credit card or direct debit card from a checking account.)

If the America Online software came preloaded on your computer, make sure that you have the latest version. Table 1-1 shows the current software version number for each kind of computer platform that America Online supports and explains how to politely find out which version you have. You don't have to be (and, in fact, *shouldn't* be) signed on to America Online to find out the software version number.

Table 1-1		Version, Version, Who's Got Which Version?
Platform	*Current Version*	*How to Find the Version Number*
DOS	1.6	With the America Online software running, choose Help⇨About from the main menu. The version number is in the pop-up dialog box.
Macintosh	3.0	In the Finder, click the America Online icon once and then choose File⇨Get Info from the Finder menu or press ⌘+I. The version number is in the pop-up information dialog box (see Figure 1-2).
Windows	4.0	With the America Online software running, choose Help⇨About America Online from the menu bar. The version number is near the top of the screen (see Figure 1-3).

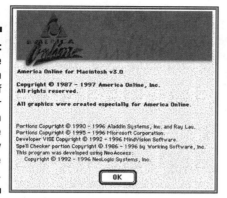

Figure 1-2:
Check the version number of your Macintosh software directly from the Finder.

Figure 1-3:
The latest America Online software for Windows shows off its version number.

Although knowing your program's version number seems a little nerdy, you have a good reason to find out what it is. This book covers the *newest* America Online software. If you're using an older version, you're going to get confused very quickly (and that's definitely not my goal). Also, if you're using the software for DOS, now's the time to consider upgrading to Windows.

A computer is a must

You can't get around this one: To use America Online, you must have a computer. Sorry, but that's the way these things go. Having settled that point, the next logical question is, "Okay, smart guy, what *kind* of computer?" "Well," I reply, "that's up to you."

Because America Online's special access software comes in both Macintosh and Windows versions, you have some leeway in choosing your computer. (A DOS version also exists, but for now, just pretend I didn't say that.) Choose whichever kind of machine you feel more comfortable with. Don't worry if you use Windows at work but prefer a Macintosh for home (or vice versa). You can still share documents, spreadsheets, and many other files between your computers without any (well, *many*) problems.

If you buy a new computer for your online adventures, make sure that it has the following:

- A fast processor (a Pentium for Windows or a Power PC in a Macintosh)

- Plenty of random-access memory (16MB to 32MB is a good minimum for either a Macintosh or Windows machine)

- A high-quality color monitor (15 inches is a good minimum size)

- Lots of hard disk space (1 gigabyte or more)

If all this computer jargon sounds foreign to you, pick up a copy of *PCs For Dummies,* 5th Edition, by Dan Gookin or *Macs For Dummies,* 5th Edition, by David Pogue (both from IDG Books Worldwide, Inc.).

A modem enters the picture

The next piece of the puzzle is a *modem,* the device that converts your computer's electronic impulses into whistles, beeps, and various digital moose calls. It then yells these noises through the phone line to another equally disturbed modem attached to another computer.

The term *modem* is actually an acronym (and you thought you were safe, didn't you?). It stands for modulator/demodulator, which is a computer nerd's way of saying that it both talks and listens. To find out more than you could possibly want to know about modems, get a copy of *Modems For Dummies,* 3rd Edition, by Tina Rathbone (IDG Books Worldwide, Inc.).

The main things you're looking for in a modem are a well-known manufacturer and blazing speed. My recommendations are as follows:

- Get a modem made by U.S. Robotics or Hayes. Although many other modems are available, these manufacturers stand behind their products better than all the rest.

- If you buy a new modem, make sure that it's fast. Modems that run at 28,800 and 33,600 bits per second (bps) are the rage these days. Condemning yourself to anything slower than 14,400 bits per second just won't do (I care about your sanity too much for that).

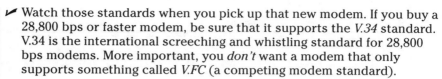

15

✔ Watch those standards when you pick up that new modem. If you buy a 28,800 bps or faster modem, be sure that it supports the *V.34* standard. V.34 is the international screeching and whistling standard for 28,800 bps modems. More important, you *don't* want a modem that only supports something called *V.FC* (a competing modem standard).

✔ Due to the involvement of too many engineers, the 56,000 bps high-speed modems don't follow a single standard yet — or at least they don't as I write this. Look for a standard to emerge sometime in late 1998, but in the meantime, don't let the lack of standardization worry you. America Online supports both of the current contenders, 3Com's *X2* technology and Rockwell's *K56flex*. See the sidebar called "A few words about modem speed" for a little more about these extraordinarily fleet animals.

Many computers include a modem as part of the deal these days. If you aren't sure whether your PC includes one, glance at the back of the machine and look for a place to plug in a phone cord. Congrats — there's your modem!

What about a phone line?

All this other stuff won't do you a whit of good if you don't have a phone line to connect it to. The phone is your link with beautiful, metropolitan Vienna, Virginia, the home of America Online. Luckily, you don't need a special phone line — just about any phone line will work.

The key words in that last sentence are *just about,* because not all phone lines are created equal. Many phone lines have been endowed by their subscribers with certain very alien services — such as call waiting — that interfere with a computer's basic rights to life, liberty, and the pursuit of a connection with America Online.

(Sorry, I've been reading American history lately and got a little carried away. If I had an "I'm so embarrassed" icon, rest assured I'd insert it here.)

To successfully use a modem, you need an *analog* phone line. If your home has a single phone line (or two plain, old-fashioned phone lines), you have an analog phone line. Fax machines need the same kind of phone line, so in times of emergency, you can unplug the fax and use its phone line to reach America Online.

A few words about modem speed

A modem's speed is measured in bits per second (bps). The more bits per second, the more information the modem stuffs down the phone line in a given period of time.

Because America Online doesn't charge extra to use a faster modem, you save a lot of money in the long run by using the fastest modem you can. Right now (as I write this book), America Online supports 28,800 and 14,400 bps modems all over the country, with growing pockets of support for 33,600 modems.

America Online also works with ultra-fast X2 and K56flex modems, although support isn't widespread yet. If you're interested in either of these high-speed technologies, check out keyword **Highspeed** for general information, or try keywords **X2** and **K56flex** for specifics.

My advice: Pay a little extra and get the fastest modem possible, because it will pay you back tomorrow and many days thereafter. It also pays to check your modem maker's Web site and find out if your modem can be upgraded to support higher speeds. Sometimes, the upgrade is free — all you need to do is ask.

At work, the story is a little different. Many office telephone systems use *digital* phone lines. You shouldn't plug a normal modem directly into one of these lines. Please, for the sake of your modem, don't try. At best, the modem won't work this time. At worst, the modem won't ever work again because it's fried. If you're planning to use America Online from the office, contact your telephone folks and tell them that you have a modem and need something to connect it to. Remember to ask nicely, or they may not give you the answer you're looking for.

Chapter 2

A Brief Romp through an Average Day

- -

In This Chapter

▶ Starting your online day

▶ Checking your mail

▶ Reading the rags

▶ Making sense of your dollars

▶ Grabbing some new software

▶ Surfing the Internet wave

▶ Shopping — need more be said?

▶ Chatting with the neighbors

▶ Relaxing with some online games

▶ And still there's more

- -

Beep Beep Beep Beep BEEP BEEP! [whack] {yawwn} <<strrreeetch>> Ah, good morning! Nice to see you're up (and looking as bright-eyed and bushy-tailed as ever, I might add). A full chapter lies ahead, so I'm glad you slept well.

This chapter is a whirlwind tour through an average online day. Think of this tour as a visual sampler, a platter of digital appetizers, each one delicious in itself, but also tempting in the knowledge that more waits to be discovered. Collectively, this chapter gives you a broad idea of what you can do with America Online — and what it can do for you.

For now, kick back and read on. If something piques your interest, take a break and try it online. Each section of the chapter includes the keywords and menu instructions you need.

First, You Need to Sign On

The online day has to start somewhere, and signing on to the service is as good a place as any. Just follow these steps to sign on to America Online:

1. **Turn on your computer, monitor, modem, stereo, food processor, and that cool cordless toothbrush/answering machine in the bathroom. Marvel at what modern technology has accomplished (and how noisy it all is), and then turn off the unimportant stuff.**

   No, you need to leave the computer *on* for now.

   If you have a Windows 95 or Macintosh machine, your computer should start blissfully and leave you with a ready-to-go desktop screen. If that's you, go on to Step 2.

   If you use an older PC with Windows 3.*x*, Windows may or may not start automatically. If Windows does fire up on its own, go ahead to the next step. To manually start Windows, type **WIN** at the DOS prompt ($C:\backslash>$), and then press Enter. In just a moment, the friendly Microsoft advertisement — er, the Windows logo screen — appears.

2. **Find the triangular America Online icon cowering among all your other software icons and double-click it to start the program.**

   In Windows 95, look in the Start button menu. On the Macintosh, find the America Online folder. When the program finishes loading, it displays the Sign On dialog box.

3. **Choose the screen name you want to use (if you have more than one, that is) by clicking the down arrow next to the Select Screen Name list box and clicking the name of your choice.**

   If this is the first time you've picked this particular screen name with the America Online 4.0 software, the program accosts you with another dialog box that demands to know if you want to store your password. For now, click Cancel and ignore the dialog box. If your curiosity is piqued by this option, then flip to Chapter 4 and un-pique it with the details awaiting you there.

   Don't panic if the Enter Password text box disappears after you choose a screen name. That means the password for that name is already stored in the access software.

4. **Press Tab to move down to the Enter Password text box and type in your password.**

   Your password appears as asterisks — not words. That's a protection feature to keep that guy looking over your shoulder from breaking into your account. What guy? Why, that one right there. (Yipe!)

5. **Click Sign On or press Enter to open the connection to America Online.**

The software goes through all kinds of cool visual gymnastics while it's connecting. Granted, it's not a Hollywood masterpiece, but at least it's marginally entertaining.

If the connection process doesn't work for some reason, make a note of the last thing that the software did (initializing the modem, dialing, connecting, requesting network attention, and so on), and then try connecting again. If it still doesn't work, close the America Online software, restart your computer, and give your software one last chance to get things right. (Aren't you glad that your car doesn't work this way?)

If your software *still* doesn't connect to America Online, breeze through Chapter 24 for the top ten problems and how to solve them.

6. **After a moment, the Welcome window appears on-screen.**

Congratulations — you're online and ready to get some stuff done.

The Welcome window sorta takes over the screen, but the Channels window isn't far away. To see the Channels window, click the Channels button on the Toolbar and select the Channel you want to see (I recommend starting with AOL Today). Check out *AOL Channels For Dummies,* the minibook way back at the end of this book — you'll know it by the gray edge on the minibook's pages.

Checking the E-Mailbox

Electronic mail (or *e-mail*) is one of America Online's most popular services. That's why the e-mail button takes a position of pride and power on the left side of the Welcome window. In the Figure, I have mail waiting in the box (an everyday occurrence in my world, and soon to be a regular feature of yours, too). If you don't have any mail waiting, the graphic shows a closed mailbox emblazoned with the simple title Mail Center.

To read your mail, either click the You Have Mail button or click Read on the Toolbar. After the New Mail dialog box pops up, click Read to start through your mail.

✔ If you're writing a mail message instead of reading one, why are you logged in? Sign off the system and click the Write toolbar button or press Ctrl+M to write your message offline. After you finish, turn to Chapter 6 and read about the myriad ways to send mail.

✔ If you do a lot of e-mail with America Online and want to save time, then I see Automatic AOL sessions in your future. Mark your place and flip to Chapter 6 for more about this incredibly useful feature.

Say the magic keyword and get there fast

Keywords are America Online's answer to the Star Trek transporter. A keyword is a single code that immediately takes you to a particular forum or service in the system. A sidebar in Chapter 5 explains all the details of keywords, but for now, I want to briefly tell you how to use them. Check out that other sidebar for more detailed information.

To use a keyword, either press Ctrl+K (⌘+K on the Macintosh) or choose Go To⇨Keyword from the menu bar. When the Keyword dialog box appears, type in your keyword and press Enter or click OK. Was that fast or what?

As you may have figured out by now, Chapter 6 tells you everything you need to know about addressing, sending, receiving, and generally dealing with e-mail. I had to put this information somewhere, and that seemed as good a place as any.

Reading the Morning Paper (And a Magazine or Two)

There's nothing like disappearing behind the morning newspaper while waiting for that first cup of coffee to turn you into a human being. With America Online, you have your choice of not one, not two, but — heck — a whole slew of newspapers and magazines. To get there, start with a channel that interests you, such as Computing, Families, Games, Interests, International, Sports, or Workplace. Each channel has its own individual newsstand area, like the News Newsstand shown in Figure 2-1.

To find out most everything you could possibly want to know about the Channels, check out the minibook with the cool gray-edged pages at the end of this book.

If newspapers are your thing, try the *Chicago Tribune* (keyword **Tribune**), the *New York Times* (keyword **Times**), or the *Orlando Sun-Sentinel* (keyword **Sun-Sentinel**). Are you more into magazines? Check out *Newsweek* (keyword **Newsweek**), *Scientific American* (keyword **SciAm**), *Slate* (keyword **Slate**), or *Sew News* (keyword **Sew News**).

To curl up with whatever publication suits your fancy, look for a link in your favorite online area (the Sewing & NeedleCraft forum offers a link to *Sew News*, for instance) or turn to a likely-looking Channel. If you go the Channel route, find the Newsstand department in the Channel window, then click on it. Once in the Newsstand department, scroll through the publications list to find the magazine or your desire. If there's no newsstand in the channel, try using the Find system (covered in Chapter 11) to track down your reading quarry.

To find out lots more about the various newsstands, check out the various channel descriptions inside *AOL Channels For Dummies* — the special book-within-a-book right after The Part of Tens.

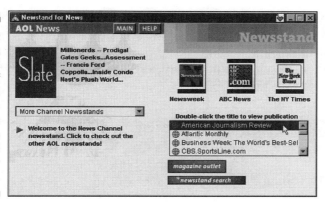

Figure 2-1:
The News Newsstand is one of several Channel-specific magazine and newspaper areas.

Eyeing the Markets

Managing your stock portfolio was never easier than this. America Online's Quotes & Portfolios service (keyword **Quotes**, or click Quotes on the Toolbar) tracks the stocks closest to your heart and pocketbook.

Columbus, Eriksson, Magellan, and you

New services appear on America Online faster than facial aberrations on a teenager. There seems to be something new every week. How do you keep up with it all? Leave it to those clever America Online programmers to think of a way: the Discover AOL member orientation center (Keyword **Discover**).

From the Discover America Online window, my personal picks for really cool buttons are Places of AOL and Talk about AOL. The Places of AOL button displays a subject-based peek at America Online's content. The Talk about AOL button brings up discussion boards and chat areas specially geared to new members. If you're new to America Online, you should definitely check out these two areas.

To satisfy a brief curiosity, you can look up a single stock by its symbol. Figure 2-2, for example, tracks America Online's stock activity by using the symbol AMER. If looking at the *big picture* is more to your liking, the Display Portfolio feature (keyword **Portfolio**) follows all the stocks you choose, tracking the current market price *and* how that translates into a gain or loss for your invested dollars.

- ✔ Don't panic, but the information in Quotes & Portfolios is delayed about 15 minutes. I guess that means you can't call it up-to-the-minute information. Hmm — how about up-until-quite-recently information?

- ✔ You can save the portfolio information to a text file by choosing File⇨Save from the menu bar.

America Online charges no extra fee to use the Quotes & Portfolios service — it's just part of the service. Flip to Chapter 12 to find out more about America Online's financial offerings.

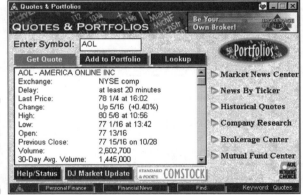

Figure 2-2: Be a stock spy with Quotes & Portfolios.

Internet On-Ramp, Next Right

At this point in your online life, you've probably heard, read, or otherwise been exposed to *something* about the Internet. If you haven't heard about the Internet yet, don't worry; you're about to.

The Internet is the worldwide network of networks that's all the rage these days. You can't get your hair done, shop for tires, or even play cricket without bumping into the Internet somehow. "Oh, is that a new cricket bat?" you ask. "Aye, a player in the rec.sport.cricket Internet newsgroup recommended it." See what I mean?

Several broad kinds of services are available on the Internet. America Online Internet Connection (keyword **Internet**) is your portal to the World Wide Web, gopher, the Internet newsgroups, and much more. You can also find an index of mailing lists available for your perusal and subscription pleasure. Of course, you always have America Online's e-mail feature, which lets you send mail anywhere on the Internet.

There's far too much to say about the Internet to do so here, so cruise to Chapter 14 and get ready for the ride of your life.

The Joys of (Nearly) Free Stuff

It seems like everywhere you turn in America Online, you find a software library. You don't have to be anywhere special; just about every service area has something to offer.

Exactly what's available depends entirely on where you are. In the *Omni* magazine area (keyword **Omni**), you can browse through the Antimatter Files and find UFO pictures, NASA photographs, and text files of selected *Omni* articles. The Food area (keyword **Food**) serves up recipes and a variety of cookbook programs (both shareware and commercial demonstrations). The Hypractv8 section (keyword **Hypr**) offers everything from virtual reality software to music, with a touch of 3D drawing and utility programs thrown in too (including lots of cool Mac software).

Thanks to America Online's Internet links, you also have access to the infinite software libraries available through File Transfer Protocol, lovingly known in Net lingo as FTP. Troll the likes of Winsite (`ftp.winsite.com` — widely acknowledged as the world's largest Windows software library), Sumex (`sumex-aim.stanford.edu` — the home of more Macintosh software than anyone could possibly need), and the Walnut Creek Archive (`ftp.cdrom.com` — a great spot to find all kinds of programs) with ease. Filling your hard drive has never been so much fun!

Whether it's fonts and clip art, games and playing tips, or something a little more businesslike, you can find the details of getting it, unpacking it (watch out for the foam peanuts!), and making it work for you in Chapter 15. For FTP info, check out Chapter 14.

Let the Fun and Games Begin!

Because all work and no play makes me really grumpy (and probably does the same thing to you), take a break from the Internet and indulge in some fun. The online world offers games to suit every age, style, and taste.

If you're a shoot-'em-up kinda person, work through your aggression (and sharpen your aim) in Splatterball (keyword **Splatterball**), the first of a new breed of interactive online games. For enthusiasts of more sedate games, America Online offers a dedicated crossword area (keyword **Xwords**), chess (keyword **Chess**), and interactive Trivial Pursuit (keyword **Trivial Pursuit**).

All this fun stuff and more is waiting in the Games channel. For more fun, flip to Chapter 13.

Shopping without the Crowds

Imagine shopping the malls on the day after Thanksgiving. After you regain consciousness, get a drink of water and then come back and keep reading.

Now imagine the same shopping trip with no crowds, no pushy children, and no whining adults. It's a dream, right? No, it's the America Online Shopping channel (keyword **Shopping**), your 24-hour shop-till-your-fingers-drop electronic mall.

Take a stroll through the Classifieds (keyword **Classifieds**), America Online's own version of a digital flea market. Or pick up some high-tech goodies at the Sharper Image (keyword **Sharper Image**). Have something a little bigger in mind? Try the Shoppers Advantage club (keyword **Shoppers Advantage**), with the best in just about everything you could want — and great prices as well.

If your credit card is already out, take a break and power shop through the Shopping channel in *AOL Channels For Dummies,* the book-within-a-book that follows Part VI, The Part of Tens, at the end of this book.

Having a Little Chat

The People Connection (select People⇨People Connection or use keyword **People**) is the home of America Online's *chat* areas. Here, you can interactively talk live with other America Online subscribers. All this chat happens in what the technology jockeys call *real time,* which is a fancy way to say that right after you type a message, the other people in that chat area see the message on their screens, wherever in the country they are.

The chat areas usually hold a maximum of 23 people. America Online does have some larger rooms — you can find out about them in Chapter 7.

When Problems Come Up (As They Usually Do)

Compared to other online services, America Online offers a truly awesome level of support. You can find online chat areas, discussion boards, and even an old-fashioned, pick-up-the-phone-and-call-a-human line. Whew — they really have you covered.

Precisely where you look for answers depends on the problem that you're having. Following is a two-step guide to help you find assistance fast:

- ✔ If you *can* sign on but don't know how to do something (for example, send an e-mail or read your Internet newsgroups), look in this book first, because that information is probably in here somewhere. If I left it out, you have my apologies (goodness knows, I tried). Now that I'm done groveling, go to the Member Services One Stop InfoShop (keyword **Help**) and look in the Step-by-Step Assistance section or the Members Helping Members discussion board.

- ✔ If you can't sign on at all, call the America Online Technical Guru Department at 800-827-3338. Wade through the menu prompts, cross your fingers, and get ready to work through your problem with one of America Online's helpful technical support folks. If you call at one of the system's peak times (like early in the evening), keep some reading material handy because you may be on hold for a while.

For general assistance and live online help, take a look at the Reach Out Zone, at keyword **Reach Out**. It covers online conduct, viruses, scams, account security, and more. When you have questions, it's definitely a great place to go.

Handling the Rude, the Crude, and the Socially Maladjusted

Few things spoil a perfectly wonderful online evening quite like an annoying oddball in your favorite chat room, a persistently pestering Instant Message, or obnoxious e-mail. When problems arise, you need to take action — and this section points you in the right direction.

The following list explains how to handle the various (and unfortunately *common*) annoyances of online life. If something comes up that's not on the list, check keywords **Help, Reach Out, Guidepager,** or **TOS** for suggestions.

- ✔ **Disrupting a chat room:** Click the Notify AOL button along the bottom of the chat window to report the problem and summon some help. Fill out the brief form, and then click Send This Report. Sometimes it's better to have that personal touch (particularly if the miscreant is *really* annoying). For those moments, click the Summon a Guide button instead of doing the form. In a minute or two, a People Connection Guide appears in your chat room and deals with your problem. (Be sure to give the guide a big *thank you!* when all the dust settles.)

- ✔ **Someone just asked for your password:** Use keyword **Guidepager** to open the I Need Help dialog box, then click the big Password button. Follow the instructions from there. If you're in a chat room, be sure to warn everyone else that someone is fishing for passwords! If you accidentally *did* give out your password, go immediately (and I mean *right-now-don't-wait-to-think*) to keyword **Password** and change your account password.

- ✔ **Annoying Instant Messages:** Don't close the Instant Message window. Instead, click and drag to highlight the offensive Instant Message text (include the sender's screen name as well) and choose Edit⇨Copy from the menu bar. Use keyword **Guidepager** to open the I Need Help dialog box, then click the Other button. In the Report A Violation window, click the IM Violations button. Follow the on-screen instructions carefully to complete your report.

- ✔ **Questionable e-mail messages:** To report e-mail problems, click the Forward button on the bothersome e-mail message, and send it to screen name TOSEmail. If someone you don't know sent you an e-mail message with an attached file, *do not download the file!* Instead, forward the message directly to screen name TOSFiles. (The odds are *very* good that the file will mess up your computer or steal your America Online password!)

For help reporting other problems, like raunchy screen names, vulgar member profiles, or tasteless America Online member Web sites, go to keyword **Guidepager** and click the Other button to bring up the Report a Violation window. Look through the options there for assistance.

But Wait — There's More!

This chapter doesn't even begin to tell you what's available out there in the wilds of America Online. Come to think of it, that's what the rest of the book does.

✔ To find out more about a specific channel, look up the area in *AOL Channels For Dummies,* the super-cool book-within-a-book waaaaaay in the back of this book.

✔ To follow the biddings of your own interests, look in Part IV.

✔ If you feel the need to follow other interests, the bathroom is down the hall.

When It's Time to Say Good-Bye

All good things must come to an end, and so it is with America Online. Signing off the system is quick and painless, though. Here's a quick list of good-bye (and good-bye–related) options in the America Online 4.0 software:

✔ To sign off the system, select Sign off⇨Sign Off from the main menu. This closes your online connection and leaves you sitting quietly in front of the main America Online software window.

✔ To switch into another screen name, select Sign off⇨Switch Screen Names from the main menu. In the Switch Screen Name dialog box (shown in Figure 2-3), double-click the name you want to use, then follow the on-screen instructions for typing your new password. In just a moment, America Online signs your other screen name on to the system — and you didn't even need to redial the phone! For more about creating new screen names, see Chapter 4.

✔ To shut down the America Online software, choose File⇨Quit on the Macintosh or File⇨Exit in Windows. You're done!

Figure 2-3:
Moving
from one
screen
name to
another is
easy with
the Switch
Screen
Name
feature.

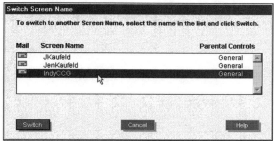

Chapter 3
Surviving the Software

U sing America Online is one thing. But before you can actually use it, you must tangle with (insert scary organ music here) *the user interface!*

No, it's not something else that you need to buy. The term *user interface* is just a fancy way of saying "the tools you use to interact with the software." It's like an automobile engineer looking at the layout of a dashboard and thinking, "Golly, that's a clever user interface." (Yes, despite their various specialties, most engineers respond to the simplest stimulus in predictably unintelligible ways — they're just that way.)

This chapter covers the three main tools in your user interface for working with America Online: the Toolbar menus, the menu bar, and the navigation bar. It doesn't matter whether you use these tools together or separately, but I do recommend using them; collectively, they make your life a little easier. (That's more than you can say for most software on the market.)

Revealing the Toolbar (And Its Way-Cool Menus)

It's always there right below the menu bar — watching you, daring you, enticing you with color buttons. But the Toolbar itself remains a mystery. What do those little pictures mean? Why are there so many of them? Why do some give you a menu, while others just do their thing? (By the way, is it time for lunch yet?)

Don't worry if the Toolbar looks a little, well, odd at first glance. That's because the America Online 4.0 software features a very different kind of toolbar (it's quite avant-garde) than most programs use today. The America Online programmers endowed the 4.0 Toolbar with a combination of old-fashioned click-the-button-to-do-something features and new-fangled click-the-button-and-watch-the-menu-appear functionality, bringing to life a sort of graphical menu filled with colorful possibilities. In a final burst of refined simplicity, those same developers added names below each Toolbar button, indicating what each entry does. (No more guessing!)

You also probably noticed the small down-pointing triangle next to some of the Toolbar buttons. The triangles aren't anything dramatic, but they *are* very helpful. A triangle next to a Toolbar button shows that when you click that particular button, a whole menu hops into view. Buttons *without* the little triangle are, well, just buttons — click 'em and they do whatever they say they will. Most of the buttons that contain drop-down menus also include a hot key (the little underlined letter in the name of the button). To use the hot key, just hold down the Alt key and press the underlined letter. With no further ado, that button's menu appears. Talk about speed!

To make particular functions easier to find, the America Online developers organized the Toolbar items into five groups according to what the various buttons do. Each group shares a background color to make it stand out from the others (and probably to enhance the group's self-confidence a bit — you know how insecure buttons get sometimes). Here's a quick overview of the various button groups, starting from the left side of the Toolbar (as shown in Figure 3-1):

✔ The first group of Toolbar buttons governs e-mail and printing. All the e-mail goodies live here, along with the vaguely dejected Print button, which doesn't understand why it's grouped with the e-mail tools. (That's okay, though, because I don't understand the reasoning either.)

✔ The second group covers a bunch of utility functions, including your Personal Filing Cabinet, chat logs, saved mail, and Favorite Places entries. As if it didn't already have enough on its plate, this group also includes My AOL, which is home to the wide range of settings that customize your America Online experience.

✔ The two buttons in the third group form your gateway to all the cool content available on both the America Online channels and the world-wide Internet. One click here and you can kiss a few hours farewell as you dive into the amazing bounty of online information.

✔ Next to the content area of the Toolbar sits a single, lonely button, banished into its own little group. This button opens the doors to chat rooms and discussion areas all over America Online. (Considering all the interaction that happens in the chat areas, it's kinda funny that the People button lives by itself on the Toolbar.)

> ✔ The last group of entries on the far right sit in the customizable area of the Toolbar. Although the America Online software plunks down some buttons here by default, this Toolbar section really belongs to you, the member. To find out more about laying claim to an area that's rightfully yours and cramming it full of icons for your favorites-of-favorites, flip to Chapter 22.

Figure 3-1:
The new
America
Online
Toolbar.

Now that you know how they're organized, it's time to dig into more details of the buttons themselves. The following sections rattle off the name and purpose of each Toolbar button. Some buttons (like Read and Print) perform one particular task, so their descriptions are pretty straightforward and short. Most of the Toolbar buttons, though, lead to drop-down menus, filled with options galore.

The description sections for these Toolbar buttons start with a quick overview of that button's overall goal in life, and then follow with details on all of the button's menu selections. By the way, the sections are in the same order as they appear on the Toolbar, so don't blame the programmers for the fact that (as my 5-year-old daughter would say) Muh-Muh-*Mail Center* comes before Fuh-Fuh-*Favorites*.

Read

This button is a direct throwback to the America Online 3.0 software. Clicking it displays the New Mail section of your e-mail box, just like clicking the YOU HAVE MAIL button on the AOL Today window or selecting Mail Center➪Read Mail elsewhere on the Toolbar. This button only works when you're signed on to America Online.

To read mail that you downloaded through an Automatic AOL session (what used to be known as a FlashSession), use the Mail Center➪Read Offline Mail menu choice.

Write

Like its neighbor Read, the Toolbar's Write button harks back to the days of America Online 3.0. It's a single-purpose button that opens up a blank e-mail window, ready and waiting for your next digital missive. This button does the same thing as pressing Ctrl+M or selecting Mail Center⇨Write Mail.

Write works both online and offline, although you can't actually send your new mail message until you sign on to America Online. For all the details about e-mail, check out Chapter 6.

Mail Center

This Toolbar button offers one-stop shopping for everything to do with e-mail, from reading new messages to managing your online address book. The bullets below explore the button menu's numerous choices:

- **Mail Center⇨Mail Center:** Pop into the Mail Center, home of all there is to know (outside of this book, of course) about doing the e-mail thing with America Online.

- **Mail Center⇨Read Mail:** Read your incoming mail; same as Ctrl+R or clicking the Read Toolbar button.

- **Mail Center⇨Write Mail:** Write a new e-mail message; same as Ctrl+M or clicking the Write Toolbar button.

- **Mail Center⇨Old Mail:** Revisit mail you already read at some point or another. Mail remains here for seven days or less, so don't be surprised if something you want to see is gone.

- **Mail Center⇨Sent Mail:** Take another look at the outbound missives (and other types of notes) you sent within the last 30 days or so.

- **Mail Center⇨Address Book:** Open up the built-in Address Book and manage your ever-growing collection of online friends.

- **Mail Center⇨Mail Preferences:** Display the Mail Preferences window and adjust the details of how America Online handles your incoming and outgoing e-mail.

- **Mail Center⇨Mail Controls:** Adjust the e-mail restrictions for your account.

- **Mail Center⇨Mail Extras:** Check out all the cool things you can do with e-mail, like sending electronic cards and such.

- **Mail Center⇨Set up Automatic AOL (FlashSessions):** Automate the process of sending and receiving e-mail with a few well-chosen settings here.

- **Mail Center⇨Run Automatic AOL (FlashSessions) Now:** Send your America Online software out to carry on an Automatic AOL session (what used to be called a FlashSession until the folks at America Online's Department of Renaming Things got hold of it).

- **Mail Center⇨Read Offline Mail:** This displays mail that you wrote offline (without signing on to America Online) and messages that arrived during an Automatic AOL session.

Print

Click this Toolbar button to make a paper copy of an online article, graphic, or Web page that tickles your fancy. The Print button sends the contents of the current window (whatever you happen to be looking at right then) over to your printer. It works the same as selecting File⇨Print from the main menu. Print works both online and offline.

My Files

Whether you want to browse or add something to your Personal Filing Cabinet, log a chat room, adjust your America Online-based Web page, or cruise through your offline newsgroup information, this button takes care of you. Here's a look at the menu items it offers:

- **My Files⇨Personal Filing Cabinet:** Opens the Personal Filing Cabinet window, your very own digital attic for storing your digital, um, stuff.

- **My Files⇨Save to Personal Filing Cabinet:** Takes the contents of the current window and saves a copy on your computer, carefully tucking it away in a file folder within your Personal Filing Cabinet.

- **My Files⇨Offline Mail:** Opens a window containing the Incoming/Saved Mail, Mail Waiting to Be Sent, and Mail You've Sent file folders.

- **My Files⇨Download Manager:** Fires up the Download Manager, your always-willing accomplice in the task of filling up your hard drive.

- **My Files⇨My Web Page:** Takes you to the Personal Publisher area, to create, edit, and marvel at a Web page of your very own.

- **My Files⇨Offline Newsgroups:** Opens a window with the Incoming/ Saved Postings, Postings Waiting to Be Sent, and Postings You've Sent file folders. Only works if you set up newsgroups to read offline (see keyword **Newsgroups** for more about that — it's kinda advanced).

- **My Files⇨Log Manager:** Calls forth the Chat and Session Log dialog box. For more about chat logging, see Chapter 7. Session log details are in Chapter 12.

My AOL

Thanks to the programmers' hard work, you have lots of ways to customize just about *anything* about both your America Online software and your online experience. There's the online profile, your screen names, access passwords, account parental controls — the list goes on and on. The My AOL Toolbar button serves up all these items in its drop-down menu, outlined in the following bullets:

- **My AOL⇨My AOL:** Opens the cheerful and friendly My AOL settings screen, which gently (sometimes irritatingly so) walks you through all the settings available to customize your America Online experience; same as keyword **My AOL.**

- **My AOL⇨Set Up AOL:** Guides you on a lush tour of the many things you can do to make your corner of the America Online world as cool as can be.

- **My AOL⇨Preferences:** Sends you straight into the America Online Preferences window, the nerve center of your America Online customization opportunities; same as keyword **Preferences.**

- **My AOL⇨My Member Profile:** Create, adjust, or simply blow away your online member profile. (See Chapter 21 for tips about building a *very* cool profile.)

- **My AOL⇨Screen Names:** Opens the screen name management window, where you can create, delete, recover, and generally annoy the screen names on your account (only works if you are signed on with the master screen name — see Chapter 4 for details).

- **My AOL⇨Passwords:** Select this to change your America Online password, which, of course, you should do every month or two, just for good measure (and to test your memory, too).

- **My AOL⇨Parental Controls:** Brings up the Parental Controls window, which explores and explains everything you ever wanted to know about the Parental Controls. Check Chapter 4 for the lowdown on the Parental Control options.

- **My AOL⇨Online Clock:** If your kitchen clock suddenly poops out, choose this option to see the current time.

- **My AOL⇨Buddy List:** Opens the Buddy List window, for viewing, editing, and otherwise working with your Buddy List.

- **My AOL⇨Personal Publisher:** Fires up the Personal Publisher, your online Web page creation assistant.

- **My AOL⇨Stock Portfolios:** Track your investment dollars in the portfolio system, delightfully delivered by this menu option.

✔ **My <u>A</u>OL⇨<u>R</u>eminder Service:** Never forget a date again (unless you forget to read your e-mail, that is!) by using the Reminder service on America Online.

✔ **My <u>A</u>OL⇨<u>N</u>ews Profiles:** Tell the News Profiles system what kind of news, sports, business, or feature information you like and watch in amazement as stories from the wire services start filling up your e-mail box.

Favorites

As you browse through America Online, it doesn't take long to develop a list of online areas that you enjoy. The more time you spend using the system, the more areas you find (trust me on this one — it's a truism of digital life), so at some point, you need a way to keep track of everything. Of course, a couple of helpful navigation tools wouldn't hurt, either.

That's where the Favorites button comes into play. Use the items on its menu to cruise through your Favorite Places and for easy navigation any-where inside and *outside* of America Online. Here are the details:

✔ **Fa<u>v</u>orites⇨<u>F</u>avorite Places:** Open up the Favorite Places window for a few quick trips around either America Online or the Internet.

✔ **Fa<u>v</u>orites⇨<u>A</u>dd Top Window to Favorite Places:** Add a Favorite Places item for the cool content area you happen to be in right now.

✔ **Fa<u>v</u>orites⇨<u>G</u>o To Keyword:** Bring up the Keyword dialog box for quick navigation around both America Online and the Internet.

✔ **Fa<u>v</u>orites⇨<u>M</u>y Shortcuts:** This corner of the menu system belongs to you — fill it with up to ten of your favorite keyword areas. Check out Chapter 22 to find out how.

Internet

Click here for easy access to the World Wide Web, the Internet newsgroups, and all the other goodies that the international network of networks has to offer. The Toolbar menu gives you specific menu choices for different Internet-based information tools, like the World Wide Web, the newsgroups, and FTP (the File Transfer Protocol), plus links to the system's main Internet site. Here's the quick list of what's waiting for you here:

✔ **<u>I</u>nternet⇨<u>I</u>nternet Connection:** Opens the AOL Internet Connection window, your doorway to the Web, the world, and beyond.

✔ **<u>I</u>nternet⇨<u>G</u>o to the Web:** Fires up America Online's built-in Web browser and loads the `http://www.aol.com` Web site.

- ✔ **Internet⇨AOL NetFind:** Starts the built-in Web browser, then directs your attention to the helpful and fact-filled NetFind search system.

- ✔ **Internet⇨Newsgroups:** Sends you straight to the Usenet Newsgroups window, where a sometimes-strange (but always interesting) world of information awaits.

- ✔ **Internet⇨Search Newsgroups:** Opens the America Online Web browser and drops you into NetFind's special newsgroup search system.

- ✔ **Internet⇨FTP (File Transfer):** Get a head start on filling your hard disk to overflowing with a trip to the Internet's voluminous file libraries, all available directly through America Online's FTP window.

To find out more about America Online's connection to the Internet and what you can do out there, check out Chapter 14.

Channels

There's a *lot* of great stuff on America Online — so much, in fact, that you need a map of some kind to ensure that you don't accidentally get lost. The America Online *channels* perform that task for you by organizing all the online content areas into a much smaller collection of subject-oriented channel windows.

When you're signed on to the system, the Channels Toolbar button offers a drop-down list of America Online content channels. To see a channel, click the Channels button, then click your particular choice from the options below to display a channel:

- ✔ **Channels⇨AOL Today:** Take a look at what's timely and cool all over the system.

- ✔ **Channels⇨News:** Keep up on the latest in news, sports, features, and weather here.

- ✔ **Channels⇨Sports:** Thrill the sports fanatic in you with scores, schedules, and more from events all over the world.

- ✔ **Channels⇨Influence:** Get the news *behind* the news in the worlds of business, entertainment, art, books, and more.

- ✔ **Channels⇨Travel:** Plan a trip, arrange a trip, or just dream about a trip in this warehouse of globe-trotting information.

- ✔ **Channels⇨International:** Click here to enjoy a peek at online life from other perspectives (and in other time zones).

- ✔ **Channels⇨Personal Finance:** Manage your money with the news, information, and discussion awaiting you here.

- ✔ **Channels⇨Workplace:** No matter what your job, this channel covers you with business news, research sources, lunch chats, and discussion areas for everything from accounting to vending (okay, technically it's from accounting to veterinarians, but that just doesn't ring).

- ✔ **Channels⇨Computing:** Turn here when you need the latest trouble-shooting tips, software notes, or file downloads.

- ✔ **Channels⇨Research & Learn:** When your mind reels with questions, turn to this Channel for answers. The resources are organized both by topic (history, science, and so on) and by type (dictionary, encyclope-dia, and others).

- ✔ **Channels⇨Entertainment:** News, reviews, discussion, and more about the wild world of movies, music, books, and TV await you here.

- ✔ **Channels⇨Games:** Relax here for a while (or a whole night if you aren't careful) with the online games, game shows, and game information.

- ✔ **Channels⇨Interests:** Explore your hobbies and interests in this digital potpourri of magazines, discussion areas, chats, and more.

- ✔ **Channels⇨Lifestyles:** When you long for a good discussion about the ebb and flow of life, try the message boards, information areas, and chat rooms in here.

- ✔ **Channels⇨Shopping:** Shop, shop, shop, shop. (What else can I say?)

- ✔ **Channels⇨Health:** Keep a sharp eye on health concerns for both you and your family with this channel's information areas.

- ✔ **Channels⇨Families:** Worried about your kids? Concerned about your parents? Wrestling with a relationship? This channel delivers informa-tion and discussion you can use to keep the home fires burning bright without torching the house in the process.

- ✔ **Channels⇨Kids Only:** Finally — an area that's just for kids! Explore, play, meet, and chat here with kids from all walks of life.

- ✔ **Channels⇨Local:** Drop in here to explore online links and information areas about your particular corner of the world.

For all the details about the channels, flip to *AOL Channels For Dummies* — the very cool book-within-a-book following The Part of Tens. It's the section with the gray-bordered pages — you can't miss it!

People

This friendly-looking Toolbar button links you to the wonderful world of the People Connection and AOL Live!, home to more great conversation than a convention of talk-show hosts. The People Toolbar button takes you directly to chats and presentations all over the system, plus it includes other people-related things like locating members online and searching the member database. By the way, this button only works when you are attached to America Online.

Here's the lowdown on what's available under People:

- ✔ **People▷People Connection:** Drops you into the People Connection main window, America Online's home for 24-hour conversation.

- ✔ **People▷Chat Now:** Dive straight into a randomly selected lobby of the People Connection.

- ✔ **People▷Find a Chat:** Seek out a particular chat room by searching on its name.

- ✔ **People▷Start Your Own Chat:** Click here to create a new member chat room.

- ✔ **People▷AOL Live:** Hear celebrities, scientists, singers, and (yes) even authors as they hold forth on all kinds of fascinating topics.

- ✔ **People▷Instant Message:** Drop an Instant Message onto a friend's desktop with this menu item; just like pressing Ctrl+I.

- ✔ **People▷View Buddy List:** Display your Buddy List and find out which of your friends are spending a few relaxing hours on the system.

- ✔ **People▷Send Message to Pager:** If someone you know subscribes to the right pager service, send them a full text-and-numbers page directly from AOL! (Check the information in here for details about what pagers and services the system covers.)

- ✔ **People▷Search AOL Member Directory:** Discover that special someone by sifting through the millions of profile entries in the America Online member directory.

- ✔ **People▷Locate AOL Member Online:** Find out whether a particular screen name is signed on to America Online right now. If the person is signed on, the system tells you whether that person is in a chat room, a private chat room, or just wandering around the service somewhere. This item is the same as pressing ⌘+L on the Macintosh or Ctrl+L in Windows.

- ✔ **People▷Get AOL Member Profile:** Learn more about the person you just bonked on the head with an Instant Message or bumped into in a chat room. Same as pressing ⌘+G on the Macintosh or Ctrl+G in Windows.

- ✔ **People▷Internet White Pages:** Search the Internet for people and businesses with this powerful online tool.

For all the best information on the ins, outs, ups, downs, and all-around-the-towns of the People Connection, flip to Chapter 7.

Quotes

Opens the America Online stock quoting system to track your market investments (and, depending on the day, send you into blissful ecstasy or hair-ripping wails of angst). This button does the same thing as keyword **Quotes.** This button only works while you're signed on to America Online.

Perks

Take a quick look at what's new, exciting, and generally fun on America Online by clicking the Perks button. If you don't feel like clicking the button, try using keyword **Exclusives** instead. Like the other buttons in this lonely end of the Toolbar, Perks only works while you're attached to America Online.

Weather

Check out the weather for wherever you are or wherever you're headed. The button brings up the America Online weather center, just as keyword **Weather** does. As with so many other options on the Toolbar, Weather doesn't work if you aren't signed on to the system.

Sailing around the Navigation Bar

Just below the Toolbar is a thin little group of controls known as the Navigation bar. Even though it's small, the Navigation bar plays a vital role in your time on America Online by acting as both your native guide and skillful scribe.

The bar includes only a few controls, but what they lack in number they make up for in power. Here's a quick breakdown, from left to right, of the cool things awaiting you there (for a complete multimedia experience, follow along in Figure 3-2 as you read these bullets out loud — but don't let anybody see you do it, okay?):

✔ **Browser buttons:** The five buttons on the left of the Navigation bar provide the basic features you need to steer through the Web. (The buttons work with America Online–based information areas, too, but it takes some practice before you get the hang of it.) The right- and left-pointing triangle buttons are Back and Forward. Back takes you to the Web site or information area you last saw, while Forward returns you to the page you were on when you clicked Back. The X-in-a-circle button is Stop, which whacks your America Online software over the head,

Figure 3-2:
The Navigation bar may be small, but it's jam-packed with the good stuff.

Keyword button

Browser buttons

Address Window

Find button

Go button

making it lose its concentration for a moment and stop whatever it's doing right then. The curly arrow is Reload, which tells your Web browser to reload the current page (it doesn't work with America Online areas). Finally, the little house button is Home. Click the button, tap your heels, and sing "Somewhere over the Rainbow" to display the America Online Web site (or whatever site you have configured as your Home page).

✔ **Keyword button:** Click to open the Keyword dialog box (same as pressing Ctrl+L).

✔ **Address window:** This handy box saves you time and energy by accepting both America Online keywords and World Wide Web addresses. This always-present box does the same thing as the Keyword dialog box (the one that comes up when you press Ctrl+K in Windows or ⌘+K on the Macintosh). Just type a keyword or Web address into the box, then either press Enter or click Go. America Online immediately whisks you away to the appointed online destination.

✔ **Go button:** After you have typed a keyword or Web address into the Address box or selected an item you already saw from the Address box's pull-down menu, click this button to actually go there.

✔ **Find button:** Opens a menu with options to find just about anything (short of your car keys, that is) and anyone on America Online and the Internet.

For a detailed romp through the options on the Find menu, check out Chapter 11.

Running through the Menus

Beauty, as the cyberbard says, is only button deep — and there's more to the America Online interface than mere pretty buttons. How about that menu bar up there? What's it do? Actually, quite a lot. I can't *imagine* trying to figure out America Online without the menu bar.

This section looks at the menu areas one by one, giving you a brief description of both the whole menu area and the individual items that populate it. If you're an old hand with America Online, remember that *most* of the menu items you know and love have moved to the new Toolbar, covered earlier in this chapter.

File

The File menu governs everything dealing with documents (such as magazine articles, bulletin board postings, and forum announcements), files, and other trivialities such as exiting the America Online access program (but who'd ever want to do that?). The most interesting File menu commands are:

- ✔ **File⇨New:** Starts the built-in text editor and gets ready to create a new plain-text document. I often keep a blank document window open when I'm browsing through the system and use it like a notepad for keywords, screen names, and anything else I want to remember. It works really well!

- ✔ **File⇨Open:** Opens a document (a plain-text file — not a WordPerfect or Microsoft Word .doc file), graphic, or sound file that you downloaded or saved to your computer's disk drive.

- ✔ **File⇨Open Picture Gallery:** Displays the Open Image Gallery window, which offers a quick way to view, change, and use the graphic files in any folder on your computer. Pick a folder, then click Open Gallery to view a nice thumbnail display of the graphic files there. Click a particular picture to see it full-size.

- ✔ **File⇨Save:** Saves the current document (article, discussion board posting, and so on) as a plain-text file on your computer's disk drive. If a graphic is on the window (a photo accompanying the news story, for example), the America Online software automatically offers to save a copy of it, too.

- ✔ **File⇨Save As:** Saves the current document under a new filename. If the current document is an article, discussion board posting, or something else in an online area, then this command behaves just like File⇨Save.

- ✔ **File⇨Save to Personal Filing Cabinet:** Saves the current document (article, discussion board entry, or other text item) into a folder within your America Online software's Personal Filing Cabinet. For the whole scoop on the Personal Filing Cabinet, yank open Chapter 6 and check out "Organizing Your E-Mail Mess(ages)," which explains this electronic organizational wonder.

- ✔ **File⇨Print Setup:** Opens the Printer Setup dialog box, where you can change the options for the default printer or temporarily select a different printer.

✔ **File➪Print:** Prints the current document. If you choose this option and don't have a printer connected to the computer, your computer may seem to lock up for a minute or two. Be patient — the machine should come back to life, probably complaining that your nonexistent printer is either turned off or out of paper. (Silly computer.)

✔ **File➪Stop Incoming Text:** Tells America Online to stop sending the current text document to your system. Works in e-mail, articles, discussion board postings, Internet newsgroup postings, and other text windows like those.

✔ **File➪Exit:** Closes the America Online access software.

Edit

Just about every Macintosh and Windows program has an Edit menu. This menu contains your basic text-editing tools; apart from that, the Edit menu is nothing to write home about. Your main choices in this menu are:

✔ **Edit➪Undo:** Undoes the last change you made. I use this command a lot when I'm writing e-mail messages. My fingers enjoy playing tricks on my brain, so they take charge of the mouse and randomly delete text. After my brain goes spastic for a moment, it brings the hand digits back under control and uses Undo to recover the nearly lost text.

✔ **Edit➪Cut:** Removes highlighted text from the screen and puts it on the Clipboard.

✔ **Edit➪Copy:** Copies the highlighted text from the screen to the Clipboard, leaving the original text in place.

✔ **Edit➪Paste:** Inserts text from the Clipboard into the current document.

✔ **Edit➪Select All:** Highlights all the text in the current document.

✔ **Edit➪Find in Top Window:** Searches the current window for a given piece of text. Open a Web page, an article in the News section, or a discussion board posting and give this menu choice a try.

✔ **Edit➪Spell Check:** Scours the e-mail message, newsgroup posting, bulletin board entry, or other text document you're creating.

✔ **Edit➪Dictionary:** Opens a search screen that scours the online Merriam-Webster dictionary (keyword **Collegiate**) for whatever *correctly* spelled word you enter.

✔ **Edit➪Thesaurus:** Brings up the online version of the Merriam-Webster Thesaurus (keyword **Thesaurus**) to help you track down synonyms for your favorite word.

✔ **Edit⇨Capture Picture:** If your computer includes a video camera (like the Connectix QuickCam, for instance), this item lets you shoot pictures on the fly, right from your America Online software. If you don't have a camera, then, well, it doesn't do a whole lot.

If none of these menu items sounds familiar to you, get a copy of *Windows 95 For Dummies,* 2nd Edition, or *Windows 3.11 For Dummies,* 3rd Edition, both by Andy Rathbone; or *Macs For Dummies,* 5th Edition, by David Pogue; all available from IDG Books Worldwide, Inc. You can thank me later.

Window

This menu is a whoa-I-have-too-many-windows-open navigational lifesaver. If you misplace an Instant Message window or lose track of your Web browser, head to the Window menu and find it right away. Best of all, tracking the errant window is merely a two-step process:

1. **Choose Window from the main menu.**

   The Window menu drops down, displaying some marvelously technical options near the top and a numbered list of your open windows at the bottom. On the Macintosh, the windows aren't numbered, but they're still listed at the bottom of the menu.

2. **Click the name of the window you want to display.**

   The until-so-recently-lost window immediately pops to the top of the heap. Is this a great country or what?

If you're completely fed up with all those open windows (or if it unexpectedly starts raining), close them all with a quick visit to the Window⇨Close All Except Front menu choice. Like it says, selecting this option makes all the open service windows go away, except for the window you're currently looking at. It also helpfully minimizes the Welcome window.

As for the other items in the Window menu, don't worry about them. They're for people who actually *care* about the difference between tiling and cascading windows — definitely folks with too much time on their hands.

Help

If you have trouble getting onto America Online, check the Help menu for assistance. This menu isn't particularly good at helping you with problems after you've signed on to the system, but it does have some specific ideas about getting there. Help menu options include:

- Help⇨**Offline Help:** Displays the Help system's Contents page.

- Help⇨**About America Online:** Shows the version information for your America Online software. (Sometimes the America Online technical support folks may ask you to open up this window — it's a techie thing.)

For help *after* you sign on to the system, check out these Help menu goodies:

- Help⇨**Member Services Online Help:** Sends you directly to the free Member Services window. Same as using keyword **Help.**

- Help⇨**Parental Controls:** Brings up the Parental Controls window to adjust the controls for your various screen names. You must sign on from the master screen name (the one you created when you signed up for America Online) to use these controls. Same as using keyword **Parental Controls.**

- Help⇨**Help with Keywords:** When keywords get you down, try this help menu for tips and tricks for making the little animals behave.

- Help⇨**Accounts and Billing:** View and change your account billing information with this helpful window. Same as using keyword **Billing.**

- Help⇨**AOL Access Phone Numbers:** Search the world (literally!) for local America Online access phone numbers. Also includes notes about international access and the surcharged 800 numbers (still cheaper than long distance). Same as using keyword **Access.**

Chapter 4

Making Yourself at Home

A new America Online account is like a college dorm room on the first day of the school year: completely bare, devoid of anything beyond the marvelously institutional look of gray linoleum tile surrounded by lime green concrete-block walls. But when its inhabitants move in, that room becomes unique; it becomes more like home.

Making yourself at home in America Online means setting things up just the way you want them. That's what this chapter is all about. The chapter covers topics such as screen names, the Member Profile, and setting your personal preferences. It also explores the parental controls, the online version of a good, old-fashioned grounding.

If you're completely new to America Online, start with the next section and continue through the chapter from there. If you're looking for details about specific preference settings, screen names, the online profile, or parental controls, flip ahead to the detailed sections later in this chapter. If you're hungry, go get something to eat (and order me a vanilla malt, would you?).

What's in a (Screen) Name?

When you join some online services, you mechanically receive a clever, memorable name from a computer that's quite proud of itself for calling you 71303,3713. After all, the computer has no problem remembering it — why should you?

America Online, though, was started *by* humans and designed *for* humans. As a direct result, *you* (a human) get to choose the name you use on America Online. You can be yourself if you want to: Anne, Paul, or Susan. Of course, you could also be a little more daring and become BlasterMan, SuperMom, or LoveBug. The choice is almost entirely up to you (but more about that later).

Every America Online account has space for five different screen names: one primary name, plus four others. The primary name is the one you choose when you sign on to the service for the very first time. This name is special — it's kind of like your permanent file in school. (The mysterious record always spoken of in dark, terrifying phrases such as, "You realize, of course, that this incident will go in your *permanent file.*") The primary name is *permanent* — you can't ever change it. The other four names, though, can come and go as you please.

Technically speaking, America Online doesn't place too many limits on screen names. Screen names need to be between three and ten characters long and must start with a letter. After the required first letter, you can use letters, numbers, and spaces to create your online identity.

Here's a quick overview of the technical rules covering America Online screen names:

- You can have five screen names in your account — one that's primary and four others.
- The primary name is permanent, and you can't ever change it; the other screen names can come and go as you wish.
- Choose your primary name carefully; it's going to be with you forever.
- Screen names are three to ten characters long, start with a letter, and contain any combination of letters, numbers, and spaces your imagination can dream up.

Now be nice!

A creative screen name is your tool for carving out a unique identity in the world of America Online. You're *supposed* to be creative — that's the whole point. However, a subtle line separates *creative* and *obnoxious*.

Here's a simple guideline for creating a good screen name: Make it as creative as you want, but if you blush at the idea of explaining it to your children, parents, spouse, or significant other, your screen name is probably beyond the bounds of good taste.

One final thought about choosing a screen name: Make it appropriate. A screen name for official business e-mail is quite different from one for a character in the Free Form Role Playing area. If you want to be BoogerDigr, that's your choice, but your new e-mail address (boogerdigr@aol.com) may look a little funny on a business card.

Dealing with Screen Names

Managing the screen names in your account isn't just a job — it's a creative adventure. The following sections go through everything you need to know to keep your screen names in order.

These instructions *don't* apply to your account's primary name. You can never change that. So there.

Creating a new screen name

I think the people who started America Online must have read Shakespeare. In the play *Romeo and Juliet,* Romeo can't decide on a screen name. Juliet tries to calm him with the observation, "What's in a name? That which we call a rose by any other name would smell as sweet." His confidence thus buoyed, he tries making a new screen name for himself in his father's account.

Kids — *don't* try this at home. Romeo and Juliet did, and look what happened to them. (If you don't know what happened to Romeo and Juliet, you can find out on the Internet. Just page ahead to the section, "The OCF Online Library (Gopher)," in Chapter 25, to read the classics.)

Making a new screen name isn't hard at all. Just follow these steps:

1. **Sign on to America Online under your account's primary name.**

   Only the primary name can create new screen names.

2. **After safely connecting to the service, choose My <u>A</u>OL⇨Scree<u>n</u> Names from the Toolbar (or use keyword Names).**

   The Create or Delete Screen Names dialog box opens. If you haven't read the screen names sidebar "Now be nice!" yet, this is an excellent time to do so.

3. **Double-click the Create a Screen Name option in the dialog box.**

   The Create a Screen Name dialog box appears on-screen.

   If America Online protests that Your account already has the maximum of 5 screen names, then you must delete an existing name before creating a new one. For more about that, see "Deleting an old screen name" later in this chapter.

4. **Type your new screen name in the text box and then click Create a Screen Name.**

   If the screen name you typed is available, America Online creates it and tells you. Otherwise, the system suggests that you choose something else, as shown in Figure 4-1.

Figure 4-1:
Drat — you
have to
choose
something
else.

5. **If America Online tells you that your desired screen name is not available, click OK to make the information dialog box leave you alone, and then go back to Step 3 and try again.**

   The big computers at America Online sometimes feel creative and attempt to help you make a valid screen name. The outcome is a lot like having your three-year-old "help" you make a cake from scratch. Figure 4-2 shows the computer's suggestion for poor Romeo. At this point, I think Juliet's earnest advice is by far the wisest: "O, be some other name!"

Figure 4-2:
Don't let the
computer
"help" you
make
screen
names.
Baaaad
idea.

> **Create an Alternate Screen Name**
>
> Each account may have up to five screen names at one time. A screen name may be from 3 to 10 characters (letters, numbers, and/or spaces). The first character in the screen name must be a letter, and will be capitalized automatically. The rest of the characters will appear just as you enter them.
>
> E.g. "Ski Racer", "JohnDoe123"
>
> The screen name you have chosen is already in use. You may have the following alternate name, or you may enter another name of your choice:
>
> Romeo39540
>
> [Create a Screen Name]   [Cancel]

After you and America Online agree on a screen name (which may take several tries), the Set Password dialog box appears, asking you to set a password for the new screen name.

6. **Type the password twice and then click Set Password.**

   You type the password first in the box on the left and then again in the box on the right. Once the password is accepted, the Parental Control dialog box appears.

Whatever you type for your password doesn't actually appear in the boxes. (Yes, it's *supposed* to happen that way.) Instead, the boxes display a little star for each letter. It's a security thing. Because it doesn't show you what you're typing, America Online makes you enter the password twice. If the two entries don't agree, America Online warns you, and then it lets you try again. By the way, America Online passwords must be between four and eight characters long.

See the sidebar "Psst — what's the password?" for some important thoughts and warnings about passwords.

7. **Select an access level for your new screen name by clicking the General, Teen, or Child radio button in the Parental Control dialog box. Click OK to finish making the screen name.**

After setting the access level, America Online congratulates you on a screen name well-created.

Although the Parental Controls dialog box offers some guidelines for picking the right access level, the actual decision is up to you as a parent. America Online doesn't require kids to have a particular access level — it's not their job. You, the parent, have the full and final say in the matter.

You can always change this setting later if you find that it's either too restrictive or too loose. To find out how, and to get more information about the other Parental Controls, see "Parental Controls: Taking Away the Online Car Keys" later in this chapter.

8. **To use the new screen name, sign off America Online by choosing <u>G</u>o To⇨Sign Off and clicking Yes in the dialog box that appears.**

The sign-on screen clears and the Goodbye dialog box bids you a fond farewell.

9. **Click the down arrow next to the Screen Name list box and choose your new screen name from the list.**

10. **Press Tab to move to the Password box and type the new password you created.**

11. **Click Sign On.**

Poof — it's the new you!

Deleting an old screen name

Even screen names reach the end of their usefulness. And when that time comes for the screen names in your account, delete them and go on about your business. Just follow these steps to delete a screen name:

1. **Sign on to America Online with your primary name.**

2. **After connecting, choose My A̲OL⇨Scree̲n Names from the Toolbar (or use the keyword** Names).

   The Create or Delete Screen Names dialog box appears.

3. **Double-click the Delete a Screen Name option in the dialog box.**

   The Delete a Screen Name dialog box pops up.

4. **When America Online displays the aptly named Are you sure? dialog box, take a deep breath, then click Continue.**

   The Delete a Screen Name dialog box appears, looking just the tiniest bit somber in its fateful duties.

5. **Click the screen name you want to delete, and then click Delete.**

   Be *darn sure* that you want to delete this screen name before clicking that button. Although you can theoretically restore deleted screen names, it's an inexact science. Translated into English, that means that restoring a deleted screen name is up to the impish whims of the America Online computers. Maybe they'll let you restore the name, but then again, maybe they won't. Who knows how these machines think?

6. **After doing the dirty deed, America Online issues the brief, generic obituary shown in Figure 4-3.**

You can't delete the primary name.

Figure 4-3:
He's history
(so to
speak).

Psst — what's the password?

Just like music and cooking, there's an art to making a good password. Here, in two sentences, is my accumulated knowledge on the subject.

The best passwords string together two common but unrelated words (such as GRAINFUN) or add a number to the end of a word (TRAIN577, for example). Your password should *not* be your name, birth date, spouse's name, dog's breed, shoe size, or anything else that someone can find out about you.

By the way, if you're setting up a screen name for a child or a password-phobic adult, you can configure the America Online software to automatically enter that screen name's password. Discover the details in the "Making Your Preferences Known" section, later in this chapter.

Changing a screen name

What if you have a screen name and decide you want to change it a little bit? Well, you're out of luck. To paraphrase the wisdom of Yoda, the Jedi master from *Star Wars,* no *change* is there, only *delete.*

Your only option is to delete the existing screen name entirely and create a new one from scratch. Sorry to break the news to you like this, but that's life in the big online services, I guess.

Restoring a deleted screen name

Having second thoughts about deleting your favorite screen name, eh? Well, who could blame you? (After all, that really *was* a great screen name!) Thank goodness America Online offers the Restore a Screen Name option. If all goes well, after a couple of quick clicks, your old screen name (complete with its online profile) will be back as good as new.

Notice that I said "if all goes well." As you may suspect, things *can* go wrong with the restoration process — like the simple problem of the America Online computers saying No, you can't have that name back. Precisely why they do this, I don't understand. It probably has something to do with zebra migrations, cat hairballs, and the number of lawyers worldwide telling the truth at any given moment in time.

Now that you've had fair warning that the process might not work, here are the steps to restoring a deleted screen name:

1. **Sign on to America Online with your primary screen name.**

2. **After you connect, select My A̲OL⇨Scree̲n Names from the Toolbar (or use keyword** Names**).**

   The Create or Delete Screen Names dialog box appears.

3. **Double-click the Restore a Screen Name option in the dialog box.**

   The Restore a Screen Name dialog box pops up.

4. **Look through the listed screen names and click the one you want to restore, then click Recover.**

   Assuming that the America Online computers feel cooperative, the system restores your screen name and gleefully pats you on the back to celebrate.

   If the name you want isn't on the list or if the America Online computers decide that you can't recover it, well, you have my condolences. See the earlier section on creating a new screen name, because that's your next stop.

Turn a Bit and Let Me See Your Profile

When you see people on the street or in the office, the first thing you notice about them is their physical appearance. Beyond that, they're a mystery until you meet them, talk with them, and invest some time getting to know them.

In the world of America Online, you determine how you "look" when you choose a screen name. In the chat areas you get to meet people and talk. But America Online has something else, too — something really neat that I personally wish existed in real life: the *Member Profile*.

A Member Profile is a collection of tidbits and trivia about the owner of a particular screen name. For example, my Member Profile appears in Figure 4-4. Despite what you may think, I'm an average, all-American game player, computer jockey, musician, husband, and father of two. And I write books (but you already knew that). If I'm chatting with someone online and the other person wants to know a little more about me, all he or she has to do is choose People⇨Get AOL Member Profile from the Toolbar (or press Ctrl+G in Windows or ⌘+G on a Mac), type my screen name into the Get a Member's Profile dialog box, and click OK. Presto! My Member Profile appears on-screen.

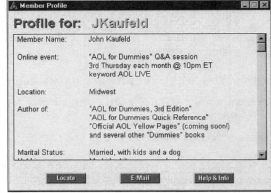

Figure 4-4:
Now you
know all
about me.

So where does all this profile information come from? From you — that's where (well, mine came from Cleveland, but that's another story). It's up to *you* to create a Member Profile for your screen name. If you don't create one, other members can't find out about your likes, interests, and hobbies. In short, you'll barely exist on Planet AOL.

✔ Please, oh please, fill out your Member Profile. Leaving it blank is like moving into a new neighborhood because you heard it had lots of fun people and then acting like a hermit.

✔ There's another reason to fill out your Member Profile: so that people who share your hobbies and interests can find you. A special command for searching all the Member Profiles is available. It's revealed in Chapter 11.

✔ Although this falls under the heading of *common sense,* I want to drive home a point. *Do not* put your phone number, address, or other truly personal information in your profile. On a scale of good to bad, doing that is reeeeaaaaaally bad. Parents, check your kids' profiles every now and then just to make sure that they didn't put anything (too) weird in there.

✔ If you use more than one screen name, you need to fill out a Member Profile for each one. Every screen name has its own Member Profile.

✔ Some parts of the service (such as the Space Fleet Online simulations, keyword **SFO**) rely on information in your Member Profile as part of the game. To find out more about these interactive online entertainments, refer to Chapter 13.

To create (or update) your Member Profile, follow these steps:

1. **Make sure that you signed on to America Online with the correct name.**

   Every screen name has its own Member Profile.

2. **Choose My <u>A</u>OL⇨My Member Profile from the Toolbar.**

   The Edit Your Online Profile dialog box appears. If you're *creating* a Member Profile, the dialog box is blank. If you're *changing* the Member Profile, your current information appears in the spaces (just like mine in Figure 4-5).

   My profile window looks like a mess because I customized it — added new categories and things like that. Although it's dangerously close to nerd territory, if having a profile that's truly your own sounds intriguing, check out Chapter 21 for the scoop.

3. **Fill out the Member Profile form. After you finish, click Update.**

   Don't worry if you type past the end of the boxes for Hobbies, Occupation, and Personal Quote. You have plenty of room to type — the text scrolls through the box until you can't enter any more text. At that point, the box is full. Use your directional arrow, Backspace, and Delete keys to correct any typing or editorial errors.

Figure 4-5:
Here's my
Member
Profile
"under con-
struction."
The strange
boxes and
such are
part of the
secrets to a
custom
profile (see
Chapter 21
for more
on that).

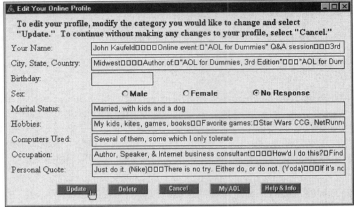

After you click the Update button, America Online replies with a little dialog box telling you that your profile is being updated. It takes a little while (usually ten minutes or so, but *much* longer if the system is busy) before your newly entered (or updated) Member Profile is available for the world.

Making Your Preferences Known

You know, America Online is starting to look kind of cozy now. Fine-tuning a few personal preferences should finish the job.

The *preferences* are your chance to tweak the America Online software so that it behaves exactly the way you want. (No, you can't have preference settings installed in your kids — I tried, but it didn't work.) These options cover every aspect of the software from sign-on to sign-off, plus a whole lot of stuff in between. The following sections explain all the preference settings and how to change them. The individual preference settings are listed in alphabetical order, despite the fact that they're scattered haphazardly throughout the Preferences dialog box itself.

Although America Online remembers your settings from session to session, you can change them anytime you want. For instance, if I'm working late and want to keep the noise level down, I hop into the Preferences window (explained in the next section), click General, and then turn off the Enable Event Sounds option. Later, when I'm ready for some noise, I turn it back on (and crank up the speakers, too). For more about the General preferences, keep on reading.

Finding the preferences

You can work on your preferences in two ways. If you're somewhat new to the preferences and want a lot of hand-holding while making your changes, use the My AOL dialog box. To get there, either select the quaintly redundant My A̲OL⇨M̲y AOL from the Toolbar or use keyword **My AOL**. If you're *really* new, check out the sidebar in this chapter called "Hitting the highlights in one easy step" for a cool tip about setting the important stuff all at once.

When you feel more comfortable with the preferences, dive straight into the Preferences window (seen in Figure 4-6) to make quick adjustments. To open the window, select My A̲OL⇨P̲references on the Toolbar.

Figure 4-6:
The
Preferences
dialog box,
in its
option-filled
glory.

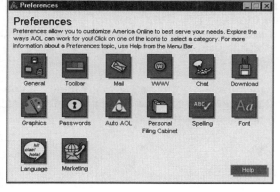

Automatic AOL

The America Online software includes a lot of tools to make your online life easier, but none of them holds a candle to Automatic AOL and Automatic AOL sessions (the new name for FlashSessions). Automatic AOL sends and receives e-mail and Internet newsgroup postings with incredible ease, saving you both time and effort (and money, if you use either the Light Usage or Limited pricing plans).

Automatic AOL helps you manage time by downloading all of your e-mail and Internet newsgroup postings onto your computer and then signing you off of America Online. From there, you can work off-line, reading and responding to your incoming messages and postings. All of your replies are saved on your local computer as well. When your replies (and whatever new messages you feel like writing) are ready to go, the Automatic AOL session signs you back onto the system and sends them all out in a nice big batch.

Clicking the Automatic AOL button on the Preferences window takes you directly to the Automatic AOL setup window. You end up with the same window by selecting Mail Center⇨Set up Automatic AOL.

For all the details about Automatic AOL sessions and the joys and mysteries of setting these preferences, flip to Chapter 6.

Chat

The interesting settings in the Chat Preferences dialog box are the notification options and the capability to alphabetize the chat group member list.

The notify options tell America Online to let you know when new people join the chat area or when current attendees leave. After hours and hours of personal testing, I liked arrival notification (Notify me when members arrive), but the departure setting (Notify me when members leave) got on my nerves. Try turning on one or both notifications for yourself and determine how the results strike you. You can turn on these settings by clicking in the appropriate check boxes.

The Alphabetize the member list option is *genuinely* handy. If you turn off this setting, the chat area member list is an absolute morass of mixed-up names. Run, don't walk, to turn on this setting.

Download

These settings govern some trivial details about the download process. I recommend turning *off* the Delete ZIP files after decompression option but leaving everything else turned on. An option is turned on if an X appears in the little check box. Click in the check box to toggle the setting on and off (or if you just like watching the little X appear and disappear).

Font

In the past, no matter where you typed in America Online — e-mail, Instant Messages, chat rooms, and so on — you had a choice of, to paraphrase Henry Ford, any font you wanted, as long as it was Arial. (Yes, the Macintosh-based America Online users are snickering, because they could change fonts two or three software revisions ago, but I digress.)

With America Online's 4.0 software, the curtain rises on a brave new world of fontographic choice. Dress up your e-mails, Instant Messages, and chat text with any font installed on your computer!

Hitting the highlights in one easy step

When you're new to America Online, working with the options is a bit overwhelming. You have so many things to choose from — where should you begin? What should you change first?

In an effort to reduce your stress and make the preference setting process ever so slightly simpler, America Online collected the most-used settings into the cool Set Up AOL Now dialog box. With a clear menu and descriptive instructions, this dialog box leads you through the most popular settings to change, including your Member Profile, screen names, passwords, and the General and Mail preferences. It also helps you build Buddy Lists (more about that in Chapter 7) and set the Parental Controls.

To open the Set Up AOL Now window, select My AOL⇨Set Up AOL from the Toolbar. The option is also available behind the Set Up AOL Now button on the My AOL window (on the Toolbar, select My AOL⇨My AOL to get there).

The Font preference setting lets you choose the default typeface (Arial, Times New Roman, and so on), size, style (bold, italic, or underlined), and color for most everything you type. Both e-mail and chat windows include their own font controls, so if you decide on something a little different, it's easy to change your settings on the fly.

General

The next stop on the preferences tour is the General area, shown in Figure 4-7. Although this area is nothing to jump up and down about, some settings in here are worth mentioning.

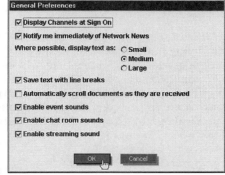

Figure 4-7:
The General
Preferences
dialog box.

The first useful option is right there at the top, Display Channels at Sign On. If you're distressed that the Channels window pops up automatically every time you sign on, here's the remedy: Turn off this setting.

The next useful option is the text display size setting. On my computer, I changed this setting to Small, because the default text size came out pretty large on my screen. Conversely, if you're having trouble reading articles or chat area text, try setting it to Large. To change the setting, click the radio button next to the text size you want.

My other favorite settings govern event sounds. If you have a sound card in your computer, I suggest turning on the Enable event sounds, Enable chat room sounds, and Enable streaming sound settings. Click the check box next to each item to do so. Why do it? Well, it's more fun that way — what better reason do you need?

Graphics

The America Online 4.0 software offers a very important option in the Graphics Viewing preference setting.

Almost every time you wander into a new area within America Online, the system sends some art files down to your computer. They're the pretty buttons, background graphics, and so on that make America Online look so cool. All that downloaded art is hanging out on your hard drive, though, taking up space. If you want to regain a little of that space, try adjusting the lengthily named preference setting called Maximum disk space to use for online art.

This setting gives you the ability to limit the size of your art database. The default is 30MB (or megabytes, short for million characters), which is fine when you have plenty of hard drive space available. If your disk drive feels smaller every day, try nudging the maximum size down to 15MB or 20MB.

Only adjust the size of the art database if you really, *really* need the extra space. It doesn't take America Online much time at all to outgrow that little space. So what happens when the art database grows bigger than the maximum size you set? An electronic version of the old-fashioned spring cleaning, that's what. The America Online software throws out art that you haven't used for a while to make room for the new stuff. It happens automatically, although it makes you wait a minute or two while it throws things out. (I think it wants you there for moral support.)

For an idea of how big your art database currently is, use File Manager (Windows 3.*x*) or Explorer (Windows 95) to check the size of a file called MAIN.IDX in the IDB subdirectory of the America Online software. That file contains the art database, plus a few other digital odds and ends.

Language

Unless you travel the world extensively and enjoy a fluency in several languages (or if you have a wicked practical joke streak in you), there's no need to change the Language preference setting. On the other hand, if you suddenly get an urge to add support for another language to your America Online software, this is the place to do it.

Mail

E-mail is one of the most useful features of America Online. Keeping track of your e-mail, though, is one of the most hair-reducing features. Thankfully, help is waiting in the Mail Preferences dialog box, shown in Figure 4-8.

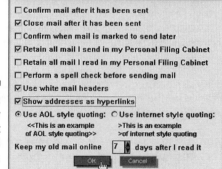

Figure 4-8: Here's how I like to set the mail preferences.

First, if you hate the Your mail has been sent box that appears automatically every time you send an e-mail message, I have some good news: You can turn it off! To make that annoying little window go away, click the check box next to Confirm mail after it has been sent. Presto! No more mail confirmation windows!

On the other side of the scale, an option that you simply *must* turn on is Retain all mail I send in my Personal Filing Cabinet. This one is a real winner, particularly if you're using America Online with your business. Turn this puppy on, and the access software automatically puts a copy of all outgoing e-mails into the Mail You've Sent folder (which itself is available by selecting Mail Center⇨Read Offline Mail⇨Copies of Mail You've Sent).

Imagine: No more worrying about whether you replied to someone's message or wondering what you said. Life just doesn't get much better than that, now does it?

The mate to this setting, Retain all mail I read in my Personal Filing Cabinet, isn't quite as excellent as its counterpart but still deserves consideration. Like its sibling, this option is *great* for the times that you need to account for all your correspondences.

One word of caution, though: All this filing uses space on your computer's hard disk, so regularly go through the messages and delete the useless ones. For more about the Personal Filing Cabinet, see Chapter 6.

Marketing Preferences

I'm not particularly big on junk mail, pop-up sales windows, and "I'm taking a moment of your time right now" telephone calls. Frankly, I don't like them. My feelings are born from a combination of personal privacy issues, environmentalism, and the desire to enjoy dinner without the phone ringing off the hook.

If you feel the same way, here's your chance to strike back. By the same token, if you *like* junk mail, telemarketing phone calls, and their various ilk, here's an opportunity to get more of exactly the kind you want.

The Marketing Preferences window isn't like the other preference settings. Instead of offering a few distinct options, it brings up a smorgasbord of preference settings that cover e-mail, postal mail, online pop-ups, telephone solicitations, and more. Invest a few minutes in browsing the various preference settings — it can only make your life better.

If you're a direct mail hermit like me, you'll be interested in two documents in the Marketing Preferences dialog box. These documents contain information about the Direct Marketing Association's Telephone and Mail services. Briefly, the documents explain how to obliterate all traces of your earthly existence (at least as far as the direct mail merchants are concerned). I highly recommend reading these documents and doing what they say.

Passwords

Clicking the Passwords button opens a dialog box for storing your screen name passwords. Storing your password offers two distinct (and completely separate) benefits. First, you can tell the America Online software to automatically enter your password every time you sign on to the system. That makes signing on a quicker process because your computer never mistypes your password.

The second benefit is a new feature of the America Online 4.0 software. By storing your password, you can *password protect* your Personal Filing Cabinet. This keeps prying eyes (like parents, roommates, and siblings) out of your stored e-mail and newsgroup messages.

As far as I'm concerned, the jury is still out on this feature. This feature is nice if you're making a screen name for someone who doesn't really care about passwords anyway and would probably write the password on a note taped to the monitor. The flip side, though, is that after you store the password, *anyone* with access to that computer can sign on to America Online with that screen name. *Anyone.*

On the other hand, password protecting the Personal Filing Cabinet might be a real boon in some cases — particularly where you share a single computer among several people.

With those thoughts in mind, here's my suggestion: I don't recommend using this feature to automate the sign-on process because it's a big-time security risk. However, I can think of many cases where the automatic sign-on or the protected Personal Filing Cabinet is either handy or helpful. With that in mind, here's how to store a password and choose how it's used:

1. **From the Preferences dialog box, click Passwords.**

2. **Click the Password box for the particular screen name you want.**

3. **Type the password.**

   As before, the stars appear in place of the actual password. If you mistype something, backspace over the whole entry and start again.

4. **To use the password during sign-on, click the Sign-On check box. To use it to protect your Personal Filing Cabinet's contents, click the Personal Filing Cabinet check box.**

   When you have everything checked (and perhaps double-checked), go on with the next step.

5. **Repeat the process for any other passwords you want to store. Click OK after you're done.**

   If you change a password in the future, you must return here and change it as well.

Personal Filing Cabinet

The Personal Filing Cabinet, that collector of Automatic AOL mail, Favorite Places, and all kinds of other stuff, is a really useful tool. The options in the Personal Filing Cabinet Preferences dialog box make it even better.

The two warning preferences instruct the America Online software to let you know when space is dwindling in the Personal Filing Cabinet and when the Cabinet is trying to single-handedly take over your hard drive. There's no need to change these options — the default settings should be fine.

For safety's sake, I recommend leaving both of the Confirm check boxes turned on. However, if you get highly annoyed with all the "Are you sure?" messages while cleaning out the Personal Filing Cabinet, feel free to turn them off here.

Spelling

Now that the America Online 4.0 software knows its spelling words and grammar rules, it's only logical that a few new preferences would arrive on the scene as well. Lo and behold, they have, in the form of the Spelling preference settings.

As with several of the other preference settings in here, there's nothing that you particularly need to adjust — the default settings are fine for almost everyone. In fact, the only reason you may want to change some of the settings is if your computer isn't very fast and performs spell-checks with all the speed of a drugged snail. In that case, try turning off some of the options under the Advanced button, because they include many grammatical checks that demand processing power.

Toolbar

The Toolbar looks bolder, brighter, and better than ever in the America Online 4.0 software. Sporting a whole new look (and those funky click-to-show-the-menu buttons), the Toolbar still harbors a few tricks up its sleeve. Those tricks live here, in the Toolbar preferences dialog box.

From the top, the Appearance option lets you pick between the normal Toolbar, complete with text and button pictures, and a "lite" Toolbar, which contains only the button text. By turning off the pictures, you regain some screen real estate, which means a lot if your computer has a small monitor.

The Location setting flips the Toolbar (and the Navigation bar, as well) back and forth between the top and bottom of the window. Where you leave it is entirely up to your personal preference, although I must say that it looks really funny along the bottom of the screen.

Navigation and History Trail, the last two settings on the window, probably won't tweak your interest very much — although the History Trail item might, if you share your computer with someone else. Turning on the Clear History Trail setting erases all the entries in the drop-down location box on the Navigation bar (try saying that three times fast). Basically, it keeps someone else from finding out where you went while you were online. Turn it on and watch your siblings, roommates, or coworkers whine.

WWW (World Wide Web)

Although most of the stuff in here borders on techno-weenie, there's one thing that I want to mention: the Empty Folder button.

Although not really a preference setting, Empty Folder is a button you should hit every now and then if you enjoy surfing the Web. Every time you view a Web page, the America Online Web browser keeps a local copy of what you see in a *cache,* a temporary storage area for use by the program, within a particular folder on your computer. This isn't a nefarious plot to use up your hard disk space — all the popular Web browsers do it. On the plus side, the cache makes your Web browser respond faster when you're bouncing back and forth between a couple of Web pages. The downside, though, is that the cache fills up after a while. Unfortunately, a full cache slows down your Web browser a bit (which is precisely the kind of help that the World Wide *Wait* doesn't exactly need).

Luckily, emptying the cache is easy. Just follow these steps:

1. **Click the WWW properties button in the Properties window.**

   The AOL Internet Properties dialog box appears.

2. **Click the Advanced tab at the top of the window.**

   All the settings on the window change (but, thankfully, the room doesn't start spinning like it did that time a few years back).

3. **Click the Settings button.**

   A slightly smaller Settings dialog box hops onto the screen, looking much like Figure 4-9.

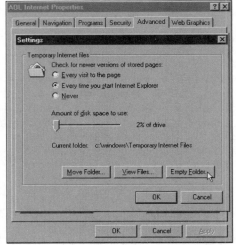

Figure 4-9:
A single
click gets
rid of those
pesky
temporary
Internet
files.

4. **Click Empty Folder. When the software worries that it didn't hear you correctly, reassure it that you really _do_ want to delete all the temporary Internet files by clicking Yes.**

   At this point, your hard drive probably sounds like it's going crazy. Believe it or not, that's a good sign. After a few moments (perhaps a minute or more, depending on how long ago you last emptied the cache and how large your hard drive is), everything quiets down.

5. **Keep clicking OK buttons until you find yourself back at the America Online Preferences window.**

Parental Controls: Taking Away the Online Car Keys

Like any major city or tourist destination, there's a lot to see and do on America Online. Unfortunately, the similarities don't end there. Every big city has a _don't go there_ side and a small population of less-than-moral people. If I said that America Online was immune to this, I'd be a fool (and no editorial comments from the people in the audience who know me personally).

Whether you like it or not, people and things that we need to shield our kids from are out there in the online world. That's what the Parental Controls (My AOL⇨Parental Controls, or keyword **Parental Controls**) are all about. They enable you to exercise some control over what your kids can and can't do on America Online.

Before going into the details, here are a few thoughts to set the stage:

- ✔ Different people have different views about what kids should and shouldn't see. Please understand that I'm not trying to get on a moral high horse and tell you what's right and wrong for your kids. I'm not passing judgments about what's available out there, but merely explaining the tools available and giving some very general advice for parents whose kids know the Internet better than they do.

- ✔ To make the Parental Controls work, only you, the parent, should know the password to the master screen name (that's the screen name you created when you first signed up for America Online). Create another screen name specifically for your child to use. Remember that each America Online account can have up to five screen names — one master name plus four others.

- ✔ Are you curious why I'm making such a big cloak-and-dagger deal out of who's using which screen name? Here's the reason: The master screen name is special. *Only* the master screen name can set the Parental Controls and create new screen names in your account. If your child uses the master screen name for online access, then he or she can simply turn off whatever parental controls you turn on. Whoops! Instead, create a screen name especially for her, place the controls on it, and then keep the master screen name for yourself.

The main Parental Controls screen appears. These settings offer the simplest degree of control. Choose from the three options (Child Access, Teen Access, and General Access) to set default controls governing what that screen name can access both within America Online and outside on the Internet (when accessing the Internet with America Online's built-in Web browser and other Internet tools).

How do you choose the right controls for your kid? Well, it depends. Consider the age and maturity of your child. Granted, our kids are all above average in intelligence and everything else, but for this one moment try to be especially objective. How responsible is your child? And how naive? How trustworthy? Yes, they're tough questions, but this decision is a very important one.

- ✔ For children 12 or younger, I recommend using the Child Access option. That lets them get into Kids Only, the area within America Online that's specifically designed for that age group, plus kid-friendly Web and Internet sites. You can feel pretty comfortable that your little one won't run across anything incredibly weird.

- ✔ The teen years are more challenging. (Stating the obvious is one of my strengths.) If you use any controls at all, start with the Teen Access setting. If your online child finds that too restrictive, try applying some specific custom control options (discussed below). If you use the

Custom Controls, I recommend blocking Member Rooms in the Chat control, FTP in the Download control, and any Internet newsgroup containing the magic word *sex* in the Newsgroup control. That combination maximizes the widely acceptable stuff while blocking off the Internet's most colorful content.

✔ If you feel comfortable giving your kids free run of the world, that's cool. Nothing says you *must* use the controls — they're just available tools.

You can change the settings at any time, so don't worry about ruining your children forever by making the wrong choice. Pick the settings, talk to your children, and see how everything works. If you need to make adjustments, do so. Most of all, work with your children and let them know that you're interested in their online world. That makes a bigger impact than any control ever can.

Custom Controls

Sometimes (well, *frequently* in my case) the one-size-fits-all solutions just don't fit. If your child needs more access here and less access there than the Child Access or Teen Access controls allow, then turn your attention to the Custom Controls option at the bottom of the main Parental Controls window. This button leads you to the do-it-yourself side of the Parental Controls, where you, the parent, take complete control over what your kids can and can't do online.

Clicking the Custom Controls button brings up the Custom Controls window shown in Figure 4-10. The six options on the window govern the most important interactive parts of America Online. Each option is described in its own section later in the chapter.

Figure 4-10:
The Custom Controls give you incredible flexibility to tailor your child's online access.

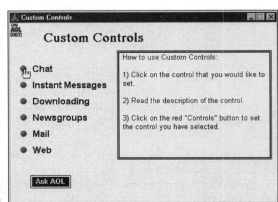

None of these controls help protect a child who has access to the master screen name in your America Online account. To take advantage of the Parental Controls, you *must* create a separate screen name for your child.

Chat controls

The People Connection chat rooms are a big attraction on America Online. On your monthly bill, though, the word *popular* often translates into *expensive* because losing track of time while chatting the night away is so easy.

To keep your kids (or even yourself) out of the chat rooms, follow these instructions:

1. **Sign on with the master screen name and then choose My AOL⇨Parental Controls.**

   The Parental Controls window hops energetically onto the screen.

2. **Click Custom Controls and then click Chat. Finally, click Chat Controls at the bottom of the window.**

   The chat controls window shown in Figure 4-11 appears.

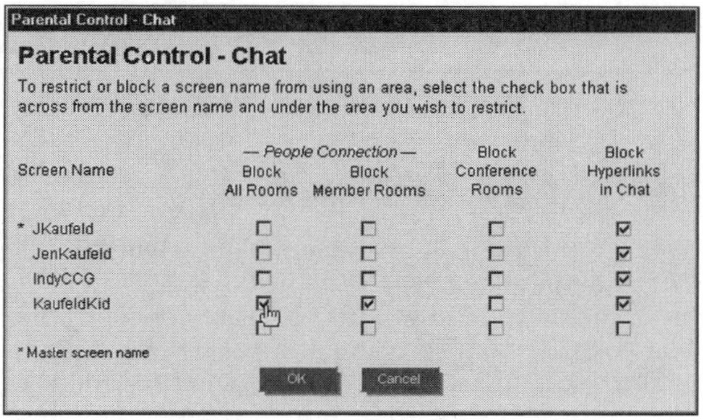

Figure 4-11: Keep younger kids out of the chat rooms with a couple of well-chosen controls.

Parental Control - Chat

To restrict or block a screen name from using an area, select the check box that is across from the screen name and under the area you wish to restrict.

| Screen Name | — People Connection — | | Block Conference Rooms | Block Hyperlinks in Chat |
	Block All Rooms	Block Member Rooms		
* JKaufeld	☐	☐	☐	☑
JenKaufeld	☐	☐	☐	☑
IndyCCG	☐	☐	☐	☑
KaufeldKid	☑	☑	☐	☑
	☐	☐	☐	☐

* Master screen name

[OK] [Cancel]

3. **Click the check boxes next to your child's screen name for each chat control you want to turn on.**

   Table 4-1 explains each of the four options, including a *Severity* option that offers an opinion on how draconian that particular setting is.

4. **When you're done, click OK.**

   America Online responds with a brief note that your changes are saved.

5. **Click OK and then close all the Parental Control windows.**

   Another one's done!

Turning off the chat options is as easy as turning them on. Just repeat the preceding steps and click each check box again, removing the mark for it.

Table 4-1	Parental Control Options	
Control	**Severity**	**Description**
Block All Rooms	5	Completely blocks access to the People Connection interactive chat areas.
Block Member Rooms	2	Prevents access to private chat areas, but allows the use of the regular People Connection areas.
Block Conference Rooms	10	Blocks *all* interactive rooms throughout America Online, including the discussion rooms in Learning and Reference (see Chapter 7 for more). Use this *only* as a last resort!
Block Hyperlinks in Chat	2	Prevents the screen name from clicking on a hyperlink that someone types into a chat room.

Instant Message controls

Instant Messages are the immediate communication windows that appear out of nowhere (sometimes scaring the living daylights out of you, depending on the hour of the day and how hard you were concentrating at that moment) and let you carry on a private, one-on-one chat with someone else on America Online or on the Internet (through America Online's Instant Messenger software — see keyword **Instant Messenger** to find out the scoop about that).

With the advent of the America Online 4.0 software, the Instant Message system also displays images from a computer-attached video camera and even handles voice calls just like a telephone. These new features are the ones that really concern me. On the good side, though, these features are *blocked* by default — you have to manually turn them on through the Instant Message controls if you want the kids to have access to them.

Depending on the age and maturity of your child, you may or may not want them to use Instant Messages at all, let alone the new Instant Images and Instant Message Phone features. (Personally, I turned the whole Instant Message thing *off* on my kid's accounts, but my kids are also in the under-ten bracket.) To limit your child's access to the Instant Message system, follow these steps:

1. **Sign on to America Online with your master screen name and select My AOL⇨Parental Controls.**

   The Parental Controls window appears, eager to help.

2. **Click the Fine-tune with Custom Controls button, then click Instant Messages. When the IM Controls button appears at the bottom of the window, click it.**

   The Instant Messages control window hops onto the screen, just like Figure 4-12.

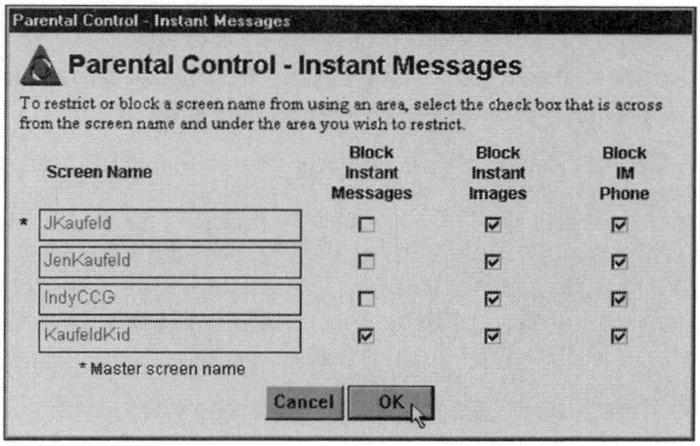

Figure 4-12:
Keep
Instant
Messages
off your
child's
screen with
the Block
Instant
Messages
option.

3. **Click the check boxes next to your child's screen name for each of the Instant Message controls you wish to set.**

   Block Instant Messages prevents your child from sending and receiving Instant Messages. Block Instant Images and Block IM Phone cover the new Instant Message features mentioned earlier.

4. **When you're satisfied with the control settings, click OK to save them. Close the Custom Controls window (click the X button in the upper right corner of the window) when you're done.**

   The Instant Message controls are in place (and you can breathe a little easier).

Download controls

Of all the Parental Controls, these are probably the least important. Granted, there are some things in the world that I don't want my kids downloading from America Online or the Internet, but that's hardly my biggest concern about online life.

If it's a bigger worry in your life than in mine, follow these steps to limit your child's access to downloadable programs and such:

1. **Sign on to America Online with your master screen name and then choose My AOL⇨Parental Controls.**

   If everything works just right, the Parental Controls window appears.

2. **Click the Custom Controls button and then click Downloading. When the Download Controls button appears at the bottom of the window, click it.**

   The vaguely impressive Downloading control dialog box leaps into view.

3. **To turn on the download controls, click the check boxes next to your child's screen name. When you're done, click OK.**

   An energetic dialog box pops up, letting you know that your changes are saved.

   I wouldn't bother with Block AOL Software Downloads, but turning on the Block FTP Downloads option is a good idea. FTP (file transfer protocol) copies files through the Internet, and there's no telling what your inquisitive kiddo might find out there.

4. **Click OK and then close the Parental Control windows.**

   Download controls are now in place!

As you may have guessed by now, to undo the download controls you simply repeat the steps to create them. The big difference is that this time you click the check boxes *off* instead of turning them on.

Newsgroup controls

Of all the custom Parental Controls, this one is the most valuable. The Internet newsgroups are an incredible resource, filled with discussions on almost every topic imaginable. However, not all the conversations out there are designed for eyes under 18.

To block out the most (I'm being kind here) exotic material that the newsgroups offer, follow these steps:

1. **Sign on with the master screen name and then select My AOL⇨Parental Controls.**

   The Parental Controls window appears.

2. **Click the Custom Controls button in the lower right corner of the window, then click Newsgroups.**

   A window listing your screen names pops into view.

3. **Click the radio button next to your child's screen name and then click Edit.**

   The screen name list is replaced with the Blocking Criteria window.

4. **For most kids, I recommend setting the controls just like Figure 4-13. When you're finished, click OK.**

   The example setting blocks your child from any Internet newsgroup with, shall we say, stimulating words in the name. This one setting quickly blocks off most of the content that many parents are concerned about.

   This setting does *nothing* to keep your kids out of the more explicit areas of the World Wide Web. For that, see the Web controls section later in this chapter.

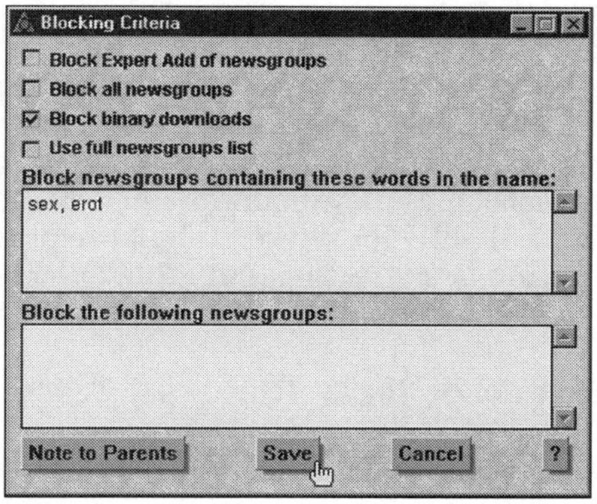

Figure 4-13: These two little words keep your kids out of so much trouble that it's amazing.

5. **Close all the various open windows and continue with your regularly scheduled day.**

   Your child is now safe from most of the newsgroups.

To undo these restrictions, work back through the steps above. In Step 4, delete the entries in the Block newsgroups text area. Remember to click OK when you're done!

Mail controls

E-mail is a powerful communications tool, but it can also be powerfully annoying. With the new America Online Mail controls, though, you can take command of your e-mail box and, more importantly, protect your kids from mail they shouldn't get.

The Mail controls fall into two distinct groups: General limitations on all mail, and specific restrictions based on a set of e-mail addresses. Here's a look at your options by group:

- ✔ **General limitation controls:** These options establish simple, wide-ranging limits on all mail coming to a particular screen name. The three options are Allow all mail (anyone on AOL or the Internet can send e-mail to this screen name), Allow mail from AOL Members only (blocking all Internet-based e-mail), and Block all mail (so much for the e-mail thing — it was nice while it lasted).

- ✔ **Specific address-based controls:** Unlike the blanket controls, the address-based controls filter mail based on a list of e-mail addresses that you, the parent, enter into the system. The options on this side of the fence are Allow mail from AOL Members and addresses listed (any AOL member can write to the screen name, but only approved Internet addresses can do so), Allow mail from the addresses listed only (you can receive mail from any AOL or Internet e-mail address, provided you put the address into the list on the dialog box), and Block mail from the addresses listed (allowing all mail except items from the listed addresses).

These six controls have a lot of flexibility — hopefully enough for everyone. My favorites on the list are Allow mail from AOL Members only (great for easily blocking Internet junk mail) and Allow mail from AOL Members and addresses listed (because it's a slightly looser version of the previous option). The Block All mail option is interesting, but I think it's more powerful to define who *is* acceptable instead of blocking those that aren't.

To put up some e-mail controls, follow these steps:

1. **Sign on with the master screen name, then select My A̲OL⇨Parental C̲ontrols.**

   The Parental Controls window appears.

2. **Click the Custom Controls button at the bottom of the window, then click the Mail Controls button.**

   A window listing your screen names hops into action.

3. **Click the radio button next to your child's screen name, then click Edit.**

   The screen name list vanishes, while the Mail Controls window appears.

4. **Click the radio button for the proper level of Mail control. If necessary, enter any America Online screen names or Internet e-mail addresses in the Type mail address here box, then click Add.**

   Because these are radio buttons, you can only choose *one* Mail control setting at a time (even if you really want a combination of two).

5. **When you're done, click OK, then close the Custom Controls window.**

   Your mail controls are now in place and running.

Web controls

Few things in the world change faster than the World Wide Web (although the flux-filled policy statements of many career politicians do come close). While the Web is filled with thousands of clever and informative sites, it's also the home of many pages best left unseen by little eyes. To keep curious youngsters pointed toward the truly educational things instead of the woo-hoo-hubba-hubba-educational ones, try applying some Web controls.

These controls limit the sites that America Online's built-in Web browser can connect to. The decisions of which sites are in and which are out come from a company called Microsystems, Inc., which rates Web sites by the type of content they contain. For the Web controls, sites fall into the Kid Approved listing (for ages 6 to 12) or the Teen Approved list (for, well, teens). The system's other two options are all-or-nothing plays — either grant all access to the Web or give none at all.

For younger kids, stick with the Kid Approved site listing. Once your child blossoms into the terrible teens, give him or her either Teen or Full access (provided he or she can handle the responsibility of it). Because so much of America Online's content is Web-based, I can't recommend completely shutting down Web access for any account.

To apply the Web controls, follow these steps:

1. **Sign on to America Online with the one and only master screen name, then choose My AOL⇨Parental Controls.**

   The Parental Controls window soundlessly enters the room.

2. **Click the Custom Controls button and then click Web at the bottom of the list. When the Download Controls button appears at the bottom of the window, click it.**

   The simple, yet powerful Web controls dialog box appears.

3. **Find the screen name you want to impose Web controls on, then click the radio button under the appropriate control.**

   Because they're radio buttons, you can only pick one setting per screen name.

4. **When you're ready, click OK.**

   The Web controls are ready to serve and protect.

Part II
The Basics of
Online Life

The 5th Wave   By Rich Tennant

In this part . . .

The only thing standing between you and a brain-numbing quantity of mundane details is the America Online access software. You and this program are a team — you'll probably be amazed at what you can accomplish together.

This part shows you how to put the software into action by exploring the fine art of navigating through America Online, sending e-mail to the world at large, enjoying an online chat, and using the Download Manager to grab programs from the system's online libraries. It even includes a section filled with places to find help, should you ever need more than you have right here in your hand. In short, Part II covers the basic stuff you need to get your citizenship papers in the Great Online World.

And best of all, I've made *sure* that it isn't boring at all. Really.

Chapter 5

Navigating the System and Marking Your Favorite Destinations

In This Chapter

▶ Looking through the digital windows

▶ Staying organized with Favorite Places

*Y*ou don't need to travel much before you start collecting a mental list of places that you enjoyed, locales that you disliked, and restaurants that you never quite found, despite splendid directions from the hotel concierge. It's human nature — we know what we like and, when in doubt, we usually choose the known instead of the unknown (particularly because we can go there without getting lost).

Human nature being what it is, by now you wandered the highways and byways of America Online, got lost among the windows a few times, and probably discovered several (perhaps many) likable haunts on both America Online itself and the Internet. Remembering your favorite spots and finding your way back to them, though, is a problem sometimes — after all, computer monitors only have so much physical space for little sticky notes before you can't see the screen anymore.

That's where this chapter fits into your life. It looks at the main windows of your online world, explores the gentle art of navigating the system, and then explains how to rid your monitor of sticky notes thanks to the built-in Favorite Places option. If you're tired of stumbling across something cool and then losing the note that got you there (or if you're just tired of getting lost), then kick back, put your feet up, and flip through this chapter. It's here to help.

Your Windows on the World

Everywhere you go in America Online, you're faced with windows. Welcoming windows, channel windows, information area windows — sheesh, spring cleaning around here must be a *total* nightmare.

Although the windows are a little confusing at first, they make America Online the special place that it is. Unlike other online services, America Online was designed with the Macintosh and Microsoft Windows graphical way of life in mind. And it shows.

This section introduces and explains the basic America Online navigation windows. It's designed to make you comfortable with the service's look and feel. The details of the content areas themselves come later, in Part III. For everything you ever wanted to know about the channels, turn to *AOL Channels For Dummies* in the dark-bordered pages near the back of this book — that's the special book-within-a-book that's all about channels. For now, though, sit back, grab a bottle of spray cleaner, and head for the windows of your digital world.

The Welcome window: Hi there — thanks for signing on today!

Every time you sign on to America Online, the Welcome window hops right up and offers a great big Hiya — welcome to the system! This window is like an electronic version of the Wal-Mart door greeter, only better. This greeter doesn't just wish you well; it even knows the news and keeps tabs on your e-mail box. Not even Californians have it this good.

Figure 5-1 shows the Welcome window on an average day. It's a pretty straightforward affair with three different areas: navigation buttons, highlighted services, and anchor services.

Highlighted services

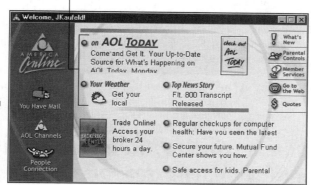

Figure 5-1:
How's this
for a warm
welcome?

✔ Clustered on the left side of the window are the *navigation buttons,* your shortcuts to the rest of America Online.

• The mailbox button tells you whether you have mail or not. Clicking this button either opens your mailbox or sends you on a jaunt to the Mail Center (depending on whether you have unopened e-mail).

• Channels displays the Channels window (discussed in the section entitled "The Channels window: Road map, cheerleader, and commentator rolled into one").

• Finally, the People Connection drops you into a chat room (nothing like a grand entrance, eh?).

✔ Along the bottom center of the window are brief descriptions of the *highlighted services,* along with little buttons that take you to each one. These entries change all the time, so don't worry if your screen doesn't show exactly the same items as Figure 5-1.

✔ Cascading through the upper center and right side of the window are the *anchor services,* places that send you hither and thither on your quest for hot AOL happenings, the weather forecast, the leading news stories. The remaining anchor services (What's New, Parental Controls, Member Services, and others) are on the right.

For a special treat, click the America Online logo in the upper-left corner of the Welcome window. Who knows what might happen? (Okay, so it really leads to the Daily Delights area, but keep it to yourself. We don't want *everyone* to know.)

In Windows, you can't make the Welcome window go away — ever. The best you can do is minimize it, so instead of being an annoying window in the middle of the screen, it's only an annoying icon cowering in the corner. To do this in Windows 3.*x*, click the down arrow button on the right side of the window's title bar (the bar that says Welcome and your screen name). The window pops down to the lower left corner of the screen, never to bother you again. In Windows 95, click the minimize button (the leftmost of the three little buttons at the right end of the title bar) to accomplish the same thing.

The Channels window: Road map, cheerleader, and commentator rolled into one

If you're looking for the right place to start your online expedition, it just doesn't get any better than the Channels window, shown in Figure 5-2 with the AOL Today channel open and alive. From here, any of America Online's 19 channels is a quick jump away.

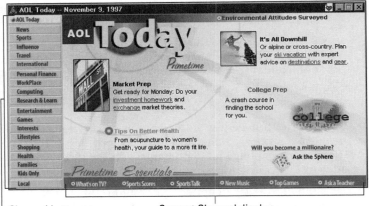

Figure 5-2: A smorgasbord of options awaits you among the channels.

└─Channel buttons   Current Channel display

Occupying the left side of the window are the *channel buttons,* offering single-click connections to the 19 content channels in America Online. Each button displays the menu of services available in that channel area. In another new development, the Channels window in the America Online 4.0 software includes not only the channel buttons, but also a big space where the channel window itself shines through.

To make things ever more consistent and easier to understand, the 19 channels look significantly more alike than ever before. Each channel window includes buttons for its various departments, plus some links to featured areas within the channel. The featured area buttons change periodically, but unless something groundbreaking happens, the departments remain the same.

In the lower right corner of the channels window is the *keyword* for this particular area. See the sidebar "Psst — what's the keyword?" later in this chapter for more about these useful little thingies.

Because I have your attention, here are a few other things you should know about handling the channels before I let you go:

✔ Getting back to the Channels window is never hard. Just click the Channels button on the Toolbar, select the channel you want to see, and {poof!} you're there.

✔ You can also get to the Channels window from the Welcome window, thanks to the cleverly named Channels window button (but you probably knew that already).

✔ If your Channels window has a bunch of colorful buttons strewn all over it instead of the high-tech look shown in Figure 5-2, then you're not using the newest software. Refer to Chapter 1 for more about the whole software thing and how to get the latest version.

To pick up a lot of detailed information about what each channel contains, flip to *AOL Channels For Dummies* — a special book-within-a-book in the gray-bordered pages near the back of this book.

Individual content windows: The heart of America Online

The digital foot soldiers of America Online are the individual content areas. Hundreds, if not thousands, of them are out there, and each one has its own unique interface window. Some of the windows have lots of artwork and feature buttons (like Figure 5-3). Others are plain to the point of being utilitarian (see Figure 5-4 for a to-the-point example). Both do basically the same things, except the fancy ones do it with more panache.

Psst — what's the keyword?

Almost every service in America Online has a *keyword.* It's like a magic carpet that whisks you wherever you wish to go. Using keywords saves you time, and that saves you money.

To use a keyword, press Ctrl+K in Windows or ⌘+K on a Macintosh. Doing so brings up the Keyword dialog box. Type the keyword and then click OK. If everything is working as it should, you'll immediately jump to that keyword's window.

Jot down the keywords for your favorite services on the Cheat Sheet in the front of this book and then use that list as a memory jogger or to plan your online sessions.

Figure 5-3:
A truly fancy service window.

Feature and Function buttons   Service areas   Keyword

Service Areas

Figure 5-4:
The essence of simply presented content.

A fancy service window always contains some *feature and function buttons*. These graphic buttons lead you to special parts of the service, help you search the service's archives, or otherwise do something truly fun for you. Read the button descriptions carefully — don't rely too much on the picture to tell you what the button does.

Somewhere on the window (sorry I can't be more specific — it migrates all over the place) is the service's keyword. If you're not familiar with keywords, you should be. Look in the sidebar entitled "Psst — what's the keyword?" for more information.

Last on the tour is the list of *service areas* — see Table 5-1. Most of the time, both kinds of content windows contain this list, but not always (fancy content areas sometimes replace the list with a series of buttons). The list is in whatever order the service feels like using (in other words, don't bank on things coming up in alphabetical order). To get into an area on the list, double-click its entry.

Don't expect every service to look just like every other service. Some are very plain; others are quite fancy. Just relax and go with the flow — you're doing fine.

Table 5-1		Service Areas
Icon	*Name*	*Meaning*
🗁	File Folder	Leads to an individual service window, which in turn contains still more icons.
🗩	Chat	Takes you into a conference chat room within a content area.
🗋	Document	Shows a document explaining something about the service.
📖	Open Book	Displays a searchable database (mostly found in the various Reference sections).
🗇	Disks	Opens a library of downloadable software.
⊞	Globe	Usually points to an item on the World Wide Web.
🖽	Bulletin Board	Opens up a window of discussion boards.
⌁	Special	Might be just about anything — it defies description.

Organizing the Places of Your Heart

There's a new button in town — and it's appearing on a Toolbar near you. Say hello to Favorites and its sidekick, the Favorite Places window — both of them riding hard to organize the online areas you know and love.

The Favorite Places system won't bring any law into your digital life (hopefully Congress won't either), but it promises a *lot* of order. Instead of having just ten favorite places socked away in your My Shortcuts menu (see Chapter 22 for the details about that), you can store as many favorites as you want! Is that just too cool or what?

Figure 5-5 shows a hard-working Favorite Places window in action. The heart entries link to services within America Online or to Web pages and gophers on the Internet. For instance, the item highlighted in Figure 5-5 is the Card Collecting forum on America Online. The entry right below it, Intertext, is a Web page. Manila folders (such as Support Areas, Gaming, and Fun Spots) apply some order to the impending chaos.

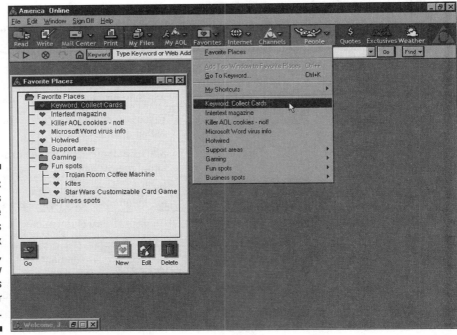

Figure 5-5:
The famous Favorite Places dialog box and its twin, the new Favorites Toolbar menu.

Figure 5-5 also shows a new feature of the America Online 4.0 software: The Favorite Places *menu item list* that automatically appears underneath the Favorites button on the Toolbar. When you add an online area to your Favorite Places, it automatically appears in both the Favorite Places window and the menu list under the Favorites Toolbar button. (Life's getting better all the time, isn't it?) Items in both places work the same way, so I end up in the Collectable Cards forum whether I double-click its heart entry in the Favorite Places window or just select it from the Favorites drop-down menu.

Here are a couple other random musings about the Favorite Places system that wandered out of my brain at the last moment:

✔ To use the new Favorite Places system, you must have Version 2.5 or later of the America Online access software for Windows. Any older America Online software just isn't this cool.

✔ Even though all the items in your Favorite Places window are also displayed in the Favorites drop-down menu, you can only make changes to the entries through the Favorite Places window. The Favorites drop-down menu notices the changes on its own, so don't worry about that.

✔ You're not limited to the folders shown in Figure 5-5. I created those myself to meet my exceedingly peculiar needs. You have the freedom — yes, even the right — to create equally peculiar folders for yourself.

Using folders in the Favorite Places window

I almost forgot to mention this, but luckily two of my brain cells, spurred into action by the caloric heat of a half-digested Oreo, reminded me to mention that double-clicking is the key to using the Favorite Places window:

✔ To open a folder, double-click it.

✔ To close the folder when you're done with it, double-click the folder again.

✔ To take off for a favorite place, double-click it.

Flip back into single-clicking mode when using the drop-down menu under the Favorites Toolbar. Because it's a menu and not a list of items in a window, you *single-click* to select destinations there.

Adding a favorite place

Including a new favorite place is a cinch. You can do so in two ways: the Easy Way and the Other Way. This section tells you how to handle them both.

The Easy Way is for areas inside America Online or Internet-based Web pages and gophers that you've browsed your way into. Here are the steps:

1. **Display an area that you're fond of, either inside America Online or on the Internet.**

 2. **Click the heart-on-a-document icon in the window's upper-right corner.**

   A little dialog box appears (see Figure 5-6), demanding to know what you intend to do with the link to this online area.

   Not every window in America Online has one of those cute little heart document icons. It's unfortunate, but true. If the window you're looking at doesn't have one, you can't add it to the Favorite Places list.

3. **In the little You have selected a Favorite Place dialog box, click Add to Favorites to include an entry for this online area in your Favorite Places list.**

   Your new entry takes up residence at either the top or the bottom of both the Favorite Places window and the drop-down menu under Favorites, just like Figure 5-7 shows. (Which end of the list it lands on seems to depend entirely on how your America Online software feels at the moment. Strange, isn't it?)

Figure 5-6:
The America Online 4.0 software makes it easy to collect favorites as well as share them through e-mail and Instant Messages.

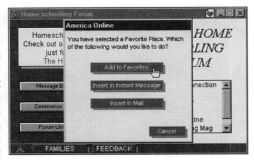

TIP

If you click Insert in Instant Message, a new Instant Message window appears, complete with a ready-to-use link to this favorite place. Clicking Insert in Mail does much the same thing, except that a blank e-mail message pops up, with the link in the body and a friendly Check this out notice in the Subject line.

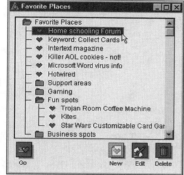

Figure 5-7:
The new entry lands at the top of the list.

Use the Other Way when someone dashes up and says, "I just found the neatest Web page — you've *gotta* check it out!" The Other Way assumes that you have the address of a Web page and want to manually include it in your Favorite Places. Here's how it's done:

1. **Select Favorites⇨Favorite Places from the Toolbar.**

   The Favorite Places window appears.

2. **Click the folder in which you want to store the new item.**

   If you don't know where to put the item, click the Favorite Places folder at the top of the window. That's as good a place as any — and you can always move the entry somewhere else later.

3. **Click New at the bottom of the Favorite Places window.**

   The Add New Folder/Favorite Place dialog box (designed by the Use No Articles Programming Team) appears.

4. **Type a name for this entry in the Enter the Place's Description box, press Tab, and then type the entry's address in the Enter the Internet Address box.**

   Figure 5-8 displays a finished entry, ready to be saved for posterity.

5. **Click OK to add the entry to your Favorite Places window.**

Figure 5-8:
The digital
Dumpster
Diver gift
site is ready
to join my
favorite
places.

Add New Folder/Favorite Place

⊙ **New Favorite Place**   ○ **New Folder**

Enter the Place's Description:

Connect-Time's Dumpster Diver digital gift

Enter the Internet Address:

http://cgi.connect-time.com/cgi-bin/dumpdive

[OK]   [Cancel]

Adding a folder

Adding all kinds of favorite places to your system is great, but you need some organization to keep everything in order. That's why those clever America Online programmers included folders.

Folders can live in the Favorite Places area or inside other folders (see Figure 5-9). Either way, creating a folder is easy. Here's how (assuming that you already have the Favorite Places window open):

1. **Click the Favorite Places button on the Toolbar.**

   The Favorite Places window pops to attention.

2. **Click the Favorite Places folder at the top of the window.**

   The Favorite Places folder is highlighted (this is a good sign).

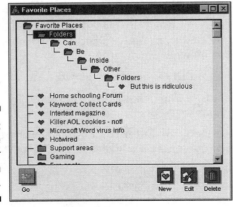

Figure 5-9:
An example
of folder
creation run
amok.

3. **Click the New button.**

   The Add New Folder/Favorite Place dialog box appears on your screen (yet another good sign).

4. **Click the New Folder radio button.**

   The dialog box suddenly shrinks to half its previous size, shedding those unwanted pounds and inches in no time at all.

5. **Click in the box under Enter the New Folder's Name, then type the name of your new folder. Click OK when you're done (see Figure 5-10).**

   Your new folder appears at the bottom of the Favorite Places list.

6. **Move the folder wherever you want it in the list.**

   If you're not sure how to move the folder, look in the next section.

Figure 5-10:
Now there's
a safe place
for my stuff.

Moving folders and favorite places

Creating folders and favorite places is one thing, but organizing them is another. The little buggers tend to land wherever the America Online software feels like putting them. Moving them around is easy, though, once you get the hang of it.

The technique is the same for both folders and favorite places. After you open the Favorite Places window, here's what to do:

1. **Decide which item you want to move and where it's headed.**

2. **Put the mouse pointer on the chosen item, and then press and hold the mouse button.**

   The technical term for this maneuver is *click and drag,* but there's no reason to mention it, so I won't.

3. **While holding the mouse button down, move the item to its destination (see Figure 5-11) and then release the mouse button.**

   The item settles down, safe and sound in its new home (see Figure 5-12).

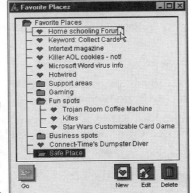

Figure 5-11: The Safe Places folder on the move.

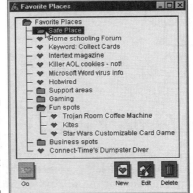

Figure 5-12: Coming in for a perfect landing!

Modifying folders and favorite places

There comes a point in every life when it's time to make some changes. When *that time* in the life of your Favorite Places window arrives, have no fear. Although change is never fun, at least it's easy in the Favorite Places window. Open the Favorite Places window and then follow these steps:

1. Click the folder or favorite place and then click Edit.

For a folder, the Rename dialog box appears. For a favorite place, the description and Internet address dialog box appears.

2. **Make your changes (usually to the name of the item) and then click OK.**

   If you change your mind and don't want to make any changes, double-click in the upper-left corner of the box.

Deleting folders and favorite places

Favorite Places entries, like other impetuous flashes in the dark sky of fading youth, have a limited life span. When it's time to delete one, just do the deed and go on as best you can. Solemnly open the Favorite Places window and then morosely proceed through the following:

1. **Click the item you want to delete.**
2. **Click Delete and then OK in the pop-up dialog box.**

The entry is no more. Remember, ask not for whom the Delete button clicks — it clicks for thy once-favorite place.

Chapter 6

E-Mailing the World, One Mailbox at a Time

*I*n my humble opinion, e-mail is *the* communications medium of the '90s. It seems like everybody has an e-mail account at the office, at home, or both. Messages travel quickly, arrive safely, and rarely get delayed by any of the obscure national holidays that shut down the post office so frequently.

Through America Online, you can send e-mail to virtually anyone on the planet. (No, I'm not kidding — I'm not even exaggerating.) One way or another, your e-mail message flies on the wings of technology from your online mailbox to its destination, whether it's headed to another America Online e-mail box or an Internet e-mail address.

This section tells you how to join in the fun, from sending Internet mail to organizing your incoming messages. No matter what you want to know about e-mail and America Online, this chapter is the place to look.

Sending E-Mail to an America Online Subscriber

Because you're surrounded by these people every time you sign on, the odds are good that you'll send at least a few messages to other America Online subscribers. That's what the e-mail system was designed for in the first place, so trading messages with other members is pretty easy. The mail system also has some special features, like *unsend,* that are only available when writing to another America Online person. (If unsending a message sounds interesting, check out the "Stupid mail tricks" sidebar for more information.)

Before you can send e-mail to someone, you must know the person's screen name. Upper and lowercase doesn't matter, but spelling *does.* For example, you could enter my screen name as **JKaufeld** or **jkaufeld** and the mail would still go through. But if you try **JKaufield**, don't expect a reply — at least not from me — because the name is misspelled.

Before sending your first few messages, take a second to look through these tips and suggestions for making your e-mail stand head and shoulders above the crowd:

✔ Writing e-mail messages is a little different from any other kind of communication. Good e-mail takes a bit of care, the right words, and a willingness to type until the message is clear. If you're new to e-mail, don't panic — I was new once, too.

✔ Please don't type your messages in one huge paragraph. That makes them *really* hard to read. Press Enter (or Return) a couple of times every now and then to break the behemoth into smaller, more digestible chunks.

✔ According to America Online's official *Rules of the Road* (also known as the *Terms of Service* agreement by lawyers and other people who create official-sounding language because they enjoy it), you can't send unsolicited advertisements through the e-mail system. If someone specifically asks to receive information from you, that's perfectly okay.

✔ Did you ever use the *e-mail to postal mail* and *e-mail to fax* features in the America Online e-mail system? If so, then I have some bad news for you. Both of these beloved and adored features recently passed through that thin veil and sloughed off that digital coil — in other words, they're history. The e-mail system now handles only e-mail. Sorry to be the one to break the news to you, but it had to happen sometime. At least you read it in a book instead of hearing it second-hand in some chat room.

Enough of this talk — it's time to hit the keyboard and start e-mailing! To send a mail message, follow these steps:

1. **If you're signed on to America Online and use the pay-as-you-go pricing plan, sign off now.**

   Unless you're a really good typist, you need to send a very short message, or you just don't care how high your America Online bill is this month, don't compose messages online if you pay for access by the minute. Doing so is a serious money-waster.

2. **Create a new mail message by clicking the Compose Mail button on the Toolbar or Ctrl+M.**

   A blank e-mail window mystically appears on-screen.

3. **Type the recipient's screen name.**

   To send the same message to more than one screen name, keep typing screen names into the To box and separate them with commas.

   If the screen name is in your Address Book, click the Address Book button and then double-click the entry for that person or group. When you're done choosing addresses, click OK to make the Address Book go away.

   You can freely mix America Online screen names and Internet e-mail addresses when addressing a message. Just separate each entry with a comma, and America Online's e-mail system will make sure that the message goes to the right place. When you include a group of recipients from the Address Book, the America Online software automatically adds commas for you. Isn't that helpful?

4. **Press Tab to move the blinking cursor into the CC: box. Enter the screen names of people who should get a copy of the message but should not be listed as a main recipient.**

   Odds are, you won't ever use the CC feature, but I had to mention it anyway. It's just the kind of guy I am.

   Don't bother putting your own screen name in the CC area. You automatically get a copy of every message you send. Choose Mail➪Check Mail You've <u>S</u>ent to see them. Copies are only kept for about 30 days, so if the message is *really* important, print it out and keep the paper.

5. **Press Tab again to put the cursor in the Subject box. Type a brief (32 characters or less) description of the message.**

   Write your message subjects so that the other person can tell what it's about right away. If the message is *really* important, write something like *URGENT* at the beginning of the subject. Because your reader may have 35 other messages to look at, making the subject descriptive helps him or her figure out which e-mails to check first.

6. Press Tab once more to get into the message area in the bottom of the screen. Type your message text in here.

Enter the text as if you're using a word processor (for example, don't hit the Enter (or Return) key at the end of every line). Press Enter (or Return) a couple times every now and then to break the message into easy-to-read paragraphs (see Figure 6-1).

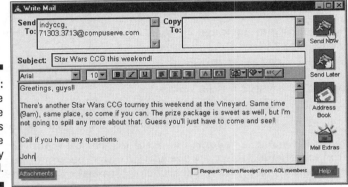

Figure 6-1:
Leave some white space in messages to make them easy to read.

To really jazz up your messages, add some cool formatting or live links to your favorite Web sites. For all the details, flip ahead to "E-Mailing with Panache" later in this chapter.

7. If you're sending a file, click Attach. In the Attach File dialog box, find the file you want to send and double-click it (or highlight it and click the oddly named Open button.)

After picking the file (whichever way you do it), the Attach File dialog box vanishes. Part of the name of the attached file appears just below the Attach button.

To attach another file to the same message, repeat the process. In fact, you can attach as many files as you like and the America Online software automatically compresses them into a ZIP file for you. Isn't technology wonderful (at least when it works)?

If you change your mind about attaching the file, click the Detach button (it's right next to the Attach — what a strange coincidence).

What if you just want to see a list of the files you attached to the message? Even though it sounds odd, click the Detach button. The America Online software assumes that you want to remove an attached file, so it promptly displays a list of all the files currently attached. After perusing the list, click Cancel to make the little window go away.

8. If you're signed on to America Online, click Send to mail the message. If you aren't signed on right now (which is important if you still pay by the hour!), minimize the mail window (click the down arrow

in the window's upper-right corner) and then sign on. When you're in, double-click the mail message icon (it's probably in the lower-left corner of the screen) and then click Send.

America Online automatically reassures you with a little message that "Your mail has been sent," but that reassurance gets pretty old if you send a lot of mail. To stop the annoying little dialog box from popping up, turn off the Confirm mail after it has been sent option in the Mail preferences window. (See Chapter 4 for everything you never — er, ever — wanted to know about preference settings.)

"Doing E-Mail the Automatic AOL Way," later in this chapter, explains the Send Later button and why it's the coolest thing since, um, well, they started tracking cool stuff.

America Online automatically keeps copies of all your outgoing mail for about 30 days. To review these old messages, select Mail⇨Check Mail You've Sent from the menu bar. If you're truly attached to your correspondence, tell your America Online software to squirrel away copies of all outbound messages in your Personal Filing Cabinet. To find out more about this setting, along with the many other fascinating and tweakable items which control your America Online experience, flip to Chapter 4 and look in the "Mail Preferences" section.

Stupid mail tricks

As if it weren't enough that you can send e-mail to anyone in America Online, those zany programmers threw in some extra features designed to make your mind do loops. Look for these options along the bottom of the Mailbox window or on the right-click pop-up menu. (Right-click on a mail message's entry in the Online Mailbox to see the menu.)

Status: Want to see if your buddy hasn't read the mail lately or is just ignoring you? Click the mail message you sent and then click Show Status. America Online returns a dialog box with the screen name of the person who read the letter and the time and date it was read. If it's still in unread limbo, the time and date are replaced with (not yet read).

Unsend: If you send a message that you quickly regret, America Online lets you reach through the system and pretend the message never happened — provided the other person hasn't read it yet. To unsend a message, click the message you're embarrassed about and then click Unsend. If the message hasn't been read yet, America Online yanks it out of the other person's e-mail basket and throws the message away. If it's too late and the person read the message, it's truly too late — Unsend won't work now. This button only appears in the Sent Mail page of the Online Mailbox.

Ignore: When junk mail (or any other mail you don't want to see) fills up your box, this option makes a great antidote. As its name implies, the Ignore option disregards the current message, automatically consigning it to the Old Mail page of the Online Mailbox without actually opening it. If you get a lot of junk e-mail, then the Ignore option promises to warm your heart. To ignore a message, right-click the message's entry in the Online Mailbox, and then select Ignore from the pop-up menu.

Sending Internet E-Mail

Using America Online as your e-mail link to the Internet is really easy. In fact, you can pretend you're just sending mail to another America Online user, except the person has a very weird screen name.

To send mail through the Internet, you go through exactly the same steps you did to send e-mail to another America Online user. The only difference with Internet e-mail is in how you address the message.

The key to sending Internet e-mail is getting the address right. Most Internet mail addresses look a little bizarre to uninitiated human eyes, but that's not an issue — in a moment, you'll be initiated. Instead of being simple, straightforward things like **JKaufeld**, Internet mail addresses look like **imrappaport@stagetheatre.com**. The part that's to the left of the @ is the person's ID (the Internet term for screen name). The other half is the address of the computer the person uses for e-mail (in this case, it's one of those other online services). Put the whole thing together, and you get an Internet mail address.

These addresses get really complicated sometimes (the one for a friend of mine in France contains about 50 letters, numbers, and various punctuation symbols). One way to get the address just right is to have your friend send a message to you first. When it arrives, carefully copy the address into your Address Book. Now you don't have to worry about the gory, technical address stuff anymore — just pick the entry from your Address Book and you're done.

Because you're on America Online, you have an Internet e-mail address too; it's your screen name with **@aol.com** glued onto the end. If your screen name is **Have Fun**, your Internet e-mail address is **havefun@aol.com**. The Internet address doesn't use the space or the capital letters in the screen name — it just ignores them.

By the way, remember to use the person's *screen name* or *Internet address* instead of their *real name* when sending an e-mail message. Both America Online and the Internet use advanced technology, but the computers still aren't good enough to know everyone by their names (and I, for one, hope they never get to that point!).

E-Mailing with Panache

In the image-conscious '90s, looking good is almost as important as sounding good. Thanks to advances in the America Online software, e-mail messages are more powerful and flexible than ever. The new formatting buttons put you in charge of the text size, style, alignment, and even color while creating e-mails. The possibilities for font size, color, and alignment are endless (but, for your message's sake, I hope your design skills are better than mine).

Most of these formatting tips work with Instant Messages as well. Don't let your e-mails have *all* the fun — add some formatting and dress up your Instant Messages, too.

The buttons just above the message area control the formatting magic. They're grouped into sets by what they do. Here's a quick rundown of the sets, from left to right:

- ✔ The first set handles font and text size. Pick any of your installed TrueType fonts, then select the size that meets your purpose. If the person receiving the message has that same font installed and uses America Online's 4.0 software, then he or she sees your message in the font you chose.

- ✔ The next set does text formatting. These are the bold, italic, and underline buttons, as their labels demonstrate.

- ✔ The third set covers text alignment. Like any good word processor, the America Online e-mail system understands left, center, and right justification, plus so-called newspaper justification, which is even on both sides. This final option isn't available in Instant Messages. (I guess they aren't smart enough to handle it.)

- ✔ The fourth set handles text color. Change the color of the text itself with the first button. Use the second to change the background color of the entire message (not just a small portion of it). And remember that blue text on a blue background doesn't show up very well!

- ✔ The final three buttons are new to the America Online 4.0 software. The Camera inserts a graphic image into your e-mail, so you can both tell Aunt Sarah about the holiday party and show off the digital pictures. To insert a graphic, click the camera button, select an image file, and {poof!} the graphic appears in your message. The Heart button opens your Favorite Places window, making it easy to drag-and-drop Favorite Places links into your e-mail messages (see the next section for more about that). Finally, clicking the ABC button checks your spelling (yes!) to prevent embarrassing speeling misteaks.

The font, formatting, color, and alignment buttons all work the same way. To use them with new text, click the buttons for your choices and start typing. The software applies the fonts, formatting, and whatever else you chose to the text as you type. To format text that's already in the message, click and drag across the text you want to change, and then click the various formatting buttons. Presto — the old text looks new! To remove some formatting, highlight the text in question and click *off* the format options that you don't want.

Linking with Ease

Almost every time I wander America Online or surf the Web for a while, I run across something that's really neat and worth sharing with my friends. In the past, I laboriously copied the Internet address or America Online keyword into a mail message — and sometimes messed it up in the process. Today, though, I never miss an address because I let the America Online software insert the link for me.

Before trying this, you need to understand how the Favorite Places area works and what it does for you. If you're not familiar with Favorite Places, flip to Chapter 5 and find out more about it before attempting this link thing.

When you want to include a link to either an America Online keyword or an Internet site in an e-mail message, follow these steps:

1. **Go to the keyword area or Internet site so it's in a window on your screen.**

   If the keyword area doesn't have a Favorite Places icon on its window, then you can't send a link to it. Sorry — it's just how life goes sometimes.

2. **Click the Favorite Places heart in the upper-right corner of the window.**

   A small dialog box appears and wants to know what it should do with your Favorite Place link.

3. **Click the Insert in Mail option.**

   After a few moments of thinking, the America Online software displays a fresh e-mail window with your link ready and waiting in the message body.

4. **Address the message, type a subject and body, and then send the message just as you normally would.**

   The new 4.0 software really makes this mail-the-link thing easy, doesn't it?

Incoming Missive, Sir!

Sending mail is only half the fun. After you send something, you get a reply! If you think a mailbox full of junk mail is a lift, just wait until you sign on to America Online and find a message or two in your e-mail box. Someone out there cares!

To check your online mailbox, click the Read button on the toolbar. This whisks you away to the New Mail window.

To read a message, either double-click the message in the New Mail window or click it once and then click Read. Your message hops up into its own window. To reply only to the person who sent the message, click Reply. To share your comments with the sender *and* everyone else who received the message, click Reply to All. To send a copy of the message to someone else (even out to the Internet, but not to a fax or postal mail address), click Forward. After you're done with the message, close the window by double-clicking in its upper-left corner.

✔ To keep a message in your inbox after you read it, click the message in the New Mail window once and then click Keep As New. Unread messages live in your America Online inbox for 30 days after arriving. After that, they turn into very small pumpkins and are shipped to your local grocery store, never to be seen or heard from again.

✔ To save an important message, either print it out or save it as a text file in your computer. To print, click the Print button (it looks like a page coming out of a printer) on the Toolbar. To save it as a text file, choose File➪Save As from the main menu, type a filename for the information, and then click OK. The text is now safe and sound on your disk drive.

✔ After you read a message, it hangs out in the Old Mail area for about two days after you first look at it (in the Mail Preferences, you can tell the America Online computers to store incoming e-mails for up to seven days — see Chapter 4 for more about that). To reread an old message, choose Mail➪Check Mail You've Read from the menu bar. Doing so brings up the Old Mail dialog box. Double-click the message you want to read.

Organizing Your E-Mail Mess (ages)

I absolutely *live* on e-mail. Maybe it's my job or the peculiar people I work with (or perhaps it's my nerdy side showing again — I hate it when that happens), but I spend a lot of time each day fielding incoming messages and unleashing my own outbound correspondence flood. Thankfully, my faithful digital assistant, the Personal Filing Cabinet, keeps all my e-stuff organized.

The Personal Filing Cabinet tracks incoming and outgoing e-mail, discussion board postings, and e-mail and newsgroup messages retrieved with Automatic AOL sessions. It even covers file downloads, too. Best of all, it's built right into the America Online software, so there's nothing to download and nothing to buy.

To open the Personal Filing Cabinet, select File⇨Personal Filing Cabinet on the menu bar. The window hops onto the screen, looking much like Figure 6-2. The file folders along the left side of the window represent different storage areas. The buttons along the bottom control the Personal Filing Cabinet itself.

Figure 6-2: The Personal Filing Cabinet uses electronic manila folders to store your digital information.

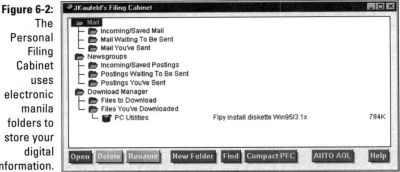

There's a lot to work with here, but this area is easiest to understand when you play with it. Before I turn you loose, here are some basic ideas about how the Filing Cabinet works:

✔ To open a folder, double-click it. To close it, double-click again. When you open a folder, the software displays all the items the folder contains (which can be a lengthy list sometimes). Don't be surprised if you have to scroll up and down to see everything in a folder.

✔ To view something inside a folder (be it a piece of e-mail or a newsgroup posting), double-click it. Double-clicking an entry in the Download Manager area displays the description for that file, but only if you're currently signed on to the system.

✔ To create a new folder, click the top folder of the area (like Mail, for instance) and then click Add Folder. Type a name for the new folder and then click OK. The new folder appears underneath the top folder. Isn't automated organization amazing?

✔ Folders can be inside other folders, just like in the real world.

✔ Moving things from one folder to another is easy. Just point at the item you want to move, hold down the mouse button, and drag the item to its new home. When the mouse arrow is pointing to the item's destination, release the mouse button. The Personal Filing Cabinet gently puts the item in place.

✔ If you misplace an e-mail message, click Search to have the Personal Filing Cabinet ferret it out. You can search on the item's title or the full text of messages. Pretty spiffy, eh?

✔ In the Mail option of the Preferences (Members⇨Set Preferences and then click the Mail button), you can tell America Online to automatically store copies of all the mail you send and receive in the Mail folder of the Personal Filing Cabinet. Personally, I think this idea is really cool, but it can take a lot of disk space. Try turning this feature on and see if you like it.

Catching People with Your Address Book

You start meeting people right away in America Online. Join a discussion, drop in for a chat, or attend a live presentation, and suddenly you have online friends. You also have a problem: How do you keep track of the members in your newfound social club?

It's time to invoke the familiar refrain, "Luckily, the America Online programmers thought of that." Yup, those clever folks from Virginia did it again. Step right this way and meet the America Online Address Book.

As address books go, this one's pretty simple. It handles entries for single screen names or big, honking mailing lists (assuming that you're into large, noisy name collections).

- ✔ For an individual, the Address Book holds the person's real name, screen name or Internet e-mail address, and notes describing the entry. There's also space for a picture, just in case your friend sent a digital likeness of himself.

- ✔ For a mailing group, the entry consists of a descriptive title and list of the assembled crowd's e-mail addresses.

The Address Book lists both individual entries and groups together in one master alphabetized list. Yes, you read it right — *alphabetized!* After years of waiting, Address Book entries are finally alphabetized! Hooray!! (I probably shouldn't be this excited about the Address Book, but it's the nerd side of me showing through — down, nerd, down!)

Adding Address Book entries

Before you can use the Address Book to send messages, you have to put some addresses into it. With that marginally deep thought in mind, here's how to add new items to your Address Book:

1. **Open the Address Book by choosing Mail⇨Edit Address Book or clicking the Address Book button on a new mail message.**

   The Address Book window pops up, all bright and cheery.

2. **To add an entry for a person, click New Person. To build a group entry, click New Group.**

   A blank New Person or New Group dialog box appears.

3. **Fill in the appropriate spaces in the dialog box, then check your work carefully, especially the e-mail address entry (or addresses, as the case may be).**

   When making a group entry, type the America Online screen names and Internet e-mail addresses one after the next, with commas separating them, just as in Figure 6-3.

Figure 6-3:
Mix and
match
America
Online
screen
names and
Internet
e-mail
addresses
in the same
group.

Capitalization doesn't count here, but spelling definitely does! For instance, you can enter my screen name any way you want (JKaufeld, Jkaufeld, jkaufeld, or jKaUfElD all count), and America Online figures out that you mean me. But if you put in **jkaufield,** the system gets all confused and won't send the mail to me.

4. **When you're done, click OK.**

   The new entry pops into the Address Book window, in (as I previously gloated about) alphabetical order.

Repeat the process until your Address Book overflows with friends, acquaintances, business associates, and other online contacts.

Deleting Address Book entries

So now you have an Address Book full of stuff and it's getting unwieldy — plus you can't remember who half these people are. No problem — that's what the Delete button is for. Deleting is a quick and painless process. Here's how to do it:

1. **Start the Address Book (if you haven't done that already) by choosing Mail⇨Edit Address Book.**

   Of course, you can also click the Address Book button in the e-mail message window if that's where you happen to be when the inspiration hits.

2. **Scroll through the Address Book list until you find the entry that you want to dispose of.**

3. **Click the description once to highlight it and then click Delete.**

4. **When the software wrings its little hands and asks if you're *serious* about this deletion business, click Yes.**

   If you just wanted to see what the Delete button did and how the program would react when you used it, click No. Apologize to your software for even *thinking* of tricking it like that. Shame on you.

Changing Address Book entries

Because things change at a ridiculous pace, particularly in the online world, keeping your Address Book up-to-date is a never-ending task. That's why your Address Book has a Modify button.

Here's the scoop on changing an existing Address Book entry:

1. **Open the Address Book (if it's still closed) by choosing Mail⇨Edit Address Book from the menu bar or by clicking the Address Book button in a brand-new mail message.**

2. **Click once on the entry you need to change.**

   This highlights the entry.

3. **Click Edit.**

   The Address entry window comes back. It's the same window you used to create the entry originally.

4. **Make your changes to the Description and Screen Name List.**

   Everything is open for change, so make whatever modifications you must. If you're working with a list, you can freely add and delete screen names as you desire.

   All the standard Windows text editing tricks work here: highlight, delete, insert, click and drag, and the rest. Edit (and play) as much as you want.

5. **After you're done with the changes and are pleased as punch with them, click OK to save your work.**

   Click Cancel if you want to abandon your carefully wrought editing and keep the record the way it was before.

   Whichever button you click, the Address Group dialog box vanishes, and you're back to the Address Book screen.

Doing E-Mail the Automatic AOL Way

"Do you want to save money? Do you want to save time? Well, then, step right up, folks, step right up and see the working man's miracle, a techno-logical time-saver: Automatic AOL. This little beauty lets you type your e-mails offline, that's right, *offline,* folks, not signed on at all — step back, son, you bother me. Save yourself some money right then and there. But it doesn't stop with that, no siree. It doesn't want to save you a *little* money, folks; it wants to save you a *lot.* That's why it au-to-matically gets your new mail when it's sending the old stuff off. Read your messages, write your replies, and then tell the little fellow to go do it all again. Every time you use it, you can't *help* but save money. Like money in the bank, folks, that's Automatic AOL for you."

Okay, so America Online probably didn't use old-time carnival barkers to announce Automatic AOL, but they sure could have. This technology is incredibly useful, and it's built right into your America Online access software. There's nothing else to buy; no salesperson will call. Even if you belong to the *all you can use* unlimited online time plan, Automatic AOL still simplifies life by managing all your online communications in one easy tool. And if you still pay by the hour, Automatic AOL is your key to low monthly America Online bills!

To work with Automatic AOL, choose Mail⇨Set Up Automatic AOL from the menu bar. The Automatic AOL dialog box pops up in the middle of your screen. For all its power and usefulness, Automatic AOL is pretty easy to set up and use.

You don't have to be signed on to the system in order to configure Auto-matic AOL — in fact, it's probably a good idea if you aren't.

Here's what Automatic AOL does for you (be sure to sit down before reading the list — it's pretty amazing):

✔ Sign on with one, a few, or all of your screen names and gather new mail for offline review.

✔ Send outgoing mail that you wrote offline and saved with the Send Later button.

✔ Automatically download files attached to mail messages (or not, depending on your preference).

✔ Retrieve postings from Internet newsgroups that you marked for off-line reading.

- ✔ Retrieve items from your favorite America Online discussion boards (the ones listed in the Read My Message Boards window at keyword **My Boards**).

- ✔ Post your comments back to Internet newsgroups and discussion boards.

- ✔ Bring down files that you marked to *Download Later* in either e-mail messages or America Online file libraries.

- ✔ Perform all these actions at regular intervals (every half hour, hour, two hours, and so on) or whenever you tell the program to do so.

Automatic AOL is pretty flexible, so you can do whatever you want. For instance, your Automatic AOL session can retrieve new mail, leave attached files online, send outgoing mail, and not mess with the Download Manager at all. And you can change the settings at your whim whenever you want.

You can choose from two ways to set up Automatic AOL: Either click the Walk Me Through button (which asks you questions and does the settings based on your answers) or follow the steps below. Do whichever is more comfortable for you. Heck — do them both if you want to.

Here's how to set up Automatic AOL by yourself:

1. **If you haven't already done so, sign off America Online.**

   Feel free to get a glass of your favorite soft drink and a handful of snackies before continuing. Food makes software configuration less painful.

2. **Choose Mail⇨Set up Automatic AOL from the menu bar.**

   The Automatic AOL dialog box appears.

   If this is the very first time you've ever used Automatic AOL, then the software throws you right into the Automatic AOL Walk-Through dialog box. If you want the America Online software to take you step-by-step through the whole configuration process (which isn't necessarily a bad idea), click Continue. Otherwise, click Expert Setup and go on with the next step below.

3. **Click Select Names.**

   The Select Screen Names dialog box appears.

4. **Click the check box next to each screen name you want to use with Automatic AOL. Enter the password for each screen name you choose. Click OK after you're done.**

   Type the passwords carefully. If a password is misspelled, Automatic AOL won't work correctly (and you don't want *that* to happen, do you?).

5. Tell the software what actions Automatic AOL should do.

Table 6-1 has a brief breakdown of the settings, what they do, and how I suggest you set them.

6. After all your settings are completed, close the window by double-clicking in the upper-left corner.

Congratulations — Automatic AOL is ready to go.

Table 6-1	**Automatic AOL Activities**	
Setting	*Recommendation*	*Description*
Send mail...	Turn it on.	Sends any mail messages you wrote offline and saved with the Send Later button. Another must-have feature of Automatic AOL. Use it.
Get unread mail...	Turn it on.	Copies new mail messages from America Online to your computer so you can read them offline. Definitely use this option — it's a time- and money-saver.
Download files attached to unread mail...	Turn it off.	Automatically downloads files attached to mail messages, which can be good and bad. If you get a lot of files by e-mail, this feature is useful. In that case, go ahead and turn it on.
Download files marked...	Turn it on.	Invokes the Download Manager and gets any files you have marked. If you download lots of shareware, this feature really shines.
Send postings...	Find out more.	Posts replies to your read offline list of Internet newsgroups.
Get unread postings...	Find out more.	Retrieves new messages from your read offline list of Internet newsgroups.

You may have noticed that I ignore the Schedule Automatic AOL button. Although I think that this feature is interesting, I don't want my computer deciding on its own that it's time to call America Online and check for mail. If automating the process sounds like a hot fudge sundae to you (it sounded like asparagus to me), look in the America Online access software help menu for help setting the scheduling options.

I leave out two other settings as well, namely the ones relating to Internet newsgroups. Using Automatic AOL with newsgroups is a slightly complex process (much like assembling a child's tricycle on Christmas Eve — if you're a parent, I know you can relate). If you *really* want to do newsgroups with Automatic AOL, sign on to the system, go to keyword **Newsgroups,** and get the details from the item Setting Up Newsgroups with Automatic AOL.

Using Automatic AOL is even easier than setting it up. To start Automatic AOL, choose Mail⇨Activate Automatic AOL from the menu bar. The Activate Automatic AOL Now dialog box appears. If you're happy with the settings you made earlier, click Begin. If you want to briefly review things, click Set Session instead. An information window pops up to give you the blow-by-blow commentary of the Automatic AOL session in progress. When it's done, close the Automatic AOL Status dialog box.

To read incoming mail, choose the appropriate screen name from the main America Online window and then choose Mail⇨Read Offline/Saved Mail from the menu bar. You can read, reply, and do whatever else you wish with the messages. After all your replies are done, set off another Automatic AOL session to send them on their way.

If your teenagers have their own screen names, they probably *won't* want to be part of your time- and money-saving Automatic AOL. Why? Well, it's a privacy thing — and you remember how important privacy was when you were young. Because you don't need to type in a password to read mail that came in through an Automatic AOL session, anyone in the family could read the teen-mail by selecting the screen name and hitting the Mail menu.

Chapter 7

Chatting the Day (And Night) Away

• •

In This Chapter

▶ Connecting with people from all over

▶ Showing off with Member Profiles

▶ Chatting the night away

▶ Keeping your password private

▶ Making a private room

▶ Attending the theater

• •

*I*nteracting with your fellow members is at the very heart of America Online. I never saw an online service that's as *into* the idea of community as America Online — and darn it, people in a community should talk to each other. The People Connection exists so that you can chat informally with other people, make friends from all over the world, and redeem yourself in the eyes of your mother, who still thinks you shouldn't spend so much time alone with your computer.

This chapter introduces the People Connection chat rooms and goes into detail about how the whole chat thing works. It also explains the AOL Live theaters, home to some of the finest online presentations ever shown, um, online. Turn off the TV, let the newspapers stack up by the door, and get ready to boldly go where a whole lot of people anxiously await your arrival.

Ambling into a Chat Room

Getting into a People Connection chat room is *really* easy. In fact, you've probably fallen into one more than once by just wandering around the system and clicking a few random links.

To formally set sail for the Wonderful World of Chatting, use keyword **People Connection** or click the People button on the Toolbar and then select Chat Now from the drop-down menu. After a moment of intense thought, the America Online software launches you into a randomly selected chat room. Once you saunter in, look around, and generally get comfy, your screen should resemble Figure 7-1.

Chat Text   People List

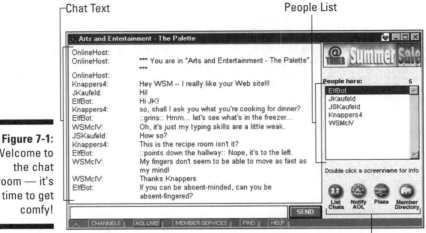

OnlineHost:
OnlineHost: *** You are in "Arts and Entertainment - The Palette".
                     ***
OnlineHost:
Knappers4:   Hey WSM -- I really like your Web site!!!
JKaufeld: Hi!
ElfBot: Hi JK!
Knappers4:   so, shall I ask you what you're cooking for dinner?
ElfBot: ::grins:: Hmm... let's see what's in the freezer...
WSMcIV: Oh, it's just my typing skills are a little weak.
JSKaufeld: How so?
Knappers4:   This is the recipe room isn't it?
ElfBot: ::points down the hallway:: Nope, it's to the left.
WSMcIV: My fingers don't seem to be able to move as fast as
                     my mind!
WSMcIV: Thanks Knappers
ElfBot: If you can be absent-minded, can you be
                     absent-fingered?

Figure 7-1:
Welcome to
the chat
room — it's
time to get
comfy!

Control Buttons

Because the People Connection rooms are, after all, for chatting, the *chat text area* fills most of the window. Opposite the chat text is the *people list,* a roster of the members sharing the chat room with you. Along the bottom of the window is the *message box,* where you compose those witty comments of yours before hitting Enter (or Return) or clicking Send to share them with the room.

Underneath the people list are the *control buttons.* List Chats is your doorway to other public and private chat rooms. Notify AOL opens the Community Action Team window (for those times when *you're* the only mature person in the chat room). The Plaza button simply defies explanation — you have to try it yourself and find out what happens. Member Directory takes you straight to the Member Directory window, just like choosing Mem̱bers⇨Member Directory from the main menu.

✔ A standard chat room holds 23 people at a time. If you try to get into a room that's full, America Online either offers to send you to another chat room (particularly if you're heading for a Lobby or the New Member Lounge) or digitally shrugs you off, saying that the room is full. If America Online shrugs, all you can do is wait a few moments and try again.

✔ Even though America Online randomly stuffs you into the first available chat room when you first enter the People Connection, it's easy to wander off to some other destination. Just click List Chats, then double-click one of the hundreds (or on some nights, thousands) of chat rooms.

✔ If your kids use America Online, then you definitely need to know about the Parental Controls for chat rooms. Check Chapter 4 for the details.

Why you simply must fill out your profile

Before getting too far into the fun and frolic of the People Connection, you need to know about Member Profiles. Your Member Profile is a little online dossier that you write yourself. It contains whatever you want other America Online subscribers to know about you, such as your real name, your birthday, the computer you use, and so on. You don't have to fill out every line — leaving some parts blank is perfectly okay. The sidebar figure shows a really good Member Profile.

Why fill out your profile? Well, if someone meets you in a chat room or reads a message you posted and wants to find out more about you, he or she checks your Member Profile. People often search the Member Profiles looking for other America Online members with the same interests. My wife was interviewed for a magazine article because the writer read her profile and liked what was there.

Making a profile isn't hard at all. Flip to Chapter 3 for all the details. To make a truly amazing profile, check out Chapter 21 for tricks of the profile masters.

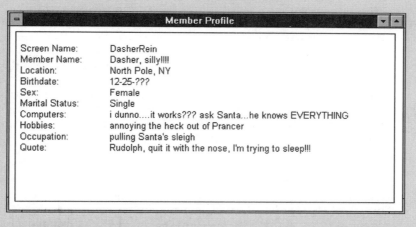

Screen Name:	DasherRein
Member Name:	Dasher, silly!!!!
Location:	North Pole, NY
Birthdate:	12-25-???
Sex:	Female
Marital Status:	Single
Computers:	i dunno....it works??? ask Santa...he knows EVERYTHING
Hobbies:	annoying the heck out of Prancer
Occupation:	pulling Santa's sleigh
Quote:	Rudolph, quit it with the nose, I'm trying to sleep!!!

Chat Room Addiction Counseling: Enter Here

It's only fair, both to you and to noncomputer portions of your life, to say this right up front: Chatting in the People Connection is almost too much fun for words. If you like people, thrive on conversation, and enjoy typing a lot, you may as well put a pillow and blanket next to the computer, because you've found a new home.

The People Connection chat rooms are America Online's answer to clubhouses, bars, meeting halls, the corner pub, and your living room (except that chat rooms are a little tidier under the chairs). Put simply, chat rooms are digital gathering spots where you and 22 other folks type about life, the universe, and what's for dinner.

When you first arrive in a room, the chat text area is blank except for a brief note from a computer named OnlineHost announcing what room you're in. After a few moments, the chat text area comes alive with messages. (Don't try to talk with the OnlineHost — it never answers.)

The key to a successful chat room conversation is knowing how to read your screen. Flip back to Figure 7-1. The chat text area is a mess, isn't it? That's because whenever anyone types a message in a chat room, everyone can read it. It's like a conference call where everyone talks at the same time *all* the time.

To follow the flow of a chat room, you have to skip around. The chat text in Figure 7-1 shows at least three different conversations. Here's a breakdown of the action.

At the top of the window, Knappers4 compliments another room member, WSMcIV, on his Web site. WSMcIV is deep in conversation with someone else at the moment, but he replies to Knappers4 near the bottom of the window. Meanwhile, I wandered into the room and ElfBot welcomed me. Near the middle of the window, Knappers4 and ElfBot carry on a little conversation about food. Around the same spot, WSMcIV and JSKaufeld chat about typing. At the bottom of the window, ElfBot tosses out a half-hearted joke (at least it came out that way) based on WSMcIV's last comment.

Tossing your own thoughts into the chat room maelstrom is really easy. Basically, start typing. Whatever you type appears in that long, thin box along the bottom of the chat room window. When you're done typing, press Enter (or Return) or click Send. In a moment or two, your words of wisdom appear in the chat text area for all to see. A single chat room comment only holds 92 characters, so choose your letters, numbers, and punctuation marks carefully (or split your thought into two lines — that works, too).

If you type a comment but your text *doesn't* appear in the box at the bottom of the chat room window, click the mouse anywhere in the box. Once you see the blinking toothpick cursor way over on the left side of the box, go ahead and start typing again.

There's a lot to tell about chat rooms, but little of it follows any kind of organization. With that bit of rationalizing out of the way, here are some randomly assembled thoughts and tips about the wild world of chatting:

✔ To get someone's attention in a chat room, start your comment with his or her screen name. If the person doesn't respond in a minute or two, try it again. If all else fails, send the person an Instant Message asking whether he or she saw what you typed.

✔ To quickly read a fellow chatter's Member Profile or send the person an Instant Message, scroll through the People Here list until you find the person's screen name, and then double-click it. A little dialog box pops up. At the bottom of the box are two buttons destined to make your life easier. Message sends an Instant Message to the selected person; Get Info displays his or her Member Profile. To get back to the chat room, close the little dialog box. Before making another comment in the chat room, click the mouse anywhere in the long box at the bottom of the window and then start typing (otherwise, what you type doesn't appear on-screen).

✔ That same dialog box (mentioned above) contains a really handy check box labeled Ignore. If a person is getting out of hand, or you just don't like listening to him or her, find the person's screen name in the People in Room list, double-click it, and click Ignore. From then on, nothing he or she types appears on your screen.

✔ If you see people writing comments like afk, bak, LOL, and ROFL!, don't worry — they're not making fun of you. That's standard chat room shorthand for things like *away from the keyboard*, *laughing out loud*, and other ever-necessary comments. For a quick primer in chat room-ese, use keyword **Shorthand** or check out Chapter 26.

Beware the Password Scammers

I wish I didn't have to include this section, but I must. Password scamming is alive and well on America Online. The good news is that America Online actively fights the jerks who do it; the bad news is that more jerks are *always* available to replace the ones who get caught.

Don't *ever* give your password to anyone — *anyone* — who asks for it, whether it happens online or some other way. Nobody from America Online will ever ask for your password. Period. Never. It won't happen. No matter what the person says, who the person claims to be, or what he or she threatens to do, ignore anyone who asks for your password — he or she lies.

Figures 7-2 and 7-3 are actual samples of password scammers I bumped into on America Online. I want to emphasize that: *I did not make these figures up — they are real.*

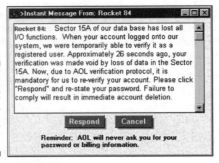

Figure 7-2:
Don't
believe it —
it's a pack
of lies!

Figure 7-3:
Don't talk to
them —
they'll say
anything to
get your
password.

If you get an Instant Message that looks like these figures, don't bother to reply or say anything catty; just get ready to ruin the scammer's day. Here's how to report a password scammer to America Online:

1. **Type a note to the other members of the chat room that says some- one is fishing for passwords.**

   Be sure to give the screen name of the person who sent you the Instant Message. It never hurts to remind everyone to *never* give out their passwords — think of it as your good deed for the day.

2. **Highlight the text in the scammer's Instant Message.**

3. **Choose Edit⇨Copy from the menu bar.**

   This copies the message text into the Clipboard, so you can easily send it to America Online.

4. **Use keyword** Guidepager **to bring up the I Need Help report-a- violation-here window.**

If you're not familiar with keywords, press Ctrl+K in Windows to open the Keyword dialog box, type your keyword (in this case the word **Guidepager**) in the space provided, and then click Go. Later, when you have more time, flip to Chapter 5 and check out the Keyword information.

5. **Click the Password button to report your password scammer (see Figure 7-4).**

    This displays the Report Password Solicitation dialog box.

Figure 7-4:
When scammers ask for your password, give them something they didn't bargain for.

6. **Type the screen name of the scammer, and then press Tab. Press Tab once more to move the cursor down to the text box at the bottom of the window. After you arrive there, choose Edit⇨Paste from the menu bar.**

    The text of your scammer's message appears in the box. If it doesn't, click Cancel and go through the steps again.

7. **When everything is filled out to your satisfaction, click Send.**

8. **Close the scammer's Instant Message window and proceed with your regularly scheduled evening.**

If you gave out your password before realizing that the person requesting it was a scammer, all is not lost. *Immediately* go to keyword **Password** and change your account password. After that, go through the preceding steps and report the scammer.

Enjoying a Little Private (Room) Time

Whether you're talking business or catching up with a friend, the People Connection's private room option gives you all the benefits of a chat room without the inconvenience of filling it with strange people. Private rooms are great for reunions, parties, brainstorming sessions, and regional meetings.

Private rooms are just that — private. Nobody can get in without knowing the name of the room (a name *you* make up, by the way). America Online doesn't keep a master list of active private rooms. People outside the room can't monitor the discussion in a private room.

Some limitations exist, but they're mostly technical. For example, a private room holds only 23 people (so you can't have a really *whopping* party). And you get unexpected guests every now and then. Someone thinks up the same name *you* used and {poof!} that person appears in your private room. Don't worry, though — that doesn't happen very often.

To create or join the discussion in a private chat room, follow these steps:

1. **Select People⇨Start Your Own Chat from the Toolbar.**

   The Start Your Own Chat dialog box appears.

2. **Click the Private Chat button.**

   The Enter a Private Chat dialog box hops nimbly onto the screen.

3. **Carefully type the name of the private room you want to either join or create and then click Go Chat.**

   The chat room window reappears, with the name of the private room emblazoned across the top.

If you're creating a new private chat room, just make up any name for it that you want. If you're joining someone else's room, type the name *exactly* as they gave it to you (assuming that they sent you the room name when they invited you in).

If you were heading into a private chat with some friends, but find yourself alone in an empty private room instead, make sure that you typed the name right (capitalization doesn't count, but spelling does). If you unexpectedly waltz into someone else's private room, blush profusely, type a brief apology, close the window, and start over at Step 1.

If you spend a lot of time chatting with folks on your Buddy List, then the new Buddy Chat feature promises to make your life a little easier. Flip to Chapter 10 for the details.

Attending Lectures (And Enjoying Them)

Chat rooms cater to small, informal groups of people. For something a little larger (such as, oh, about 500 people), America Online offers AOL Live!, where you can interact with popular media figures, captains of industry, authors (yes, even me), and lots of other fascinating folks. AOL Live! is a more controlled environment than the chat rooms, but it's still a lot of fun.

To get into AOL Live!, use keyword **Live**. The AOL Live! window appears, looking a lot like Figure 7-5. All the AOL Live! theaters look alike and work in basically the same way.

Figure 7-5:
Appearing
now in AOL
Live! . . .

When you enter one of the AOL Live! theaters, you're randomly assigned to a row with up to seven other people. To find out who else is in your row, click the People button. A dialog box that lists your row-mates appears. To say something in your row, type your thoughts in the text box along the bottom of the window and click Send (just as in the regular chat rooms). What you type appears in the chat text area, with your row number in parentheses before the comment. In-row comments are visible only to people in the row with you, so you can say just about anything you want.

To ask a question of the person onstage, click the Interact button, type your question in the dialog box, and then click Ask a Question. If the presenter answers your question and asks for more details from you, click the Interact button, type your comments, and click Send a Comment.

Sometimes the audience votes or bids on things. No, I don't know exactly *what* you vote or bid on, but I have it from the best authorities that the process is very important. To take part in this, click the Interact button, type your vote or bid (whatever it is), and click either Vote or Bid.

As with chat rooms, you need to know many other things about theaters to make your enjoyment complete:

✔ Take your newly developed chatting skills for a test drive at my *America Online For Dummies* monthly chat. It's the third Thursday of each month in AOL Live! (keyword **Live**). For 45 minutes, I answer questions and keep everyone filled in on the latest America Online news. It's a hoot (if I do say so myself).

✔ Did you miss a theater presentation that you wanted to attend? No problem — just look for a transcript. Use keyword **Intermission** (or click the Intermission button on the AOL Live! main screen) and then click Transcripts & Photos. All transcripts are plain-text files, so you can read them with any word processor.

✔ To change rows (if you're allergic to someone you're sitting with), click the Chat Rows button in the theater window and then double-click the row you want to move to. Remember that each row holds only eight people.

✔ For a list of upcoming AOL Live! events, use keyword **Live Guide**. Events in this folder are organized by date. Scroll through the list and double-click whatever event looks interesting to get the details.

Recording Your Conversations

For whatever reason (be it simple paranoia or something more complex), you may want a record of what went on during a chat. Perhaps you're attending a forum conference center presentation and need to review the chat for ideas. Or maybe you're just feeling a little cloak-and-dagger today and want to spy on your chat room friends. Whatever the reason, keeping a copy of your chats is easy.

To record the chat room you're in, choose My Files➪Log Manager from the menu bar. This selection opens the Logging dialog box, with the name of your chat room in the Room box. Click the Open button in the Chat Log area (near the top of the screen). In the Open Log dialog box, the chat room name automatically appears as your log name (you can change it if you want by typing a new name for the file). Either click Save or press Enter to open the Log file. From that point on, any new chat text appears on-screen *and* gets saved on your disk drive. Text that was already on-screen before you started the log won't be in the file.

Chapter 8

Dropping a Quick "Hello" with Instant Messages

*Y*ears ago, when the world was young and we thought desktop calculators and LED watches were still pretty neat, saying *hi* to your friends meant either calling them on the phone or sending them a quick note through the (gasp!) postal mail. As time went by, immediate gratification won over genteel manners, and thus phone calls became the norm.

The online world took immediate gratification to a whole new level by delivering messages anywhere in the world within moments. It also introduced new problems, because the friends that used to live next door now live in the next time zone (or, worse, the second continent on the left just past that ocean over there). E-mail still flies through the wires with the greatest of speed, but it's not interactive — you can't enjoy the back-and-forth exchange of ideas that a good, old-fashioned phone call provided.

Programmers abhor missing features, so the clever developers at America Online came up with the *Instant Message* system. Instant Messages blend the immediacy of e-mail with the interactivity of a phone call by letting you type back and forth with someone else on the system. It all happens right now — or, as the computer people say, in *real time* (as opposed to fake time, I suppose) — like a private, one-on-one chat room.

This chapter explores the Instant Message system and details how to send and receive Instant Messages (or IMs, for short), plus how to shut the little buggers off when you want to concentrate for a while.

In the near future, look for new tricks with Instant Messages, like the ability to send pictures (even *live* video captured from a camera attached to your computer) and voice conversations (just like the phone). But don't tell anyone where you heard about these great features first!

Online Telepathy with Instant Messages

Sometimes, you just want to drop a quick "Hi!" to someone you happen to bump into online. That's what the America Online Instant Message feature is for. It's an easy way to have a quick conversation with someone regardless of whatever else either of you is doing at the time (see Figure 8-1). Instant Messages are completely private, too — only you and your correspondent know what's passing between you.

Figure 8-1:
An Instant Message appears.

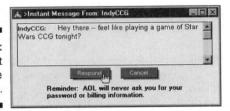

Using these little text bombs is easy — here's how:

1. **To see if someone is currently online, either check your Buddy List or use the Locate command.**

   The Buddy List system is a great tool for tracking your friends online. To find out more about it, see Chapter 10.

   You can only send Instant Messages to someone who's signed on *and* has Instant Messaging turned on in the America Online Parental Controls (keyword **Parental Controls**).

2. **Having found your target — er, friend — press Ctrl+I.**

   The Send Instant Message dialog box pops up.

3. **Type the person's screen name in the To box and then press Tab to move the blinking cursor into the text area. Type your message.**

   Keep Instant Messages short — 10 to 12 words is great. If you have something long to say, use e-mail.

If you're really in an Instant Message mode, skip step 1 entirely and use the Available? button in the Instant Message dialog box. Type the person's screen name and then click Available? to see if he or she is out there. That action gets the same results as Step 1's Locate Member Online command.

4. **After you finish typing the message, click Send.**

   If the message's recipient is signed on and accepting Instant Messages, then the Instant Message window disappears from your screen.

   If something goes wrong along the way (like the person isn't online right now or has blocked Instant Messages), then the America Online software displays an error message to keep you informed.

When your friend gets the message, he or she can reply by clicking the Reply button. His or her message then appears on your screen, and you can start a running dialogue. (That's assuming, of course, that your buddy *wants* to talk to you today.)

Turning Off Instant Messages, Because Sometimes You Just Want to Be Alone

Life on America Online sometimes resembles a huge commune. The moment you sign on, one (or sometimes several) of your friends immediately sends you an Instant Message and wants to chat. For hours.

If you want to check your e-mail in peace and quiet, or perhaps do a little online research, it's easy to hang out the *Do not disturb* sign by turning off incoming Instant Messages. The setting is temporary, so the next time you sign on to the system, Instant Messages are automatically *on* again.

To temporarily turn Instant Messages off, follow these steps:

1. **After signing on to America Online, press Ctrl+I to open a new Instant Message window.**

   A blank Instant Message window hops onto the screen.

2. **Carefully type the peculiar command $im_off in both the To field and the body of the blank Instant Message, then click Send.**

   If everything works right, America Online replies that you're now ignoring Instant Messages. If you get an error that says something about the user not being signed on, double-check your spelling and try again.

To turn Instant Messages back on without signing off the system, just repeat the process above, but use the command **$im_on**.

Teaching an old window some new tricks

The America Online 4.0 software opens up a wild frontier of communication with two new and eagerly anticipated features: Instant Images and Instant Voice. As I write this, these technologies aren't available for testing yet, but my highly placed sources (I'm tight with the night cleaning crew) assure me that the features will either be built into the new 4.0 software or be available shortly after the program comes out.

Remember the futuristic videophone things that AT&T used to show off as the future of communication? Well, Instant Images and Instant Voice turn that concept into reality — if, of course, your computer includes the right goodies.

Instant Images takes either individual graphic files or live input from a video camera and displays it right next to your Instant Message text. Instant Voice provides phone-quality (or so the developers promise) voice communication, so you can really *talk* to the person at the other end of the IM.

As I said before, though, none of this magic happens unless your computer contains the right techno-stuff. For live video Instant Images, you need a computer-capable video camera like the ones from Connectix, Intel, Kodak, Vivitar, or several other popular manufacturers. On the Instant Voice side of things, your computer requires a sound card.

To dig into the details of how these technologies work and the hardware it takes to make it all happen, check the America Online 4.0 upgrade center, at keyword **Upgrade**. Who knows — maybe we'll talk soon!

Catching a Password Scammer

Any time you collect 8 million people in one place (even if it's a virtual place), somewhere in the mix you're bound to find a few undesirable characters. At home, it's the telemarketers. At work, it's the slightly unhinged coworker who keeps calling gun shops on company time. And in the online world, it's password scammers.

These bottom-feeders only want one thing: your account password. Nobody — and I mean *nobody* — from America Online or any other company will *ever* ask for your password. It won't happen! No matter *what* the person says in their message, no matter who they claim to be, they are *lying*. Pay no attention to their drivel. Instead, get ready to report them to America Online.

If someone sends you an Instant Message or an e-mail asking for your password, credit card number, or anything else like this, report the person *immediately* with keyword **Guidepager**. This is a scam — period. Whether the person claims to be from the America Online billing department, a credit card company, or Mars (which is where he or she *should* be), it's a lie. You can find out more about this in Chapter 7, including detailed instructions for nailing — er, reporting — these scammers.

Chapter 9

Cogitating, Consternating, and Conflagrating in the Discussion Boards

• •

In This Chapter

▶ Frolicking in the folders

▶ Peeking at the messages (and adding some of your own)

• •

You can't turn around on America Online without running into a discussion. Whether you want to talk about music, mayhem, or something in between (like Branson, Missouri), America Online has a place for you somewhere.

After finding your online home, it's time to join the fray. Discussions are organized into *folders*. Each topic has its own folder. All the messages on one topic are entered (or *posted*) in the appropriate folder. Along the way, you deal with *folder windows* (which help keep the whole sordid thing organized) and *message windows* (the meat of the matter). This chapter looks at these parts of the discussion world, guiding you through the sometimes obscure path toward joining a discussion group and posting your opinions for all to see.

Winding Your Way through the Discussion Folders

Before you can join a discussion, you have to find one. To do that, cruise around in your favorite services and look for an item with a bulletin board icon (in the service list) or button (on a fancy service window) — those are strong clues that you found a discussion area.

Before getting into the details, here's a simple way to keep the following paragraphs straight in your mind, because the terms are kinda similar. Okay, ready? Here goes:

- ✔ Discussion boards contain folders (organizational helpers which can contain other folders and topics (see next bullet point).

- ✔ Topics are a collection of individual bulletin boards. Topics each contain a list of subjects.

- ✔ Subjects contain individual postings.

- ✔ Individual postings contain your thoughts.

With that firmly in mind, press onward for a more detailed explanation of the whole menagerie.

After finding a likely-looking discussion board, you encounter a window like the one in Figure 9-1. This window gives you an overview of every *topic and folder* in a particular discussion area. The board in Figure 9-1 only lists topics — individual bulletin boards focused on different discussions. Other discussion boards also include folders in this window's list as well. A single folder can hold a number of topics, and may even contain other folders. Because the online staffers in charge of each discussion area organize the boards however they see fit, the organizational details of each area vary among online forums.

Figure 9-1:
Discussion boards are the heart of America Online's communities.

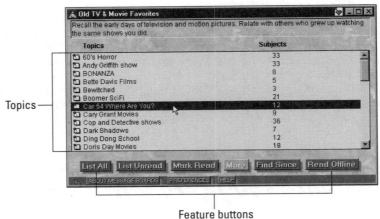

Feature buttons

Below the topic descriptions are the *feature buttons*. You usually see six buttons there. Table 9-1 lists the buttons, along with brief descriptions of what each one does. These buttons are your tools for filtering the postings in a particular message board. Use them well (particularly the Find Since button) to make short work of keeping up with your favorite boards.

Table 9-1:	Pressing the Discussion Board Buttons
Button Title	**Action**
List All	Opens the current bulletin board topic and lists all of the messages in it, whether you previously read them or not.
List Unread	Opens the current topic and displays *only* the messages you haven't read.
Mark Read	Marks all of the messages in the current topic as if you had read them.
More	Lists the rest of the topics on the bulletin in the window (available only if a particular bulletin board has a *lot* of topics on it).
Find Since	Displays only the messages written either within a particular number of days, in a certain date range, or that were added since the last time you visited the board.
Read Offline	Adds the selected topic to the list of bulletin boards you can *read offline* through Automatic AOL sessions. The list is kept at keyword **My Boards**.

Here are a couple of tips and tricks to keep in mind with the message boards:

✔ Don't fret if you double-click a message item and America Online replies with a terse message saying `This message is no longer available`. That just means that the message was posted so long ago that it was erased to make room for new ones. *Remember:* Old messages never die — they just scroll off the system.

✔ Use the Signature option in the Message Board Preferences window to automatically add a few words about yourself to the bottom of each posting. Remember that it's automatic — don't accidentally embarrass yourself.

✔ After your first visit to a topic area, save time by using the Find New and Find Since buttons to filter out old messages. That way, you don't have to wade through everything you've already read while the online clock is ticking.

Reading, Replying To, and Generally Browsing the Messages

When you find an interesting topic, double-click its entry to display a window like the one shown in Figure 9-2. These topics are discussion subjects themselves — the real meat of a discussion board.

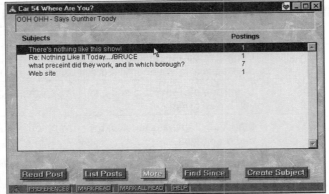

Figure 9-2:
The
discussion
is off and
running in
the subject
window.

In the middle of the screen is the Subjects list, displaying the first 40 or
so subjects that are open for debate. The Subjects list shows the title
of the subjects and the current number of responses. To see a message
within the subject, double-click the subject entry in this list, or click it once
and then click Read Post.

The feature buttons along the bottom of the window let you do all sorts of
fascinating things.

✔ Read Post does the same thing as double-clicking the subject name: It
puts you in the discussion message window and displays the first
posting in the selected subject.

When you double-click a subject (or highlight one and click the Read
Post button), the message appears in a window like the one shown in
Figure 9-3. After all that effort, this window is surprisingly easy to use.

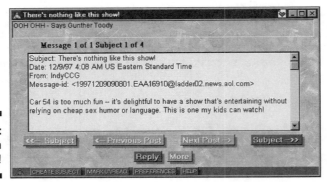

Figure 9-3:
Finally — a
message!

- ✔ List Posts generates a list of all posts within a particular topic, including who wrote the posting, how long it is, and the date and time it was written.

- ✔ The More button, like its counterpart in the topics window, only comes into play when there are so many messages that America Online can't display them all on the first try. In that case, click More to tell the system that you want to see more messages.

- ✔ Find Since works just like it does in the topics window — it displays matching messages for each subject within the current topic.

- ✔ Create Subject is your ticket to making a new discussion subject dedicated to whatever you jolly well want (is that ultimate power or what?).

- ✔ Cowering along the bottom of the window, you find the Preferences button (containing your bulletin board signature settings, plus other preferences regarding which posts are displayed, how they're displayed, and how many are downloaded).

- ✔ Mark Read and Mark All Read are down there as well to let you ignore whatever messages you wish.

The message text dominates the windows (as it should — after all, that's why you came). Every America Online message begins with a brief header giving the message's vital statistics: subject, posting date, author, and a grim-looking message ID that makes you wonder if it's harboring some secret code. The message itself follows.

Along the bottom are a whole raft of feature buttons that do just about anything your heart desires.

- ✔ The forward arrow and backward arrow Subjects buttons move you to the next subject for this discussion.

- ✔ The Previous Post and Next Post display other thoughts on the current subject.

- ✔ Use Reply to add your thoughts to this group (or *thread*) of messages within the subject.

Chapter 10

Where's Your Buddy, Where's Your Pal?

- -

In This Chapter

▶ Creating, deleting, and changing Buddy Lists
▶ Maintaining your privacy
▶ Making your preferences clear
▶ Gathering your buddies for a chat

- -

Meeting new friends is always fun. After all — what would your life have been like these past few years without your best friend (or your cadre of best friends)? When you meet a new friend on America Online, you can keep track of his or her screen name with AOL's Buddy List feature and avoid the frustrating experience of meeting a new best friend one day and losing her forever the next — and all because you forgot her name!

In this chapter, you'll learn how to create, add to, and delete Buddy lists. In case you find yourself in a talkative mood, you'll also find out how to send Instant Messages to your buddies and gather them together for a cozy private chat.

Who's Your Buddy?

The Buddy List tells you at a glance which of your friends are online. It even organizes your buddies into groups, making the task of discerning the office crowd from the gang at last week's online Jell-O diving competition an easy one. (After all, the difference may be important.)

By default, every time you sign on to America Online, your Buddy List jumps into action, hanging out on the side of your screen. (If you don't want the list to always come up, it's easy to adjust the Buddy List's behavior with the Buddy List Preferences, covered later in this chapter.) As your buddies sign on and off the system, the list updates itself automatically.

The following sections cover all the important stuff you need to know about building, using, and changing Buddy Lists on America Online. For information about the Privacy Preferences and Buddy List Preferences, see the sections entitled "Privacy Preferences: Please, I Vahnt to Be Alone" and "Setting Your Buddy List Preferences" later in this chapter.

Adding someone to a Buddy List

Including people in the Buddy List is a snap. Here's how to do it:

1. In the the Buddy List window, click the Setup button.

The Buddy List control window appears, just like Figure 10-1.

If your Buddy List window isn't already on-screen, click People➪View Buddy List from the Toolbar, then click Setup in the Buddy List dialog box. You can also use keyword **Buddy** to dive directly into the Buddy List control window, assuming that you're a big keyword fan.

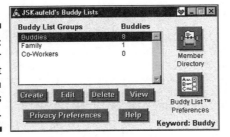

Figure 10-1: Tweak your Buddy List groups from this window.

2. Double-click the name of the Buddy List that you want to bulk up with new members.

Depending on your wishes, the Edit List Buddies window hops onto the screen, looking bright and chipper as ever. To create a new list, see "Creating a Buddy List" in the next section.

3. In the Enter a Screen Name box, type the screen name of your buddy, and then press Enter.

Your buddy's screen name takes its place in the Buddies in Group area.

4. Repeat Step 3 until all your buddies are in there. When you're done with the list, click Save.

To prove that it was listening this whole time, America Online replies that your list is updated. The Buddy Lists dialog box then returns in triumph, proudly displaying a new number of entries beside your list.

Creating a new Buddy List Group

You've met a whole slew of new people in a particular chat room, on a message board, or through an e-mail mailing list. Keep track of them by creating a unique Buddy List just for them.

1. **In the Buddy List window, click the Setup button.**

   The Buddy List control window appears, anxiously awaiting your new creation.

2. **Click Create to make a new Buddy List and add people to it.**

   The Create a Buddy List Group window hops onto the screen, ready to display the result of your creative efforts.

3. **In the Buddy List Group Name box, type a short name (16 letters or fewer) for the new list, and then press Tab.**

   The cursor jumps down to the Enter a Screen Name area.

4. **Click in the Enter a Screen Name box.**

   The blinking toothpick cursor appears there, ready to do its thing.

5. **In the Enter a Screen Name box, type your friend's screen name, and then press Enter.**

   Your buddy's screen name takes its place in the Buddies in Group area.

6. **Repeat Step 5 until all your buddies are in there. When you're done with the list, click Save.**

   America Online replies with a dialog box that says that your list has been created. When you click OK to make the dialog box disappear, the Buddy Lists dialog box returns, proudly displaying an entry for your new list (see Figure 10-2).

Figure 10-2: The Quilters proudly join my list of friends.

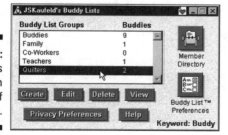

Deleting someone from a Buddy List Group

Sad to say, sometimes buddies become ex-buddies. Your interests change, their interests change, and suddenly you no longer correspond. Or maybe your friend simply changed screen names, which means you need to add his or her new screen name and delete the old one. Whether deleting a buddy from a Buddy List Group is traumatic or transitional, AOL has provided a way to get the job done.

1. **In the Buddy List window, click the Setup button. The Buddy List control window appears.**

   If your Buddy List window isn't currently on-screen, keyword **Buddy** brings the Buddy List control window to attention, too.

2. **Highlight the Buddy List Group that contains the passé screen name or absent friend, and click Edit.**

   The Edit List window opens, with the name of your selected Buddy List Group emblazoned across the window's title bar.

3. **Highlight your buddy's screen name in the Buddies in Group list, and click Remove Buddy.**

   The buddy's screen name jumps to the Enter a Screen Name field. If it was all a hasty mistake, click Add Buddy to reinstate your friend in the Buddy List Group.

4. **To remove the screen name from this particular group, click Save. A small dialog box appears, telling you that your Buddy Lists have been updated. Click OK to make the dialog box go away.**

   The Buddy List control window shows its face again. This time you'll see one fewer buddy in the Buddy List Group you just edited.

Deleting a whole Buddy List

Once a year or so, you get the urge to really clean house. Take a look at your Buddy List Groups and see if the adage doesn't also apply there. If you've been hanging onto Buddy List Groups that contain no members, groups that track outdated interests, or a list of e-mail business addresses for the job you left 18 months ago, a little window cleaning may be in order.

1. **Click the Setup button on your Buddy List window to open the Buddy List control window.**

   If your Buddy List window isn't handily on-screen, use keyword Buddy to bring the Buddy List control window to life, or select People⇨View Buddy List from the Toolbar, and then click Setup when the Buddy List window appears.

2. **Highlight the Buddy List Group you want to leave forever, and click the Delete button.**

   A small dialog box worriedly rushes to your screen, asking if you truly want to delete the entire Buddy List.

3. **Once you click Delete, the Buddy List control window adjusts to the change, displaying one fewer Buddy List Group in its collection.**

   Be very sure you want to delete a Buddy List Group before you click OK to delete the list. If you mistakenly delete the wrong list, you'll need to recreate that Buddy List Group from scratch. This has already happened to you? See "Creating a new Buddy List Group" earlier in this chapter.

Renaming a Buddy List Group

You woke up this morning and realized you'd found the perfect name for one of your existing Buddy List Groups. Never fear — changing that Buddy List name is a snap.

1. **Click the Setup button in the Buddy List window to bring up the Buddy List control window.**

   If your Buddy List window is hiding from you, keyword **Buddy** calls the Buddy List control window to your screen.

2. **Highlight the Buddy List Group you want to rename, and click the Edit button.**

   The Edit List window jumps to attention.

Watch carefully — it even does tricks!

Now that you have these cool new Buddy List Groups, what do you do with them? Well, plenty!

Want to know where your friend is hanging out online? Find him or her fast by highlighting his or her screen name and clicking the Locate button.

Quickly send your friend an Instant Message by highlighting his or her screen name and clicking the IM button. An Instant Message window opens on-screen, with your friend's screen name already filled in.

If you had a more face-to-face discussion in mind, use the Buddy Chat feature to invite your buddy to a private chat room with the two of you (and whomever else you'd like to invite). See the "Buddy Chat" section later in this chapter for all the details.

3. **Click in the Change Buddy List Group Name to box, and type in the new name for your Buddy List Group.**

   Choose a name that's representative of the whole group, or one that helps you remember why you've placed these screen names together.

4. **Click Save to make your changes a reality. A small dialog box appears, notifying you that your Buddy Lists have been updated. Click OK.**

   Once the dialog box disappears, you'll see an updated Buddy List control window that proudly displays your new Buddy List Group name.

Privacy Preferences: Please, I Vahnt to Be Alone

You don't have to be a movie star to want a little privacy every now and then. Sometimes, you just want to get away from it all and enjoy a little peace and quiet. That's why the Buddy List system includes a whole collection of privacy preferences.

If you don't want people to track your screen name with a Buddy List, that's easy to set up. Here's what to do:

1. **In the Buddy List window, click Setup. The Buddy List control window appears on-screen.**

   If your Buddy List window isn't currently visible, select People⇨View Buddy List from the Toolbar to make it magically appear. Then click the Setup button.

2. **Click the Privacy Preferences button in the Buddy List control window. You'll see the Privacy Preferences window jump to the screen, very similar to Figure 10-3.**

   Although it looks rather daunting, you'll find this window pretty easy to configure. The left side of the window shows two sections — Choose Your Privacy Preferences and Apply Preferences to the Following Features. Each section contains two or more radio buttons; clicking one to select it deactivates all the others.

3. **Click the radio button to activate whichever privacy level you prefer:**

   To completely block yourself from Buddy Lists all over America Online, click Block all AOL members and AOL Instant Messenger users.

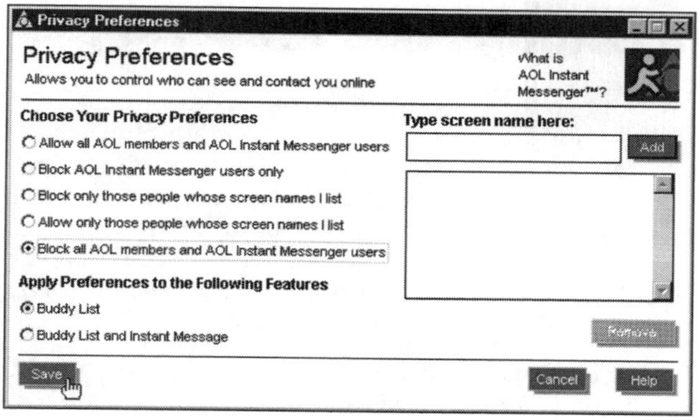

Privacy Preferences

Allows you to control who can see and contact you online

What is AOL Instant Messenger™?

Choose Your Privacy Preferences

○ Allow all AOL members and AOL Instant Messenger users
○ Block AOL Instant Messenger users only
○ Block only those people whose screen names I list
○ Allow only those people whose screen names I list
◉ Block all AOL members and AOL Instant Messenger users

Apply Preferences to the Following Features

◉ Buddy List
○ Buddy List and Instant Message

Type screen name here:

[Add]

[Remove]

[Save]   [Cancel]   [Help]

Figure 10-3:
Regain your
Buddy List
privacy.

To either allow or prevent a few members from tracking you on their Buddy Lists, click either Allow only those people whose screen names I list or Block only those people whose screen names I list. Then put the specific screen name you want to block or allow in the Type screen name here box and click Add. Add as many screen names as you want to block (or allow).

If you want to block all AOL Instant Messenger users from trying to communicate with you from the Internet, click Block AOL Instant Messenger Users only.

4. Elect to set these preferences for Buddy Lists only, or for Buddy Lists and Instant Messages.

If you decide to block both Buddy List and Instant Message users, the screen names you block appear as "not signed on" in your Buddy List window and if you attempt to send them an Instant Message. If you block only Buddy Lists, however, those screen names still show in your Buddy List window when they're online (if they were there to begin with).

5. When you've finished setting your privacy preferences, click Save. AOL sends you a dialog box that tells you you've updated your preferences. Click OK to make the dialog box disappear.

Your Buddy List privacy preferences are now active.

6. Click the upper-left corner of the Buddy List control window to close it.

Continue with your regularly scheduled online experience, free from unwanted interruptions.

Setting Your Buddy List Preferences

Some days you want sound in your world; other days the mere thought of extra noise makes your head pound. Set your general Buddy List preferences to match your mood. Opt for or against sounds when your buddies come and go, and tell the system whether you want to see your Buddy List each time you sign on. To set your Buddy List preferences:

1. **Click the Setup button on your Buddy List window to bring the Buddy List control window to attention.**

   If your Buddy List window is nowhere to be seen, keyword **Buddy** wakes the Buddy List control window, and it jumps smartly to attention.

2. **Click the Buddy List Preferences button to open the Buddy List Preferences dialog box.**

   Look for this button along the right side of the Buddy List control window — it's different from the Privacy Preferences button. You aren't deciding upon privacy issues here, but how and when your Buddy List appears and sounds.

3. **To see your Buddy List every time you sign on, click Show me my Buddy List(s) immediately after I sign onto AOL.**

   The Show me my Buddy List(s) box is checked by default. If waiting that few extra seconds for the Buddy List window to load each time you sign on really annoys you, uncheck it and use keyword **Buddy View** to see your Buddy List whenever you want to.

4. **The two remaining options deal with sound. To hear a sound when your buddies arrive, click Play sound when buddies sign on. To hear sound when your friends leave, click Play sound when buddies sign off.**

   Click only one if you want to be notified by sound only when friends sign on or sign off; click both to hear when they come and go. If your Buddy List Groups are large and their members active, the constant noises may grate your nerves after awhile. If that happens, use the Buddy List Preferences dialog box to uncheck the sound options.

   In order to hear Buddy List sounds, you need to download the Buddy Sound Installer file. The default sound for Buddy Lists is an opening and closing door; if you select the sound options and don't hear the door when the next buddy comes or goes, click the Go to Sound Library button in the Buddy List Preferences window to open the Buddy List Sounds information. Then click the Download Buddy Sound Installer "Door Theme" button to open the download window for the sound installer. Click Download Now to begin the download.

   If you want to see other available Buddy List sounds, click the Buddy List Sound Library button in the Buddy List Sounds window. Download any of the sounds in the list that tweak your fancy.

5. **When you're finished setting your Buddy List preferences, click Save. America Online produces a helpful Preferences Updated dialog box; click OK to make it go away.**

   You now find yourself back at the friendly Buddy List control window.

6. **If you're happy with the Buddy List preferences and don't wish to change anything else, click the upper-left corner of the Buddy List control window.**

   It merrily retires to windowland, to await your next summons.

Building an Online Treehouse with Buddy Chat

Instant Message conversations have their place, but for extended chatter it's nice to use the AOL chat rooms — they offer a larger text area for scrolling messages and the ability to talk to more than one person at once. With AOL's Buddy Chat feature, the system quickly creates a private chat room and invites the screen names you specify. Here's how you create a Buddy Chat of your own:

1. **Click the name of a buddy that you want to chat with, then click the Buddy Chat button in the Buddy List window.**

   The Buddy Chat window appears.

   To invite a whole bunch of buddies, click a Buddy Group entry (like Family, Friends, and so on) instead of clicking a single buddy's screen name.

2. **AOL fills in the screen names of your selected buddy or buddies, as the case may be. Their names appear in the Screen Names to Invite box. Alter the list as you like by erasing names and filling in others.**

   Invite as few as one person, or as many as you can reasonably fit into a chat room and still have a good time.

3. **In the Message to Send box, type a reason for getting together. AOL helpfully starts your message with** You are invited to; **either complete it or replace it with a phrase of your own.**

   Some invitations, like "You are invited to a public beheading," tend to turn people off. Spend a couple of seconds and make it sound inviting if you want your friends to actually attend your chat.

4. **Normally, Private Chat Room is checked in the Location part of the window. Leave it as it is to organize a Buddy Chat.**

If you click Keyword/Favorite, you need to enter a keyword into the Location text box. Friends who accept your invitation see one of your favorite places open on their screens.

Opting to invite friends to a keyword is useful if you want to attend the same scheduled chat in an area online or if you'd like to show them one of your favorite haunts. Once everyone has assembled, you can use Instant Messages to discuss the area and what you enjoy about it the most.

5. **The Location text box suggests a rather arcane chat room name, usually your screen name and then** Chat **with a few numbers tacked on the end of it. Change any (or all) of the Chat room name to make it a bit more friendly.**

   AOL chooses these chat room names to minimize the chance of having someone you don't know drop into your private chat room. If you change the chat room name to something more generic, such as I love dogs or Jane, you may receive a surprise visitor every now and then as someone else thinks up your chat room name. If this happens, simply tell them you're sorry, but their chat room name is already taken. Most of the time they'll leave as quickly as they came.

6. **When you've added, altered, and amended your invitation to your heart's content, click Send. Your Buddy Chat invitation wings its way to your friends.**

   To ensure that you're not forgotten, an invitation appears on your screen, too. Figure 10-4 shows you a sample. Click Go to enter the chat room.

   The Invitation also features an IM button. You may receive an Instant Message from buddies in a teasing mood, or from someone who had a momentary brain lapse on your screen name's identity.

7. **You arrive in the chat room you've created and await your buddies. Once you're in the room, you'll find that it works just like a normal private chat — mostly because it** *is* **a private chat room.**

   Greet your buddies as they drop into the room and have a great conversation.

Figure 10-4:
Anyone for a private Buddy Chat?

Part III
Diving into the
Fun Stuff

The 5th Wave   By Rich Tennant

It started as a wrap-
around porch, and then
Stuart found information
on medieval architecture
on AOL.

In this part . . .

*O*kay, so you're not easily impressed — e-mail doesn't do much for you, discussion boards warm your fires only a bit, and chats leave you utterly cold. You tend to repeat the question time and time again: "So what can you really *do* with AOL?" Yet, you know that the online world truly is the Next Big Thing and you want to join in the fun.

Welcome to Part III — your fieldbook for the Digital Age, offering tips for finding the who, what, and where of digital life; techniques for researching the topics that tweak your curiosity; and suggestions for picking out the *perfect* game to play while frittering the hours away. To make the part complete, I also include an Internet chapter, with the low-down on everything from gophers to the Web.

Chapter 11

Finding People, Places, Things, and Information

In This Chapter

▶ Uncovering the Find Toolbar button

▶ Searching for people

▶ Discovering great online places and resources

▶ Finding disk-filling files and programs

*I*f I could have a nickel for every time someone asked how to find things in the online world, I'd ask for a dollar instead. (A nickel doesn't buy *anything* these days.) Whatever the payment, I would be up to my eyeballs in money. That's because tracking stuff down on America Online and the Internet is (ahem) challenging — or at least it *was* challenging before those clever programmer types invented the super-cool *find systems*.

Whether you want something specific or feel like browsing aimlessly for a while, start your hunt here, with the various find systems available through America Online. This chapter reveals the find oracle's mystic secrets, starting with the Find button itself and continuing with a romp through all your find-related tools. Whether you seek an online area, Web page, favorite quotation, obscure fact, e-mail address, or business phone number, America Online's find tools make quick work of the job.

Finding the Big Search Kahuna Toolbar Button

 Your best general tool in the quest to find cool online stuff sits on the right side of the navigation bar, just waiting to offer its assistance. The Find button gathers all the various America Online search tools beneath one easy-to-use menu. From here, it's a short trip to search the member directory, the keyword list, the World Wide Web, or just about anything else.

The following bullets give you a quick introduction to the Find button's various options and where the choices lead:

- **Find⇨Find Central:** Calls up the Find Central window; same as keyword **Find Central.** This window links you to all of America Online's best search features. See the "Find it all with Find Central" sidebar later in this chapter for more specifics.

- **Find⇨Find it on AOL:** Opens the AOL Find window (just like keyword **AOL Find**). Searches for the subject you enter (like *kites* or *antiques*) across all the America Online–based content areas.

- **Find⇨Find it on the Web:** Sends you to America Online's NetFind Web search system; same as keyword **NetFind.** See the NetFind section later in this chapter for all the details.

- **Find⇨AOL Channel Guide:** Select this item for a quick overview of the 19 channel areas within America Online, plus links that take you directly to the various areas within each channel.

- **Find⇨Software:** Brings up the File Search dialog box, which sends you to the commercial and shareware search systems; just like keyword **File Search.**

- **Find⇨Chats:** Takes you into the Find a Chat window, where you can browse through the featured chat or member chat room lists, or search through the chats by room name to find *precisely* the one you want.

- **Find⇨AOL Members:** Opens the Member Directory search window; same as keyword **Member Directory.** Search for people who share your interests, location, birthday, or whatever else you can think of.

- **Find⇨Internet White Pages:** Sends you to Switchboard (keyword **Switchboard**), a searchable white pages of Internet e-mail addresses for both individuals and companies.

- **Find⇨AOL Access Numbers:** Searches for local America Online access phone numbers; just like keyword **Access.** This option works whether you're currently online or not. (Pretty cool, eh?)

- **Find⇨AOL Help:** Displays the offline America Online help screens.

Almost all the items under the Find button have direct keywords as well, so if you're more of a type-a-holic than a mouse-a-holic, feel free to use the keywords instead of mousing around through the button menu.

Find it all with Find Central

It's time for a quick experiment.

With no special equipment and nothing up my sleeve, I shall now attempt to link two ideas within the recesses of your mind. Ready to begin? First, think of the word *look*. Got it? Good. Now, use keyword **Find Central** to open up the very slick Find Central window. Softly repeat the word *look* as you gaze at the Find Central window. When you want to *look* for something, but you don't know where to start,

think of Find Central, America Online's single best starting point for the whole search experience.

From this one window, it's a snap to reach all the system's search services. Whether you seek people to meet, places to visit, or things to do, Find Central has the tools you need. Either use keyword **Find Central** or click the Find button, then select Find Central from the drop-down menu.

Finding People: Sniffing Out Friends, Acquaintances, and Other Novel Folks

Even though the world of America Online is packed with information covering every topic under the sun, it's the people that make life fun — people who populate the chat rooms, fill the message boards, and pack the audiences at online events. No matter what brought you to America Online, it's the community that keeps you here.

The tools in this section help you find people, wherever they may be. Each tool takes a slightly different spin on the problem, from locating friends currently signed on to the system, to discovering friends-to-be among the millions of other America Online members.

Locating folks to see who's around

America Online's Locate command gives you a quick way of finding your friends. If you know your pal's screen name, then the Locate command tells you whether your compatriot is signed on at the moment, and also reports if he or she is in a chat room right then. If your friend is chatting the light fantastic in a public chat room, auditorium, or conference room, the Locate system automatically offers to take you right into that chat. (Ahh . . . this is definitely one of those "Isn't technology wonderful?" moments.)

Speaking of technology, America Online *also* includes a way for you to prevent people from finding you with the Locate command (and through Buddy Lists as well). To find out more about the built-in privacy options, stealthily slink through "Privacy Preferences: Please, I Vahnt to Be Alone" in Chapter 10.

To quickly find someone online with Locate, follow these steps:

1. **Either press Ctrl+L or select People⇨Locate AOL Member Online.**

   The Locate Member Online dialog box appears on-screen, ready and willing to do its thing.

2. **Type the screen name into the dialog box and either press Enter or click OK.**

   The system searches hither, thither, and even Yonkers to see if the person you seek is currently signed on to America Online or the European AOL service.

   If the person is signed on right now (and if he or she didn't block you through the Buddy List system's privacy preferences), then America Online displays the Locate dialog box shown in Figure 11-1. The system giddily announces that it found him or her, and tells you whether he or she is currently in a public chat room, a private chat room, or just skulking around the system waiting for you. If your pal is in a public chat room, the dialog box also gives you the room name and offers a Go button so you can join him or her there. The dialog box also offers a button to send the person an Instant Message.

   If the person you seek is not online at the moment, a vaguely sad dialog box tells you. In that case, be sure to check your spelling, because America Online doesn't say `Whoops, you misspelled the screen name` — instead, it looks for a person with the screen name you typed, whether or not that's actually a valid America Online screen name.

Figure 11-1:
Hey — I'm
signed on!

Searching the member directory

It doesn't matter if you like to dress up as Ben Franklin and fly kites during rainstorms or meditate in front of the TV considering Zen and its effects on game show hosts. With more than 10,000,000 members, it's *very* likely that people just like you are out there somewhere in America Online. The trick is finding them — or being found yourself.

To ensure that you are found, fill out your online profile. If you haven't done your profile yet, then there's no time like the present. Sign on to America Online, choose My A̲OL⇨My Member P̲rofile from the Toolbar, then mark your place in this book and fill out the profile dialog box. When you're done, click Update to save your profile information and then come back to the book (yes, I'll wait for you). Now that your profile is done, you're part of the member directory. Congratulations.

If you want an incredibly fancy profile that's sure to make people stop and say "Hey, that's a really fancy profile," flip to Chapter 21.

Now that your information is in the system, try searching the member directory for friends-to-be. To do that, follow these steps:

1. **Choose Membe̲rs⇨Member Directory or use keyword Members to bring up the Member Directory dialog box.**

   The Member Directory Search dialog box appears.

2. **Type in something that describes the people you want to find: a hobby you enjoy, the city you're from, your occupation, or whatever else you can think of.**

   Short descriptions work best. Check your spelling — you don't want a typo standing between you and your friends-to-be!

3. **Click Search to see who you can see.**

   If America Online reports that it can't find anyone, check your spelling again (it never hurts) or search for some other unique characteristic. If everything works, the dialog box overflows with possible new friends. (Okay — it doesn't *really* overflow, but that's poetic license for "there are so many entries that a scroll bar appears next to the list.")

4. **Double-click anyone who looks interesting. Jot down the screen name (or add it to your address book), write a "Hi, how ya doing?" e-mail message, and see where it goes from there.**

When you reach this last step, remember that you only get one chance to make a good first impression. Make your introductory e-mail message witty, genteel, interesting, and, most of all, polite. If the person in question never writes back to you, don't take it personally — just search the member directory again and look for someone else to correspond with instead.

Finding friends with Switchboard

Even though America Online has more than 10 million members, that number pales against the countless millions who inhabit the Internet worldwide. Even though there's nothing exactly like America Online's member directory for the Internet itself, America Online's *Switchboard* system makes a good start.

Switchboard is a white pages–style listing of names, addresses, phone numbers, and e-mail addresses for United States residents. It's drawn from publicly available information, so the odds are good that both you and your friends are already listed in it. Even though you're in the system, though, there's no guarantee that the information about you is accurate, but they do try. (Ah, the joys of information in the electronic age, eh?)

In addition to address and e-mail information for individuals, the system also includes a whole section devoted to business information. The business search system works much the same way as the version for individuals, so just pay attention to the prompts as you work through the dialog boxes, and your business searches should go as successfully as your other explorations.

Searching the Switchboard system only takes a few steps. Here's what to do:

1. **Use keyword** Switchboard **to open the Switchboard system.**

   The Web browser pops up, filled to the brim with the Switchboard Web site.

   If you select Find⇨Internet White Pages instead, you end up at an introductory Switchboard page. To find a person's mailing address from there, click the Find People button, then continue with the next step.

   If you want to look for an individual's e-mail address or for business information, click the E-mail Finder or Find a Business links on the left side of the Switchboard window and carefully follow the on-screen prompts.

2. **Fill in whatever information you have about the person, such as the name, city, state, and such, then click Search.**

   Switchboard chews on your information for a while, then displays its search results.

3. **If the system found your person (or a group of people, if you did a more general search), it lists the name and address it came up with from the Switchboard database.**

   If there's more than one name, scroll through the list until you find the specific person you wanted.

   On the other hand, if the system didn't find your person, then try leaving off the first name, or shorten the name to just the first few letters. Searching for *Dave,* for instance, won't find your person if he's listed as *David.* Try using *Dav* for the search, because that matches both variations.

Finding Places: Tracking Interests and Meeting Informational Needs

Do you ever sit in front of your computer, staring at the America Online screen, knowing that what you want to know just *has* to be in there somewhere? If only you knew where to look . . . (insert wistful sigh here).

The next time that feeling strikes, fire up one of America Online's topical search systems. These routines search not only the content areas within America Online but also the wealth of stuff on the World Wide Web to match you with precisely the place you want.

When looking for a particular topic, start with the Find It on AOL system first, then use NetFind (or one of the other Web search engines discussed in the NetFind section) as a backup. To zero in on specific information (like tips, reviews, and such), use the Search & Explore options within each channel. Remember that areas inside America Online usually offer both informational and community links (like discussion boards and chat areas), while most Web sites are information-only connections.

Find It on AOL

To track down an online community for your favorite topic, open up the Find It on AOL window (keyword **AOL Find,** or select Find⇨Find It on **A**OL) and try a search. Find It on AOL takes any word you type (like *homework, finances,* or *photography*) and looks for that subject among America Online's forums and services. The system lists everything that it finds relating to your subject.

To search the subject list, sign on to America Online and follow these steps:

1. **Open the Find It on AOL window by either using keyword** Find **or selecting Find**⇨**Find It on A**OL.

   The Find It on AOL window pops up, ready for some aerobic activity.

2. **In the box at the top of the window, type the word you're looking for and then click Find.**

   After a moment, the results of your search appear in the bottom of the window, just like in Figure 11-2. If AOL finds more than 20 matches, the window shows only the first 20. To see the rest, click the More button at the bottom of the window.

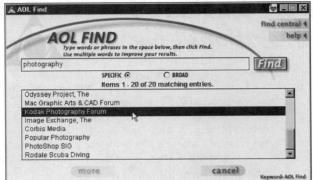

Figure 11-2:
Whether
your topic
is quite
general or
a little
esoteric,
the odds
are good
that it's
somewhere
on AOL.

If the system displays a window apologizing for the fact that it couldn't find any matches for the topic you entered, don't worry — you didn't do anything wrong. Instead, close the gee-I'm-sorry-I-failed-you window and search on a different term. You may also try clicking the Broad radio button to tell the AOL Find system to be a little less detail-oriented during the next inquiry. If you run out of terms, then take your search out to the World Wide Web through NetFind, discussed later in this chapter.

3. **Browse through the Search Results window to see what America Online found for you. To find out more about something on the list, double-click its entry.**

   When you double-click an item in the Search Results list, a new window appears with all the details about that particular area. If it looks like what you want, just click the big Go There! button at the bottom of the window. Pretty cool, eh?

4. **When you're done with the window, close it and go back to the Search Results window to look for other items of interest.**

   If you get lost on the way back to the results window, use the Window menu to jump directly there.

5. **To start another search, go back to the AOL Find window and start over at Step 2.**

   If you don't feel like looking for anything else right now, feel free to close all the search-related windows. (There's no penalty for tidiness.)

New information areas come online all the time, so search for your favorite subjects regularly. Doing so is a great way to keep up with the latest stuff.

NetFind

It seems like almost everybody (including the local plumber) offers information through the World Wide Web these days. That diversity makes the Web an incredible repository of information — like a library filled with the collected knowledge, opinions, and ramblings of a measurable percentage of the world's populace. Sounds almost too good to be true, doesn't it?

Well, you're right — there is a catch. Although the Web world is filled to the brim with cool stuff, organizationally speaking it's a mess. Imagine a library organized by a tornado, with assistance provided by every kindergartner in your hometown. Not a pretty picture, is it?

Shortly after the Web came to be, many clever people built indexes and search systems to tame this wild digital frontier. Some of these tools catalog sites and then help you search the list by a keyword you entered. Others take a slightly different approach by building a topic index that you browse by clicking on-screen menus. Both systems have their advantages, depending on what you want to find and how you feel like looking for it.

America Online's foray into the world of Web searching is NetFind. NetFind gives you the best of both worlds, by offering both a searchable database *and* a browsable subject index — although the list of subjects is somewhat limited right now.

✔ **To go topic hopping through NetFind,** just click one of the links in the Time Savers area along the bottom half of the window. Each of these leads to more-detailed lists. Just keep clicking until you dig your way down to a particular site that meets your needs. If you click your way to the bottom of the barrel without finding a good match, then try a keyword search instead.

✔ **To use NetFind's fill-in-the-blank search option,** type a word or two describing your topic into the box at the top of the NetFind window, then click the ever-exuberant Find! button. After chewing on your request for a few moments, NetFind returns with a list of matching sites. To view any of the matches, just click the site's entry. Sometimes, NetFind uncovers so many possible matches that they won't fit on one screen. In that case, NetFind presents you with a Next button at the very bottom of the window. Click that button to view the next page of matching entries.

If NetFind can't come up with anything that matches your topic, it quietly tells you of its failure and often implies that the problem is somehow your fault. Don't believe it — it lies. If this happens during your search, take your topic to another of the Web's search engines, listed in Table 11-1. Some engines, notably Yahoo!, provide automatic links to other popular search systems when they display your search results (just in case you want to try your luck elsewhere).

Table 11-1	Scour the World Wide Web with These Search Engines
Search Engine	*Web Address*
AltaVista	http://www.altavista.digital.com
Deja News	http://www.dejanews.com
Excite	http://www.excite.com
Infoseek	http://www.infoseek.com
Lycos	http://www.lycos.com
Yahoo!	http://www.yahoo.com

Browsing through some great resources

Sometimes, it's not easy to nail down precisely what you want to find. Instead of being a simple, cut-and-dried topic, your goal is more vague — sort of an I'll-know-it-when-I-see-it feeling. Even so, you still need some places to start looking. The general areas listed in the previous section may meet your needs, but sometimes a more narrowly focused source sparks your imagination in a way that a more general one can't.

The following bullets identify a selection of searchable resources from all corners of America Online. Some areas offer news, while others come bearing general introductory notes. All of them are free, which makes them my friends by default.

- The king of all general references has to be the New York Public Library Desk Reference (keyword **Desk Reference**). Just look at the list in that window — topics ranging from etiquette to personal finance, plus even more that didn't fit in the window! No matter what kind of information you seek, the Desk Reference makes a great starting point.

- Every schoolchild in the country knows that it's hard to stump the encyclopedias (keyword **Encyclopedias**). Putting these general reference guides online makes it even easier to browse and search their content.

- In addition to the encyclopedias, America Online offers many other classic references, such as a dictionary (keyword **Dictionary**) and a thesaurus (keyword **Thesaurus**). It goes a step further by offering specialized word references too, like Word Histories (keyword **Word Histories**), Other Dictionaries (keyword **Dictionary**, then click Other Dictionaries), and the finance-centered Wall Street Words (keyword **WSW**).

✔ Writers require strong research areas to find facts for their stories, but sometimes they also need information that's a little off the beaten path. For days when you either want a good laugh or feel like adding to your storehouse of the odd and mystifying, check out Straight Dope (one of my favorite areas, at keyword **Straight Dope**), Madworld (keyword **Madworld**), and Urban Legends (keyword **Hub**, then click Urban Legends).

✔ What report, theme, or presentation couldn't use a good quote to spice it up? Choose the best sound bites from the NYPL Book of 20th Century Quotations (keyword **Quotations**).

✔ When your research sends you looking for ethnic information, try areas like Native Sons & Daughters (keyword **Native Sons**), Black History Reference (keyword **BH Reference**), or Hispanic Online (keyword **Hispanic Online**). Each one includes resources, discussions, and chats that might lead you to still other resources in the Great Out There.

✔ Digging into the world of business? Check out Business Research (keyword **Business Research**) for general corporate information and a searchable library of press releases; Company Research (keyword **Company Research)** for financial reports; and the news by company ticker system (keyword **Company News**) for the latest news wire tidbits about your favorite firms.

✔ It's a frightening thought, but the Federal Government is the single largest publisher in the United States. It also generates more statistics than should be allowed by law. To dip into the wellspring of numbers bought with your tax dollars, check out the Federal Statistics Web site at http://www.fedstats.gov.

If you need to collect information about a topic on an ongoing basis, check out the News Profiles system, at keyword **News Profiles.** You define what kind of stories you want to see, and the News Profiles system scours the news wires, automatically forwarding any matching stories directly to your mailbox. Setting up a profile only takes a moment, but it keeps going and going, just like an electronic news version of that annoying pink bunny.

Finding Things Like Programs and Files

After working through the initial euphoria (and the first credit card bill) of owning your computer, the next thought that usually goes through your mind is something like "I wish the computer could do X," where *X* is some incredibly important task that none of your current software and hardware setup comes even *close* to performing. Worse yet, if you're like most people (myself included), X is quickly followed by Y, Z, and a whole horde of functions starting with peculiar math symbols that you barely remember from school.

It sounds like you need software — and lots of it, at that! Purchasing commercial programs to accomplish everything is a great idea, but your credit card is still on life support from getting the computer. Copying your buddy's program is out of the question (the software makers frown on that in a big ugly nasty way). What's a computer owner to do? Search the file libraries of America Online, that's what!

The hundreds of file libraries on America Online contain programs that process words, mangle (sorry, *manage*) data, implode unfriendly aliens — well, the list goes on and on. These programs keep your budget happy, too, because they're either *freeware* (completely free programs donated to the world by proud developers) or *shareware* (try-before-you-buy programs that require only a small payment to the author). You may even find demonstration versions of commercial applications, as well.

To help you find the software needle in these online haystacks, America Online created the Software Search system. This system quickly puts the software you need right into your hands — or, more precisely, right onto your hard drive, which is an infinitely better place for a program (software stains wickedly if you get it on your clothes).

Get into the File Search system either by selecting Find⇨Software or by using keyword **Software Search.** A little dialog box happily pops up, asking if you want to search for commercial (also known as *expensive)* programs or if you prefer to cruise through the shareware file libraries. Unless your credit card is well on its way to a full recovery, click the button for searching the file libraries. When the File Search window appears, type a description of what you need, then click Search to see what's out there. For a thorough, step-by-step walk through finding files and downloading them, flip to the first section of Chapter 15.

In the unlikely event that you can't find what you want in America Online's voluminous digital catacombs, point your Web browser to either Download.Com (`http://www.download.com`) or Shareware.Com (`http://www.shareware.com`). These two sites (both part of CNET's huge Web presence) carry software for almost any use and occasion, including business applications, utilities, games, and more. There's no cost to use the areas (and no salesman will call).

Chapter 12

Tracking News, Weather, Markets, and More

- -

In This Chapter

▶ Browsing through the news

▶ Collecting stories with a session log

▶ Checking on the weather

▶ Examining the business side of news

- -

*N*ews plays a big role in our lives. It's our link to the community, the country, and the world. America Online must think that news is very important, because it offers so many kinds of news — headlines, international, business, technology, feature; well, the list goes on — and all of it costs you nothing extra because it's part of America Online's normal service. Is this a deal or what?

Thankfully, America Online gives you lots of tools, as well, for dealing with the influx of news, weather, sports scores, and stock prices. This chapter looks at your options for picking up news, ranging from a casual romp through the channel to a detailed analysis of the markets. It's a chapter worth looking at two or three times over the coming months, because your information needs will change over time.

Getting the News

Most of the online news lives (no surprises here) in the News channel shown in Figure 12-1. This window is a general gateway featuring top headlines and links to more-targeted news in the various news departments. Each department, in turn, narrows the focus even further, giving you an ever more carefully winnowed collection of stories. (See *AOL Channels For Dummies,* a special book-within-a-book right after The Part of Tens.)

Figure 12-1:
The News
channel
hosts top
stories and
links to
specialized
online news
areas.

Some of the most interesting news areas sit deep inside the News channel's departments. For instance, it's one thing to read a relatively short news wire story about massive changes in Korea's banking system, but it's another thing entirely to review an in-depth analysis of those same events in the Economist Intelligence Unit (keyword **EIU**). Other sources, like *Newsweek* (keyword **Newsweek**), ABC News (keyword **ABC News**), *BusinessWeek* (keyword **BusinessWeek**), and the *New York Observer* (keyword **NY Observer**) provide equally deep and unique perspectives on the news that are beyond what the wire services have time and capacity to provide.

Filling your mailbox with news that you want

There's a little-known feature of America Online's news system that could save a *lot* of time if you like to watch for stories about particular topics or companies. Given all the resources in the News channel, you often don't have time to sift through tons of stories to find that all-important informational nugget. America Online's News Profiles service (keyword **News Profiles**) solves this problem for you by delivering the latest stories about topics *you* choose directly to your mailbox.

To build a news profile, go to keyword **News Profiles** and follow the instructions in the How to Create a Profile section. Start with something simple, like one topic (mine was *espionage*) or a company name. Let the profile do its thing for a couple of days so you can judge how many new e-mail messages it adds to your box. Adjust the items in your profile or the story limit setting to manage the incoming story flow.

This service comes at no extra charge with your America Online account, so it's definitely worth a look. One word of caution, though: If you track a popular topic (like *Microsoft* or *Clinton lawsuits*), your mailbox fills up in no time at all!

Rolling Your Articles into a Log

With so many easily accessible news areas, you could spend all day doing nothing but wandering from place to place, browsing through the stories. Obviously, this is going to impact your regularly scheduled day. Luckily, there's a tool built right into your America Online software that captures all the stories you see on-screen and packages them into a single file, which you can put on your laptop, print out on paper, or even download to your personal digital assistant.

The tool is the *session log* (part of the Log Manager that's built into your software), America Online's answer to a very fast-writing scribe. The Session Log automatically copies any articles that you display into a plain text file on your computer. What's an *article*? It's a news story, picture caption, bulletin board posting, or other text that appears in a window on-screen. Menu items and things like that don't count — it's only paragraphs of text that land in the log files.

Follow these steps to create a session log of your reading activities:

1. **Select My Files⇨Log Manager.**

   The Log Manager window, small though it is, hops onto the screen.

2. **Click the Open Log button in the Session Log portion of the dialog box.**

   The Open Log window, shown in Figure 12-2, appears.

3. **America Online automatically offers to name the file** SESSION.LOG, **which is fine for most purposes. Click Save.**

   If you want to save the session log files for posterity, you might change the name to today's date instead. If you reuse the same name each day (always naming the file SESSION.LOG, for example), when you click Save, Windows asks if you want to overwrite the old file with a new one. Click Yes when it asks.

4. **Browse through the news stories just as you always do.**

   From this point on, your session log file is active and working behind the scenes to capture all the stories that you display on-screen. Do what you normally do: Find a story that looks interesting, then click it to bring it up in a window. You don't need to actually scroll through the story yourself; just making it appear in the window is good enough for the session log.

Logging
Chat Log
Room:
Log file name:
Open Log   Append Log   Close Log
Session Log
Log file name:
Open Log   Append L

Figure 12-2:
Using the default name, SESSION.LOG, works well for most everyone.

5. **When you finish looking through the stories, select My Files⇨Log Manager to open the Log Manager, then click Close to save the log file.**

   Your file is safely tucked away on your computer. At this point, you can do anything you want with it, including opening it in a word processor, printing it out, or copying it to another computer or a personal digital assistant.

If you copy the log file into a personal digital assistant (such as a Sharp Zaurus or Palm Pilot), remember to erase it when you finish indulging your desire for news. Otherwise, the stories take up the very valuable (and limited) memory space in your little device.

The Weather Outside — Is It Frightful?

How much you care about the weather seems to directly depend on where you live (I wonder if anyone in Hawaii, for instance, *really* checks the forecasts, except during storm season) and which generation you belong to. My parents, for instance, were denied weather forecasts as children, so both of them actually watch the cable-TV Weather Channel radar for fun. I, on the other hand, took off on a trip into Canada without stopping to realize that late-fall-leaning-toward-winter means a much different thing when you're 700 miles farther north. (My cotton jacket froze on that trip, but I managed to survive wrapping my head in socks.)

To avoid problems like this in your life, check out America Online's Weather area, at keyword **Weather.** It's one-stop shopping for every kind of weather information imaginable (plus some that you just don't *want* to imagine). There's even a weather store, where, presumably, you can take home your very own cumulonimbus cloud and whip up a storm in the privacy of your own home.

Among other things, the Weather area (shown in Figure 12-3) offers a quick forecast for anywhere in the United States, plus detailed forecasts for both the U.S. and the world. It even includes satellite and radar images for you to look at and download (they're great for school projects or as practice maps for budding meteorolgists).

Figure 12-3: No matter what kind of weather you want, it's available somewhere in the Weather window.

Watching the Markets

Given the amount of work and worry that some people put into fretting over their stock market investments, stuffing all your cash into a mattress suddenly looks like a marginally attractive idea. At least you don't spend all your time wondering if your funds are safe, because what kind of thief is going to walk off with a big . . . um . . . did you happen to see where my bed went? Hmm — perhaps there is something to be said for putting your money in stocks after all.

If you've parked some money in stock investments, you probably want to see how your investments are performing. America Online offers two unique tools for tracking your stock market moneys. The first is the Quotes system, which pulls up the almost current (delayed by 20 minutes) price for whatever you want. The other system is Portfolios, which makes short work of watching a whole group of stocks. The following sections look at each of these tools individually.

Quotes (keyword Quotes)

The only way that checking stock prices could be easier than America Online's Quotes system is if the system read your mind — but if it did that, who knows *what* it may discover? Perhaps it's best if we just keep the Quotes system the way it is and not let computers peer into our thought processes.

Getting a stock quote only takes a moment. Here's what to do:

1. **Open the Quotes window by using keyword** Quotes **or clicking the Quotes button on the Toolbar.**

   Whichever way you choose, the Quotes window hops into action.

2. **Type the company's stock ticker symbol into the Enter Symbol box, then click Get Quote.**

   After a moment or two, the stock's information appears in the lower section of the Quotes window (see Figure 12-4).

   If the window mechanically mutters no quote information available, then double-check the spelling of the ticker symbol you entered. If worse comes to worst, click the Lookup button to find the symbol you need.

Repeat the process for however many stocks you want to see. To track a lot of stocks, it's easier to use the Portfolios system, discussed in the next section. That system gives you some extra perks as well, by offering more information about your particular investments.

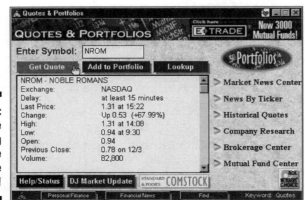

Figure 12-4: Things are looking good for the stock of the day!

In addition to the stock price search system itself, the Quotes window also offers a host of newsy goodies of interest to both serious investors and part-time plunkers. Here's a quick rundown of what's waiting there:

- The Market News Center (keyword **MNC**) offers quick graphs for everything from the Dow Jones Industrials to the Japanese Nikkei 225, plus selected news headlines.

- News by Ticker (keyword **Company News**) delivers recent articles from Reuters, the Associated Press, the PR Newswire, and the Business Wire for any company you choose. Just enter the company's stock ticker symbol, click Search, and enjoy your collection of news.

- Historical Quotes (available through a button on the Quotes window) thumbs through previous years of pricing to clearly show how a stock has performed in the past. (Remember, as the gurus say, previous performance is no guarantee that we won't all lose our socks on this sucker the next time around.)

- Company Research (keyword **Company Research**) delivers stock reports, financial statements, earnings reports, and the EDGAR 10K and 10Q reports directly to your hot little hands — and for free, too.

- For moments when you want another opinion or want to buy something *now,* the Brokerage Center (keyword **Broker**) and the Mutual Fund Center (keyword **Mutual Funds**) supply everything you need, from final analysis information through links to online brokers.

Invest carefully, and don't believe everything you hear in the Personal Finance discussion boards. To repeat this warning, and hear several others like it, flip to *AOL Channels For Dummies,* the minibook at the back of this book (you can tell you're there by the gray-edged pages), and check out the Personal Finance channel.

Portfolios (keyword Portfolios)

The other side of America Online's built-in stock tracking tools is the Portfolios system at keyword **Portfolios.** Unlike its little brother the Quotes window, Portfolios easily handles a whole, well, portfolio of stock investments. At a glance, your portfolio shows your positions for all stocks, including the number of shares, the stock's current price, the price you paid for it, and your total gain (or, horrors, loss).

All the tools you need for creating and managing a portfolio live in the Portfolios window. Your first portfolio, cleverly named Portfolio #1, is automatically created when you tell America Online that you want to add a stock to your portfolio. Open your portfolio by either double-clicking it or by clicking once to highlight it and clicking Display.

With your portfolio open on-screen, you can do any of the following:

✔ **Add another stock to the portfolio:** Use the Add Item button. You need to know the stock ticker symbol, number of shares, and the price you paid for the stock.

✔ **Remove a stock:** Click the stock to get rid of, then click Remove. When America Online asks if you're sure, click OK.

✔ **Edit an entry:** Click the entry you want to change, then click Edit. You can adjust the number of shares and the purchase price, but you can't change the ticker symbol. To do that, you need to delete the entry entirely and then create a new one.

✔ **Check the details:** Click the stock entry that you want detailed information about, and then click Details. After a moment or two of serious consideration, the system displays a window filled to the brim with expanded price information, links to recent news stories, and buttons to create historical charts.

✔ **Refresh the display:** Click Refresh to get the latest prices for all stocks in your portfolio.

You can create and manage multiple portfolios through the system as well. To do that, go to the main Portfolios window at keyword **Portfolios**, then pick your task from the items below:

✔ **Create a new portfolio:** Click Create Portfolio. When asked, type a name for the portfolio, then click OK. The new portfolio appears in the Portfolios window.

✔ **Delete a portfolio:** Click the portfolio you don't want anymore, then wave solemnly at it while clicking Delete Portfolio. When the system asks if you really, *really* want to delete the portfolio, click OK.

✔ **Rename a portfolio:** Click the portfolio with the weird name, then click Rename. When America Online asks you for a new name, type it in, then click OK.

Be careful when deleting a portfolio. Make doubly sure that you clicked the correct portfolio, because once you click that fateful OK button, that portfolio is gone forever. There's no *oops* key there, so don't let mistakes happen to you.

Chapter 13

Frolicking in the Games

Games, games, games — they're a great pastime, a relaxing way to spend an evening, and a challenging contest aimed at sharpening your mental blades. They're also one of the top reasons that people buy a computer in the first place (whether they actually admit it or not).

Being part of the America Online community brings a whole new dimension to games. Instead of playing a game *against* the computer, how about playing the game *through* the computer with a live opponent hundreds of miles away? Whether you want to challenge others or swap tales of gaming in the good old days, the games and game forums of America Online are definitely the place to do it.

This chapter looks at the free and premium (as in *not free*) games available through America Online, as well as offering some tips about online games to try and love.

Perhaps There's No Free Lunch, But Are There Free Games?

Yes, Virginia, there *are* free games on America Online. There are also pay-per-play games on the system that charge an hourly fee. No, the fee doesn't apply to all games on the system. Yes, it does cover some. Yes, you get plenty of warning before entering a pay-by-the-minute gaming area, so you can't accidentally wander into one. It'd be like "accidentally" driving your car through a shopping mall and then claiming that the pedestrians didn't get out of the way fast enough.

All the for-pay (aka premium) games come from WorldPlay (keyword **Worldplay**) and Engage Games Online (keyword **Engage**). These games include a lot of action-oriented titles like Air Warrior, Baldies, Harpoon Online, Legends of Kesmai, Multiplayer Battletech, Rolemaster: Magestorm, Splatterball, The Incredible Machine 3, Virtual Pool, and Warcraft II. (Just for fun, see if you can read that last sentence in one breath. Why should you do it? Well, why not?)

As you play the premium games, your America Online account is charged $1.99 per hour (which works out to about 3.3 cents per minute, which is the smallest amount of billable time that the America Online computers understand). The billing is automatic and begins after you pass through the This Costs Money curtain (okay, it's really a window) shown in Figure 13-1 that reminds you, in no uncertain terms, that it costs money to step beyond this point.

Figure 13-1:
Make no
mistake —
the billing
clock starts
the moment
you click I
Agree.

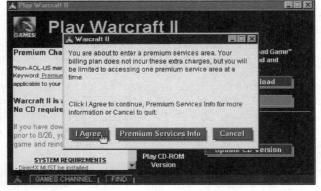

For the latest information about premium games, including hourly fees, Especial offers, and other details of online gaming, go to the Games Guide, at keyword **Games Guide.**

The free games, for the most part, live in Game Shows Online (keyword **Game Shows**), More Games (keyword **More Games**), and the Online Gaming Forums (keyword **OGF**, shown in Figure 13-2). These games lean more toward the thinking side of life than their premium game counterparts, but that doesn't mean they aren't just as exciting. Games like Strike-a-Match (keyword **Strike**), Slingo (keyword **Slingo**), and Out of Order (keyword **Out of Order**) definitely raise your blood pressure, believe me. The free games also include a huge variety of trivia titles, online role-playing games, and word puzzles.

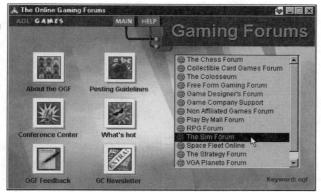

Figure 13-2:
The Online
Gaming
Forums are
guaranteed
to fill your
free time
with fun
(and free)
pursuits.

Exposing a Well-Kept Secret: Some Big Games Play for Free!

Before you start thinking that America Online put *all* the commercial games behind the no-pay-no-play curtain, check out the Westwood Studios forum (shown in Figure 13-3) at keyword **Westwood.** If you play computer games already, then the odds are good that you know about Westwood Studios. They created the series that's the standard by which real-time strategy games are judged: Command and Conquer.

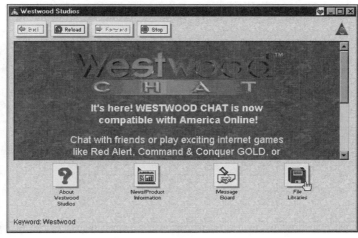

Figure 13-3:
The
Westwood
Studios
forum —
featuring
some of the
best
commercial
Internet
games.

Beyond creating an incredible multiplayer strategy game, Westwood also dedicated itself to making its games playable through the Internet. With that thought in mind, it created Westwood Chat, its own chat and game-playing system. When it first came out, Westwood Chat didn't work with America Online, but all that's fixed now.

If you have the retail version of Command & Conquer Gold or Command & Conquer: Red Alert, you can play those games through America Online with partners all over the world. And — get this — it's *free!*

To join the fun, go to the Westwood Studios area (use keyword **Westwood**), download the Westwood Chat software, and install it. Full instructions for both downloading and installing the software are available in the Westwood Studios area. (I'd include the details here, but things change so quickly in the gaming industry that what I wrote would be hopelessly outdated by the time you read it.)

Incidentally, the Westwood Chat system also supports games from Hasbro Interactive. As of this writing, Hasbro's Monopoly game was certified to work through America Online, and support for other Hasbro Interactive titles (like Battleship and Scrabble) was in the works.

Opening the door to premium games

By default, only the master screen name (the very first screen name you created on America Online) can play the way-cool premium games. All the other screen names on your account start out blocked from the games. If someone signs on with one of those other screen names and tries to play a premium game, a message pops up saying, basically, that America Online would just *love* to let them play, but some heathen scoundrel (namely the keeper of the master screen name) won't let them play. After riling the would-be player into a frenzy, the window then suggests that he or she take the issue up with the account holder.

If you *want* your other screen names to play premium games, you need to tell America Online. To do that, sign on to the system and then use keyword **Parental Controls**. When the window appears, click the Premium Services button. When the Premium Services Controls window appears, clear the Block Premium Services check box for each screen name that gets to play premium games. To clear the check box, just click it. To prevent a screen name from playing the premium games (thus protecting your credit card bill from accidental inflation), make sure that the Block Premium Services check box next to the screen name is checked.

Hopping into the Best Free Games

In our fast-paced society, time is a scarce thing at work and at home. That makes the time you devote to online gaming even rarer still! In the hopes of helping you spend most of that precious time actually playing games instead of fruitlessly wandering around looking for them, I put together the following list of popular (and mostly free) games available on America Online.

Each section includes the name of the game, the keyword for getting there, and a quick description of what the game (or game area) is like. If there's a fee for playing, there's a note about that as well.

So, with no further delay, explanation, or meandering text, here are the America Online games and game areas that you don't want to miss:

✔ Old-fashioned parlor games rule the day in the Game Parlor (keyword **Game Parlor**). This area specializes in simple-to-learn chat room games and the fun, light-hearted conversation that goes with them.

✔ If you love trivia games, then America Online's games of trivia (keyword **Trivia**) anxiously await you. This window leads to trivia games in the NTN Studio (keyword **NTN**) and Trivian Games (keyword **Triviana**), as well as the resources and community of the Trivia Forum (keyword **Trivia Forum**).

✔ To satisfy the word puzzle addict in you (or at your house), turn to the Puzzle Zone (keyword **Puzzle**), shown in Figure 13-4. This area features four different word puzzle titles, including challenging interactive crossword puzzles in Flexicon, anagram challenges from Elvis-Lives, and Clink, a stream-of-consciousness game that defies rational explanation (makes you immediately want to find out how it works, doesn't it?).

Figure 13-4:
The Puzzle Zone offers word puzzles for every skill and patience level.

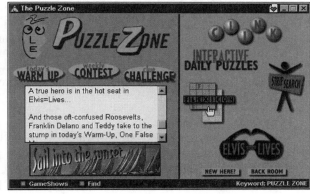

✔ Vying for the dual titles of "visually darkest online area" and "most likely to keep you coming back," you find the Antagonist, Incorporated (keyword **Ant**). Antagonist is a combination game review and online gaming site, with lively discussion and late-breaking stories in the world of both computer and console games (the Nintendos and Segas of the world). Not content to merely talk about the games, the Antagonist also includes several online games in the gothic fantasy realm (several of which cost money to play). They also offer Antagonist Trivia, which you'll find at keyword **AT.**

✔ VGA Planets (keyword **VGA Planets**) was one of the first turn-based, multiplayer space strategy games on the market. Since the time this shareware program first appeared, thousands upon thousands of players have joined the ranks. Today, VGA Planets enjoys one of the largest and friendliest game communities on the Net. Check out the VGA Planets forum to learn about the game, download a copy for yourself, and join in the fun!

✔ Fantasy role-playing games are an extraordinarily popular pastime in the gaming chat rooms of America Online. The two main forums focusing on this creativity-laden form of entertainment are the Free-Form Gaming Forum (keyword **FFGF**) and the Simming Forum (keyword **Simming**). These games are a riot to play, provided you're up to the challenge. Check the forums for more information about their various games and venues.

✔ The folks at BoxerJam Productions supply two of the most delightful game shows in the whole of America Online. Strike-a-Match (keyword **Strike A Match**) and Out of Order (keyword **Out of Order**) are both fast-playing and challenging, with a very high replay factor. Don't blame me if you get hopelessly hooked on them!

✔ Finally, I'd be seriously remiss if I failed to mention the Collectable Cards forum at keyword **Collect Cards** (shown in Figure 13-5). Collectable card games are the hottest new game trend in years. Led by games like the Star Wars Customizable Card Game, Star Trek: The Next Generation, and Magic: The Gathering, collectable card games continue to entrance new players every day with their combination of game play, collectibality, and old-fashioned horse-swapping as anxious players trade cards in hopes of collecting a full set. Learn all about the collectable card game world here, and join the fun for chats and live, online tournaments.

Keep an eye on the Game Shows Online (keyword **Game Shows**), More Games (keyword **More Games**), and the Online Gaming Forums (keyword **OGF**) areas to watch for new games joining the system. There's a lot of cool stuff coming — don't miss it!

Chapter 14
Cruising the Internet

● ●

In This Chapter

▶ Checking out the Internet Connection

▶ Getting started: a brief Internet primer

▶ Skimming the resources

▶ Using Internet e-mail

▶ Trying a mailing list (or two)

▶ Leaping through the World Wide Web

▶ Newsgroups: the Internet's answer to discussion boards

▶ Downloading the world with FTP

● ●

*T*urn on the TV news and what do you hear being discussed? The Internet. Go to lunch with some friends and what's bound to either come up at your table or be loudly debated at the one next to you? The Internet. Attend a cocktail party and what's on everyone's mind? Well, if it's boring, they may be thinking about how much better the *last* party was; but to pass the time until they can make a polite departure, they're talking about the Internet. (What's wrong with these people? Don't they have real lives?)

Rising from technoid obscurity to media-star status in just a few short years, the Internet is still a mystery to most people. Frankly, it was a mystery to me until a few years ago. In hopes of sparing you further moments of fear and anxiety, this chapter explains a little about the Internet (just enough to get you going) and a lot about America Online's powerful Internet Connection. It also unmasks the odd language of the Internet, introducing and explaining terms such as *World Wide Web, FTP,* and *newsgroup.*

A big electronic world is out there, just waiting for you to visit. Grab your modem and get ready to go Internet surfing!

Internet Connection Basics

Like everything else on America Online, the Internet is just a hop, skip, and a click away from wherever you are. In fact, it's even a little closer than that because there's a Toolbar button for it, too: the cleverly-named Internet button.

The Internet Connection itself (keyword **Internet Connection**) is designed to quickly get you where you want to go. The center of the window displays a Go to AOL NetFind button, which you use to search Web sites. Underneath that, click in the box next to Go To The Web and enter your Web address to visit a particular Web site. On the right of the window are the *Internet service buttons* — interesting stuff about the Internet that's available in America Online, including information systems like Newsgroups as well as America Online features, such as their Time Savers list of topical Web sites.

Along the bottom of the window are three featured area buttons. These buttons take you to various Internet-based areas of interest, such as e-mail finders and lists of Web sites arranged around a particular topic.

So Just What Is This Internet Thing?

Hang on to your seat — I'm about to explain the Internet in four (yes, just *four*) paragraphs. This may get a little hairy at times, but you have nothing to worry about because I'm a trained professional. Kids, don't let your parents try this at home.

The Internet basically started as a big Department of Defense project somewhere back in the '60s, slowly expanding through the '70s and '80s, and coming into its own in the '90s. It was originally supposed to help university researchers exchange information on super-secret defense projects, thus lowering the amount of time necessary to find new and ever more fascinating ways to end life on the planet. Communication links were established between computers at colleges, universities, research labs, and large defense contractors. The Internet had begun.

At the same time, though, the seeds of today's digital anarchy were sown. This research network connected lots of bright, intelligent people together. And those people started coming up with bright, intelligent ideas about fun, new things to do on the research network. "How about a discussion area where we can swap notes — kinda like a bulletin board?" {Poof!} The network newsgroups were born.

Then anarchy took over. Discussion areas originally intended for deep conversations about megaton yields and armor deflection/implosion ratios carried witty repartee about Buddha, the Rolling Stones, and kite flying. Everyone with an opinion to share was welcome, provided that they could get there in the first place.

The Internet continued to slowly bubble and ferment through the '80s, but things suddenly changed when the '90s arrived. In the span of a couple years, the Internet simply exploded. Thousands of computers and networks around the world joined in. Newspaper articles and TV news stories appeared, introducing this electronic Colossus to the normal world. Non-computer companies linked up to the network as business e-mail use blossomed. Millions of average people began poking around out there through online services such as America Online.

With that brief bit of background under your belt, ponder these important tidbits before venturing out into the online world:

- ✔ No single computer or place is called *the Internet*. The Internet is a collection of thousands, perhaps millions, of computers all over the world.

- ✔ Nobody's really in charge of it all. Nope, nobody. Some committees and groups attempt to keep everything headed in the same direction, but nobody actually leads the parade.

- ✔ No one knows how big the Internet is. Suffice it to say that it's a really, *really* big place — and it's still growing.

- ✔ Free speech is the *rule* on the Internet, not the exception. If you read something in a newsgroup or find a document through gopher that's offensive to you, you have my personal apology. But that's all the sympathy anyone's going to give you. The communications code of the Internet is simple: If something offends you, either ignore it or disagree with it, but *don't* post a message suggesting that "somebody ought to shut those people up." An action such as that is sure to fill your mailbox with angry e-mail questioning your parentage and suggesting that you do some biologically impossible things in the corner.

- ✔ The Internet is not free. It kinda looks like it is because you're just paying for connect time on America Online — you're not charged for the rest of the telecommunications time between the America Online computers in Vienna, Virginia, and the rest of the Internet world. I only bring this up so you remember that *someone* out there is paying the bill; it's good netiquette to use Internet resources wisely, particularly FTP (covered later in this chapter).

- ✔ Believe it or not, all this anarchy works if everyone's nice about it.

E-Mail the Internet Way

Perhaps you joined America Online solely to use Internet e-mail. (It wouldn't surprise me at all.) An Internet e-mail account is an absolute must these days, particularly if you're in business.

America Online's mail system is among the easiest of all commercial online services to use. You don't have to remember any special commands or be anywhere in particular to send a message through the Internet. Just create the message as you would normally, put in the person's Internet mail address, and click Send. If you need a quick review of the how-tos of America Online e-mail, flip to Chapter 6 or select Mail⇨Mail Center on the Toolbar and poke through the information there.

Here are a few notes about e-mail that I just couldn't fit anywhere else:

- ✔ An e-mail message takes anywhere from a few minutes to a few hours to make its way through the Internet and find its destination. If you send a message and it doesn't arrive by the next business day or two, consider the message lost.

- ✔ Yes, Internet mail messages *do* sometimes get lost. No, it's not the Postal Service's fault.

- ✔ The unsend feature only works on mail sent *from* an America Online subscriber *to* an America Online subscriber. It doesn't work on mail sent through the Internet (so think twice before clicking Send).

- ✔ Of course, you can receive mail through the Internet as well. Your Internet mailing address is your screen name — with any spaces in it removed — and with @aol.com appended to the end. For example, jkaufeld@aol.com is my America Online Internet mail address.

- ✔ Look through Chapter 6 for all the particulars about using e-mail both through the Internet and within America Online.

Consider getting an Internet book

If one of the main reasons you joined America Online was for the Internet services, I highly recommend getting a good book about the Internet. I personally suggest *The Internet For Dummies,* 5th Edition (by John R. Levine, Carol Baroudi, and Margaret Levine Young), and *MORE Internet For Dummies,* 3rd Edition (by John R. Levine and Margaret Levine Young), both from IDG Books Worldwide, Inc. (No, it's not because I *have* to suggest them — I really like them and have them myself.)

Join a Mailing List for Fun and Full Mailboxes

Swapping letters through a mailing list is about the simplest form of information exchange on the Internet. You don't need any special software, you don't have to buy anything, and no salesperson will call. Everything comes straight to your mailbox; you don't even have to go find it. You can find lists for everything and everybody covering hobbies, music groups, religion, mine-proofing military vehicles, motorcycle repair, world history — the list goes on and on.

Finding and joining a mailing list

Before enjoying the wonders of discussions that take place in your mailbox, you have to sign up. America Online makes that pretty easy with a searchable database of Internet mailing lists. If you know what you're interested in, you can find a mailing list for it. Here's how:

1. **Use keyword** Mailing Lists **to start the whole sordid process.**

   On cue, the Mailing List Directory window pops into action.

2. **Click the Browse the Directory button (it looks like an open book).**

   The Web browser automatically starts and displays America Online's super-cool Mailing List Directory Web page.

3. **To wander through the directory, click Directory Index.**

   As your reward for waiting, the Index fills the screen.

4. **If you know the exact name of the list you want, click its first letter in the Lists by List Title area. For a subject-based browse through the list database, scroll through the Categories section at the bottom of the window.**

   Either way, you see a display of mailing list names and titles.

5. **Scroll through the list until you find something interesting and then click its name.**

   A page of information about the list shows up on-screen (see Figure 14-1). The page describes the list topics, what kind of list it is, and how to subscribe. Feel free to either read through the information right there on-screen or print it if you like. To print it, choose File⇨Print from the menu bar and then click OK. (Oh, and turn the printer on — that always helps!)

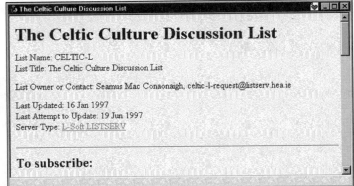

The Celtic Culture Discussion List

List Name: CELTIC-L
List Title: The Celtic Culture Discussion List

List Owner or Contact: Seamus Mac Conaonaigh, celtic-l-request@listserv.hea.ie

Last Updated: 16 Jan 1997
Last Attempt to Update: 19 Jun 1997
Server Type: L-Soft LISTSERV

To subscribe:

Figure 14-1:
Interesting
lists
abound on
the
Internet.

6. **To join the list, follow the subscription instructions on the page. To keep browsing through other lists, click the Back button on the browser bar.**

   Usually, you need to send an e-mail to either the list moderator or a program that maintains the subscriber list. If the instructions say something about putting the phrase "SUBSCRIBE listname your-name" in the body of a message, you're dealing with an automated list-keeping program. If you're supposed to send "a politely worded request," a human's doing the work.

   Don't sign up for a list and then ask to be removed a couple days later. That's considered very impolite.

7. **If you want to look for some other lists, close the information window and keep cruising through your search results.**

For those days when you'd rather search than browse, the Mailing List Directory also offers a searching option. Click Search instead of Directory Index, type your topic into the Enter a search key box, and click Search. The search engine returns a list of possible mailing lists; click any that catch your eye to read the descriptions in the same format as those listed above. Follow the subscription instructions on the page if you'd like to join the list.

Sharing your wisdom with everybody else

Belonging to a list means both reading what others have to say and tossing in your own two cents every now and then. To send a message to the entire list, write your thoughts in an e-mail and send it to the submissions or articles address — *not* to the address you used to subscribe to the list. Your important thoughts find their way out to everybody within a day or so — or at least they may.

Keep your thoughts clear and concise, with emphasis on the word *concise*. People on the Internet appreciate brevity. Remember that some of your readers have to pay for each message they receive; others are charged by the size of the message. Keep your messages short, clear, and to the point, and you will be adored by millions.

Just because your thoughts are lucid and fascinating doesn't guarantee that they'll actually be shared with the rest of the mailing list. Here's a brief guide to help you understand the three basic types of lists and how each affects the chances of sharing your thoughts:

- ✔ *Unmoderated lists* accept whatever you send; posting is automatic, provided that your contribution makes its way successfully back to the list keeper (be it machine or otherwise).

- ✔ *Moderated lists* are actually edited and controlled by someone. Everything that goes out to the list's subscribers is okayed by the moderator. If your posting doesn't meet the standards or requirements of the list, it's not distributed. You can ask the moderator why your posting didn't pass the muster, but simply whining doesn't do any good.

- ✔ *Announcement-only* lists don't accept submissions from you, the listening audience. They only send out information from a particular source. Writing an article for one of these lists is like trying to convince the recorded weather information to say something else for a while.

Unsubscribing from a list

Yes, the time does come when you must bid adieu to the things of youth and flights of information fancy. And so it is that you may, one day, wish to get the heck off that mailing list that fills your mailbox with messages each day.

To unsubscribe from a list, turn back to the information page you so carefully printed out or saved when you found the list. Buried among everything else on the page is a notation about "unsubscribing from this list" or something like that. Just follow the instructions and soon the digital torrents wash through your mailbox no more.

If you lost, erased, or otherwise can't find the information sheet, just search the mailing list database and find it there. Send your "I wanna quit" message to the list administration address, not the submission address. You don't want everyone to know you're quitting, do you?

Topic Hopping in the World Wide Web

It's huge. It's interconnected. It has a funny name. It's the most exciting, promising part of the Internet. It's also the newest addition to America Online's suite of Internet services. It's (electronic drumroll, please!) the *World Wide Web.*

The Web is a most amazing place. Where else can you find newspapers, technical information, company product catalogs, a library of folk song lyrics, far too many personal biographies, and a clock that displays the current time with fish sponges? (Not at the local mall, that's for sure.)

So just what *is* the World Wide Web? Like the Internet, it's not a single, unique "place" out there somewhere. Instead, the Web is a collection of interlinked sites (or *Web pages*). The links between the pages are what make the Web a truly cool place.

Ever hear of something called *hypertext*? (You probably know what it is but don't know that it has a name — trust me for now and read on.) Although the term sounds like a book on a sugar high, hypertext is a neat way to organize information by *linking* related topics.

Suppose you're reading an encyclopedia article about wombats and find out that the wombat is an Australian marsupial. Like most rational humans, your next thought is, "I wonder what's for lunch." While foraging for food in the wilds of your refrigerator, you casually wonder precisely what a marsupial is. Abandoning your meal in search of knowledge, you pull out the M volume of the encyclopedia and look up marsupials. You discover that kangaroos are marsupials as well, a fact that sends you racing for the A volume to determine whether the Australian government is aware that the country is brimming with marsupials.

If this keeps up much longer, you may as well move in with your encyclopedia.

What if you were using a hypertext encyclopedia on the computer? In the wombat article, the words *marsupial* and *Australian* would be highlighted to let you know that they're links to related articles. You click *marsupial* and immediately see the marsupial article. Another click takes you back to the first article so you can explore the *Australian* link. Talk about fast information — you didn't even have time to eat!

The World Wide Web works just like the hypertext encyclopedia I described. The on-screen page offers information, plus it contains links to other Web pages. Those pages have links to still *other* Web pages. That cloud of links is where the name *Web* comes from — it's a Web of links. It's an information browser's dream come true.

A quick stop at the terminology shop

The Web just wouldn't be a computer thing if there weren't a whole slew of new terms and acronyms to baffle and amaze you. Here are the top ones you need in order to make sense of the Web:

- ✔ A *Web page* is the smallest building block of the Web. It's an electronic page with information and links to other places in the Web.

- ✔ A *Web site* is a collection of Web pages. A site may have just a few pages or more than a hundred. It depends on what the site is for and how much effort the site's builder put into it.

- ✔ Every Web site has a *home page.* This is usually the first page you see when you visit that site. The term also refers to your own personal Web page (if you created one) or the page that appears when you start your Web browser (the software that you use to browse the Web — see the next section for more about the America Online browser).

- ✔ To find something on the Web, you need to know its *Uniform Resource Locator (URL).* This special code tells the browser software what kind of site you're visiting. All World Wide Web URLs start with `http://`, but `gopher://` and `ftp://` sites are out there, too.

- ✔ *HTTP* is half the magic that makes the Web work. The abbreviation stands for hypertext transfer protocol. All you need to know about it is that every Web site address starts with `http://`.

- ✔ The other half of the Web's magical underpinnings is *HTML,* the hypertext markup language. HTML is the programming language of the World Wide Web. If something has `.html` (or sometimes `.htm`) appended to its name, the odds are that it's a Web page. In everyday conversation, the abbreviation is sometimes spelled out (such as "I'm learning H-T-M-L") and sometimes pronounced as a word (as in "That hot-metal burned my hand").

- ✔ *Links (or hotlinks)* connect Web pages together. When you *follow a link,* you click a button or highlighted word and go careening off to another destination in the online world.

- ✔ Because having only one term for things often fosters understanding and comprehension, the World Wide Web is also referred to as *the Web, WWW,* or *W3.*

For more information about how the Web works, see *The Internet For Dummies,* 5th Edition, by John R. Levine, Carol Baroudi, and Margaret Levine Young (IDG Books Worldwide, Inc.).

Taking the Web browser for a spin

America Online did a lot of work to integrate the World Wide Web as seamlessly as possible. It was quite a trick, too, because you need special software (called a *browser*) to look at Web pages.

The Web browser, shown in Figure 14-2, is built right into the America Online access software. The Navigation bar, just underneath the Toolbar at the top of the screen, contains all of the goodies you need to traverse the Web. Flip to Chapter 3 for all of the details on the Navigation bar.

Figure 14-2:
The
America
Online Web
browser,
doing its
Web
browsing
thing.

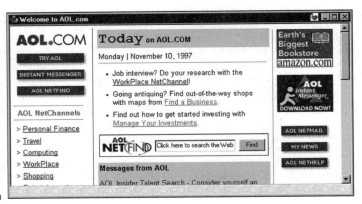

- ✔ Don't be surprised if your America Online home page looks different from the ones in the figures. World Wide Web pages change all the time — it's a natural part of life.

- ✔ Your World Wide Web browser understands gopher and FTP sites, too. Some pages have links to Internet newsgroups (more about those later in the chapter), which, unfortunately, your browser *can't* understand. If you click a link and the browser displays a window that says something like `Cannot interpret link`, that's a clue that you just clicked something that's beyond the browser's comprehension. I hope this difficulty gets fixed in the future, but as long as I'm wishing, I'd like a pony, too.

- ✔ The most common Web-oriented error you will see is something to the effect of `Sorry, I can't contact that site`. Double-check the address and try it again. If it *still* doesn't work, either America Online is too busy to be bothered with the Web right now or the Web page you're looking for isn't available at the moment. Either way, try again later.

- ✔ In case you're interested, the foam bath fish clock is at `http://www.savetz.com/fishtime`.

- ✔ Send virtual flowers to friends and loved ones from `http://www.iflowers.com` or `http://www.InternetFlorist.com`.

✔ For those who appreciate the offbeat, the odd, and the occasionally smelly, visit the Dumpster Diver site at `http://www.connect-time.com/cgi-bin/dumpdive`. Take a dumpster dive and send an e-mail to your closest friends telling them what you found.

✔ Visit Build-A-Card and send a free e-mail postcard to someone who needs a pick-me-up, to say thank you, or just because. Look for it at `http://buildacard.com`.

✔ When you find sites that you absolutely love, add them to your Favorite Places window by clicking in the little heart-on-a-page icon in the upper-right corner of the Web browser. For more about the Favorite Places window, see Chapter 5.

Opening a specific page

Even though the America Online home page offers lots of interesting links to explore, sometimes you want to hop directly to a particular page. Maybe you saw the address in a newspaper ad or TV commercial, or perhaps you're chafing at the bit to see the fish clock. No matter where it came from, explaining a Web address to America Online is a piece of cake.

Be sure to direct your attention to the new Navigation bar (parked just under the Toolbar on your screen). To go directly to a particular page, click in the Address area of the Navigation bar (the big white box), then type the address of the page you want to see, just like Figure 14-3. Be sure to include the `http://` part on the front, or America Online gets confused. When the address is in, press Enter or click Go. Shortly, the built-in Web browser comes to life, displaying your page in glorious color.

Figure 14-3:
For faster service, slide up to the Navigation bar and order your Web page there.

Newsgroups Talk about the Craziest Things

The Internet newsgroups are a collection of, oh, about 12,000 discussion topics, from artificial intelligence applications (the `comp.ai` newsgroup) to the latest Kennedy assassination theories (try `alt.conspiracy.jfk`). Newsgroup discussions get pretty wild sometimes, with ideas flying thick through the network. The language is often fairly (ahem) to the point as well, so if you're easily offended, you may not want to venture too far into the newsgroups.

I want to be *very* clear on this point, because if you can't trust me, who can you trust? When you venture into the Internet newsgroups, you're leaving the friendly, trusting, caring community of America Online and venturing out into the wild, uncontrolled reality of the Internet. It's the difference between the lawns of suburban Indianapolis and the pavement of Manhattan. The Internet has no Terms of Service agreement — anything goes (and usually does).

That's not to say that there aren't *any* rules, because there definitely are some. They're simple, unwritten, and apply to almost every newsgroup:

- ✔ You're welcome to join the discussion, provided you take the time to understand the newsgroup before contributing anything. Read a newsgroup for *at least* a week or two before posting something of your own.

- ✔ Stick to the topic of the newsgroup. Posting get-rich-quick schemes and business advertisements to the newsgroups is in very poor taste. People do it, but they're the exception, not the rule.

- ✔ You may agree or disagree with anything that's said. You may agree or disagree as loudly as you want. If you disagree, focus on the point — don't degenerate into personal attacks.

- ✔ You may *not* question a person's right to say whatever comes to mind. Yes, some points of view out there are, shall we say, distasteful, but there are people who feel that way about what you and I think, too.

- ✔ If someone disagrees with you rather abusively (known on the Internet as a *flame*), the best thing you can do is ignore the message. If you can reply in a level-headed tone, that's fine, but it's probably not going to change what the other person thinks. It's best to let the flames die down and just go on with other conversations.

By now, I hope I've scared you a little bit about the Internet newsgroups. Well, *scared* really isn't the right term. How about *educated*, instead? It's really not as wild and vicious a place as I'm making it out to be, but you need to understand that the newsgroups aren't part of America Online — they're completely outside the mores of the America Online world. If you visualize yourself stepping from your neighborhood into a completely foreign environment every time you use the newsgroups, you have the right frame of mind. The newsgroups work much like America Online's discussion areas. They're different from mailing lists, though, because mailing lists come *to* your mailbox; you have to *go* to the newsgroups. Check out *The Internet For Dummies,* 4th Edition, by John R. Levine, Carol Baroudi, and Margaret Levine Young (IDG Books Worldwide, Inc.) for a more complete explanation of newsgroups.

Finding and subscribing to a newsgroup

As I said before, you have literally thousands of newsgroups to choose from — and America Online carries them all. To keep things from getting too out of hand, the newsgroups are organized into hierarchies by topic. The main hierarchies are briefly explained in Table 14-1. Other hierarchies certainly exist, but I'll let you explore those on your own. Each hierarchy contains a bunch of related newsgroups (or, in the case of the alt and misc hierarchies, a bunch of newsgroups that are related only because they happen to be together).

Table 14-1	Newsgroup Hierarchy Names
Name	*Description*
alt	Alternative — home of free-wheeling discussions on just about any topic
aol	America Online — articles of interest to America Online members
biz	Business — topics generally relating to business on the Internet
comp	Computers and computer science — where the nerds hang out
misc	Miscellaneous — all the stuff that doesn't fit under one of the other hierarchies
news	Network news and information — discussion and information-only groups about the Internet itself
rec	Hobbies and recreation — think sports and hobbies and you have this one figured out
sci	Science and research — if you thought there were nerds in the comp group, just wait until you look in here
soc	Society and social commentary — mainly focused toward both sociologists in the audience
talk	Talk — talk, talk, talk, talk (get the idea?)

Your search for an interesting newsgroup starts by guessing which hierarchy the topic belongs in and then browsing through that hierarchy's available newsgroups. Simple enough, right? Here's how to do it step by step:

1. **On the toolbar, click Internet⇨Newsgroups or use keyword** Newsgroups.

   The Newsgroups window pops up.

2. **Click Add Newsgroups.**

   The Add Newsgroups Categories window appears.

3. **Scroll through the list of available hierarchies until you find one that looks interesting. Double-click a hierarchy to find out which newsgroups it contains.**

   A window listing all the hierarchy's newsgroups elbows its way to the screen.

4. **Scroll through all the listed newsgroups, find one that looks interesting, and double-click its entry in the list.**

   Yet another window, which may or may not tell you anything helpful about the newsgroup, appears looking something like Figure 14-4.

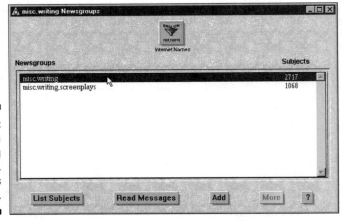

Figure 14-4:
Hmm — a writing newsgroup. Sounds interesting.

5. **For a look at the messages in this newsgroup, click Read Messages. If you're already sold, click Add to include the newsgroup in your subscription list. To pretend that you never saw the newsgroup in the first place, just close the window and go about your business.**

   Subscribing to a newsgroup may take a minute or two to allow the America Online computer to think, ponder, and snicker at its ability to make a human wait for something.

   For more about reading messages in a newsgroup, see the next section.

6. **When the confirmation dialog box pops up, click OK to reassure it that you know what you're talking about and that you really want to read that newsgroup.**

   After a great deal of digital consternation, America Online displays a brief dialog box saying that the newsgroup is now on your list. Click OK to make the confirmation dialog box go away and leave you alone.

7. **To subscribe to more newsgroups, just close the last few windows (double-click the upper-left corner of the window in Windows; single-click the box at the upper-left corner of the window on a Macintosh).**

   Congratulations — you did it!

   If someone describes a marvelous newsgroup and gives you the Internet name of it (which looks like `alt.folklore.urban`), you can use the Expert Add button and skip this whole menu-driven process. However, you must know the exact name, complete with all the required (and odd) punctuation marks. The Expert Add button is also handy for checking out newsgroups recommended by one of those clever Internet books that I suggest you buy.

Reading messages

Of course, subscribing is only the first step. Your next task is finding time to read all the stuff you subscribe to. Unlike mailing lists, newsgroup messages don't stack up in your e-mail box — they collect in some mysterious place deep within America Online. To read what's new, you have to pay another visit to the Newsgroups window. Here's what to do:

1. **Ont the toolbar, choose Internet⇨Newsgroup or use keyword** Newsgroups.

   The Newsgroups window pops up, as shown in Figure 14-5.

2. **Click Read My Newsgroups.**

   After a few pensive moments of waiting, the Read My Newsgroups window pops into being. It shows the name of the newsgroup, the number of messages you haven't read, and the total number of messages in that newsgroup.

   Even if you only subscribe to one or two newsgroups, your newsgroups list comes preset with some suggested reading, courtesy of America Online.

3. **Double-click a newsgroup to see what's new.**

   A window that's more a scrolling list than anything else (see Figure 14-5) pops into being. The window shows the article title and the number of responses in the *thread* (that's the newsgroup term for discussion).

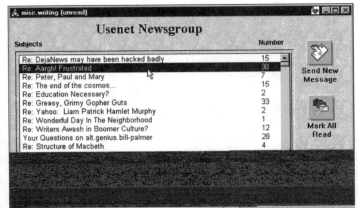

Figure 14-5:
So many
articles, so
little time.

To see all the articles in the newsgroup (whether you've read them or not), click the newsgroup name and then click List All Subjects.

4. To read an article, double-click its title.

A window opens containing the message text. Read to your heart's content and then close the window when you're done.

To reply to a message, click Reply to Group. To see the next message in the thread, click Message ->. For the previous message, click <- Message. If you're thirsty, get something to drink.

If you have a specific question for the person who wrote the article, click E-mail to Author instead of posting a reply to the newsgroup.

5. When you're done and nothing else looks interesting, click Mark All Read. Click OK in the dialog box that wonders whether you really want to do that.

This last step tells America Online to pretend that you actually *read* all the messages in the newsgroup. Therefore, you can quickly tell which messages are new the next time you wander through.

Contributing something

Reading a newsgroup is fun, but soon enough, you'll decide that it's time to post a few messages of your own. Adding a message to a newsgroup isn't hard, but it does take a couple more steps than your average e-mail message. Here's what to do:

1. Pretend you're going to read the messages in a newsgroup and go through Steps 1, 2, and 3 in the preceding section.

At this point, the window for whatever newsgroup you want to post an article to should be on-screen.

2. **Click Send New Message.**

A Post New Message dialog box appears on-screen.

3. **Type a descriptive subject in the Subject area, press Tab to move down into the Message block, and type your message.**

A check box marked Use signature (set in global preferences) sits underneath the Message block. If you want to sign all your newsgroups postings in a standard way, such as *John Doe — Ace Contractor, Incorporated* or *Sven, Lover of Adventure!*, you can write your signature once and then check the box to sign your name the same way with each posting you send. And oh — by the way — although it says the signature is set in global preferences, you'll actually find it under the Set Preferences button in the main Newsgroups window.

4. **After you're done and everything looks groovy, click Send.**

Click OK when the system asks whether you're serious about posting the article. Click Cancel if you suddenly decide that the world would be a better place without your message in the newsgroup.

When you're writing for a newsgroup, be brief and to the point. Say what you want to say and then stop. Don't go on and on and on. Whatever you do, don't ramble. I used to ramble, but I don't any more. And it's a good thing, too, what with all the newsgroup postings I write these days.

Unsubscribing from a newsgroup

Getting out of a newsgroup takes a whole lot less time and effort than getting into one. In fact, it's so quick that you'll hardly believe it.

1. **From the Internet Connection window, click Internet Extras and then Newsgroups or use keyword** Newsgroups.

The Newsgroups window reports for duty.

2. **Click Read My Newsgroups.**

The now-familiar Read My Newsgroups window appears, which you shouldn't confuse with the George Bush "Read My Lips" window or the William Shatner "Read My Books" window.

3. **Click the newsgroup you want to kick out and then click Remove.**

Click OK when the system once again questions your decision or click Cancel if you change your mind and want to keep the group.

Automating your newsgroups

Here's a little piece of advice about getting involved in the newsgroups: The words *addictive* and *newsgroups* naturally belong in the same sentence. Although they're not as bad to your America Online bill as the People Connection chat rooms, following a newsgroup does rack up your online charges if you use one of America Online's measured billing methods.

Does that mean you shouldn't do the newsgroup thing? Not at all! You just need to do it *smarter* and *quicker* by using an Automatic AOL session — the same familiar technique that prevents your voluminous e-mail traffic from overwhelming your credit card each month. With some careful tweaking, the messages from your favorite newsgroups stream right into your mailbox just like your e-mail. How could it possibly get better? Actually, I'm glad you asked.

Frankly, it could get better if doing newsgroups through Automatic AOL were slightly easier than disarming a thermonuclear device with a bobby pin and a bag of nacho chips. Unfortunately for us, it seems that the bomb folks moonlighted on the newsgroup Automatic AOL design team.

Before giving this a try, you must thoroughly understand both the newsgroups you want to keep up with and your America Online Filing Cabinet (of course, having a degree in nuclear engineering doesn't hurt either). Newsgroups are covered in the previous pages; notes about the Filing Cabinet reside in Chapter 6. The details of making it all work are too complex to attempt here — trust me. If you're still convinced that flashing the newsgroups into your computer sounds like fun, follow these steps for all the details:

1. **Use keyword** Newsgroups **to open the newsgroups window.**

   As expected, the newsgroups window appears.

2. **Double-click the How To entry in the resource list.**

   The appropriately named How To window hops into action.

3. **In the How To window, double-click Working with Newsgroups.**

   Yet another window piles onto the stack. Don't fret, though, because you're almost done.

4. **Double-click the entry for Read Newsgroups Offline.**

   A text window steps forth, revealing the secrets of this mystic feature.

If merely getting to the instructions sounds like a journey across the Himalayas (with or without a nuclear device), don't attempt to do newsgroups through Automatic AOL. The steps you just scaled were only the foothills — the peak is still waaaaay up there somewhere. Good luck, brave newsgrouper (I'm going back down the mountain for a nap).

A brief word about Parental Controls

A *lot* of truly interesting stuff is available in the newsgroups, but stuff out there could force a whole shipload of sailors into a collective blush. Thanks to the Parental Controls section, you can prevent such a thing from happening at your house.

The newsgroup Parental Controls are available under the cleverly labeled Parental Controls button on the Newsgroups window. These controls let you:

- Block the Expert Add feature, which limits a screen name to only the newsgroups that America Online chooses to list under the Add Newsgroups button.
- Block access to the newsgroups entirely.
- Prevent program and file downloads from the newsgroups.
- Block specific newsgroups you choose.
- Block any newsgroup that contains certain words in its name.
- Grant a screen name access to the complete list of available newsgroups.

If you have a child using America Online, I *highly* recommend blocking the Expert Add feature on that child's screen name. You may want to go further, but you can worry about that later.

Because little eyes and fingers often get into the darndest places, America Online offers a strong, flexible group of Parental Controls. For all the details about your online child management options, flip to the section called "Parental Controls: Taking Away the Online Car Keys" in Chapter 4.

FTP Downloading for the Nerd at Heart

If you thought the file libraries in America Online were a hoot, you haven't seen *anything* yet. Welcome to *file transfer protocol,* more commonly known as *FTP.* FTP is the Internet's answer to the Copy command. And let me tell you, it's certainly one answer.

You're about to enter (bring up geeky music in the background) the Technoid Zone, so keep a pocket protector handy. Working with FTP definitely isn't like using gopher or the Internet newsgroups. You're interacting directly with computers all over the world without the benefit of software like gopher to protect you. It's you against the computer. If using the Macintosh Finder or Windows File Manager to track down an errant file on your disk drive makes you queasy, you don't want to try FTP.

You can use America Online's FTP service in two ways: by going to the built-in FTP sites or by typing in an address on your own. At first, I suggest using the built-in options, because you can be relatively sure that they work. When you have some experience under your electronic belt, get brave and flip to Chapter 25 for some other FTP sites to try.

- ✔ I'm deliberately a little vague in my how-to-use-FTP instructions later in this chapter. The reason is simple: FTP really *is* more advanced than the other Internet services. You need to understand a lot of nerdy stuff, such as subdirectories and file compression, before FTP is of much use to you.

- ✔ If you're absolutely *dying* to learn about FTP, hang out in the On The Net (keyword **On The Net**) message boards for a while. Read the Internet Utilities message board (especially the FTP folder), ask lots of questions, and generally get your nerve up before trying FTP on your own.

- ✔ Trust *nothing* that you download from the Internet via FTP. Assume from the start that it's completely virus-infested, like a little digital epidemic just waiting to break loose on your computer. Virus-check absolutely *everything* that comes to roost in your computer from the Internet.

- ✔ Yes, I'm really serious about doing the virus checks. I do them myself.

- ✔ Watch out for files with odd extensions like .Z, .gz, or .tar.z. These are compressed files, but they're *not* good old-fashioned .ZIP files. To decompress them requires special software, the patience of Job, and often the rest of your day. If you're intent on trying anyway, get a copy of either GZip or MacGZip from the /pub/compress subdirectory of ftp.aol.com (which just happens to be on the FTP menu). If that last sentence didn't make *any* sense to you, don't try to mess with these files.

- ✔ FTP is also called *anonymous FTP* by Those Who Know. That's a fancy way to say that you don't need a special access code or anything to download files. Because the computer sending the files doesn't know who you are, it's an anonymous service. Aren't those computer nerds clever?

All it takes to use FTP is a strong stomach for the technical side of life and these instructions:

1. **From the Internet Connection, click Internet Extras and then FTP (or use keyword** FTP**).**

   The FTP - File Transfer Protocol window opens.

2. **Click the Go To FTP button, which opens the Anonymous FTP window.**

   Finally, the File Transfer Protocol window shows its face (see Figure 14-6).

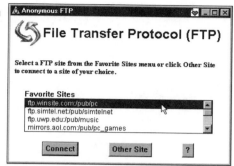

Figure 14-6:
The
Anonymous
FTP window
offers to
whisk you
away to File
Transfer
land.

3. **Scroll through the Favorite Sites list and double-click one that sounds interesting.**

   After a moment or two (or perhaps three if the Internet is having a busy night), another window pops up explaining where you're about to go. Click OK and proceed directly to the directory listing of whatever computer you just attached yourself to. (See Figure 14-7.)

4. **If something looks interesting, double-click it.**

   Different things happen depending on the icon that's next to the item. If the icon is a file folder icon, that entry is a directory; double-clicking it brings up a new window showing you what's in there. If the icon is a document, a dialog box pops up and offers you a View File Now button. To view the document without downloading it, click the button. If the icon is a bunch of disks, you're looking at a program or a compressed file that's available for downloading. Sometimes you also see the funny-looking handshake icon; it stands for a pointer to a particular subdirectory.

5. **Keep poking around and have a good time.**

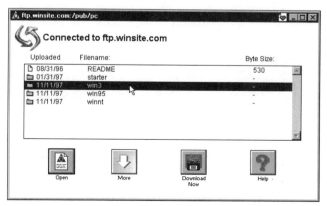

Figure 14-7:
Welcome to
the winsite.

Chapter 15

Loading Up, Loading Down, and Zipping All Around

*I*magine a Wal-Mart where everything is free — you just pick out what you want and carry your selections out to the car. Some items require a small payment directly to the manufacturer, but many don't. Sounds like heaven, right? (Well, heaven probably would be a computer superstore set up this way, but I digress.)

The scenario that I just described already exists, except that it's not a Wal-Mart — it's the hundreds of file libraries in America Online. Just find something that interests you, download the file to your computer, and then, if it's a shareware program, pay a small fee to the author because you love the application so much.

Sounds too simple, right? There must be a catch. Well, it *is* pretty simple, and there really *isn't* a catch. This chapter is your guide to getting a share of this digital bonanza. Read on and find out about finding stuff to download, how the download process works, sharing stuff you love by uploading it, and much more.

Welcome to Software Heaven. Come right on in.

Locating Likely Candidates

You're ready to storm the digital gates, eager to get your share of the software fortunes within. But where do you start? Geez — hundreds, maybe thousands, of places exist for you to look through. Nothing like having too many options to keep your mind spinning in circles, eh?

Start with one or two forums that you particularly like. If you're looking for a certain kind of file (such as fonts or clip art), use the software library search feature to see what's out there. The following sections explain both of these options.

Forum and service libraries

Almost every forum has a file library. Libraries usually are marked with the disk icon that you see in Figure 15-1 or, in fancier service areas such as the one shown in Figure 15-2, with a disk button. Both elements ultimately lead to a file list window (see Figure 15-3).

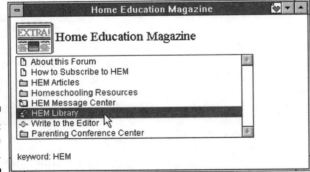

Figure 15-1: A simple file library.

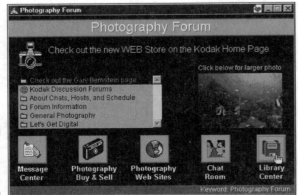

Figure 15-2: A fancier file library.

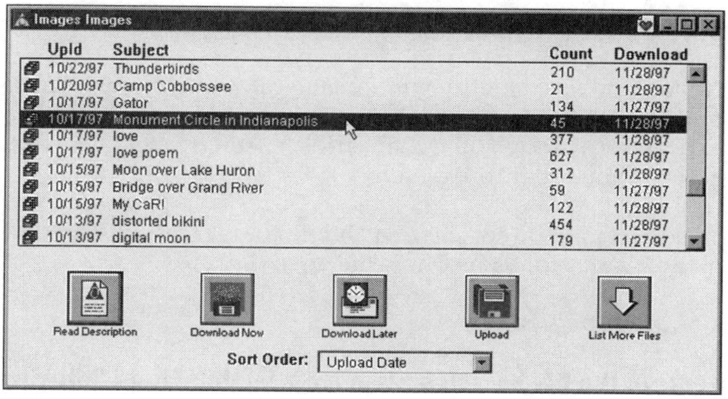

Figure 15-3:
All roads
lead to a file
list window.

✔ To learn more about a file, double-click its entry in the forum library window (or single-click the entry and then click the Read Description button). A page of information about the file appears, including its name, size, and author, plus a complete description (or as complete a description as the person contributing it provides). Incidentally, if you're using a session log, all the file descriptions that you view are saved there automatically. For more information about session logs, see Chapter 12.

✔ Downloading is a breeze with the Download Now and Download Later buttons (covered in the next section).

✔ Use the Sort Order pull-down menu to see the files by the date they were first uploaded or last downloaded, alphabetically by subject, or by download count (a relative measure of which files are the most popular). Just click the down arrow next to the Sort Order setting, choose your preferred order from the list, and wait a moment while America Online organizes everything for you.

✔ Most libraries have lots of files, but only the first 20 are displayed. That's why a List More Files button usually appears in the lower right corner of the forum library window. Click this button to display more files in the window.

For leads on good downloads, read the forum's discussion areas to see what people are talking about, or post a message that describes your interests and asks for recommendations. Also look for files that are popular. The Count column in the file list window is a good popularity gauge; this column tracks the number of times that a file is downloaded.

File library search

If you're looking for something more general, or if you just like knowing *all* your options before you start, try the software library search feature. This feature browses through all the libraries in America Online, looking intently for whatever you tell it to look for.

You must be signed on to America Online to use the software library search system. Sorry, but that's just how life goes.

Here's how to do a search:

1. **Get into the file search system by selecting Find⇨Software or using keyword** Filesearch.

   The File Search dialog box pops up, offering two places to find your software.

2. **In the File Search dialog box, click the Download Software button.**

   The File Search window *finally* appears.

   The other button in the File Search dialog box takes you to the *commercial* software area, where the price of admission is your credit card number. That's great if you need a particular program, but it's usually overkill for a home computer. Instead of plunking down the bucks for an over-packaged application, look for a shareware (or even a freeware) program that fills the bill.

3. **To limit your search to a particular period (the past week, the past month, or since time began), click the appropriate radio button in the Select a Timeframe area.**

   Barring a specific, burning need to search only the most recent uploads, leave the time frame set to All dates. When the file list appears, it's sorted by category and date anyway, with the newest files listed at the beginning of each category.

4. **To narrow your search to particular file libraries, click one or more of the check boxes in the Categories area. To search everywhere, leave all the check boxes clear (the normal setting).**

   When you feel comfortable with the search function and the kinds of files that are out there waiting for you, try experimenting with these settings to see what you can find.

5. **Type a few descriptive words about what you're looking for (see Figure 15-4).**

   If you want a specific program (like WinZip, Paint Shop Pro, or PowerTools), put the program name in this area.

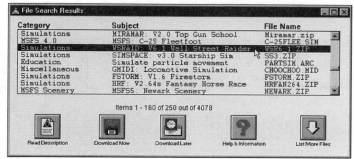

Figure 15-4:
The search
begins.

6. Click the oversized and relaxingly colored Search button at the bottom of the window (see Figure 15-4).

After a moment or two, the File Search Results dialog box appears, looking somewhat akin to Figure 15-5. The File Search Results dialog box is a whole lot like the forum's file list window, right down to the buttons along the bottom.

Figure 15-5:
The results
are in!

7. Scroll through the list to see what your search uncovered. Double-click interesting-looking entries to see a full description of the file.

At this point, you're ready to do some downloading, which (surprisingly enough) is covered in the next section.

Incidentally, Paint Shop Pro, PowerTools, and WinZip are *great* shareware applications for everybody who uses Microsoft Windows and America Online. If you don't have them yet, test your new downloading skills on them.

Downloading a File Right Now

You finally found a promising file, checked its description, and decided that you simply *must* have a copy. Cool with me. You're ready to do the dirty deed, then — time to download a file.

Here's the procedure:

1. **Click the name of the file that you want to download and then click the Download Now button (see Figure 15-6).**

   If you're in the file list window, Download Now is a square button with a cool graphic of a disk "beaming down" as in *Star Trek*. In the file description window, the button is simply labeled (you guessed it) Download Now.

   Clicking this button accesses the Download Manager's filename dialog box (but not the whole Download Manager itself — that's covered in the next section of this chapter).

   The file's name is displayed in the File Name box (see Figure 15-7).

Figure 15-6:
Ready to download your file, Captain.

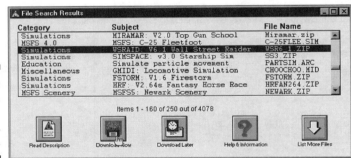

Figure 15-7:
Name the file, and it's on the way!

2. **If you want to change the file's name or the directory where it's going to land, go right ahead; after you finish, choose OK.**

   Clicking OK starts the download. To keep you updated on its progress, America Online displays a bar chart.

   The dialog box also has two control buttons: Finish Later and Cancel. If you suddenly need your computer for something more urgent than downloading this file, click Finish Later. America Online remembers that you already received part of the file, so when you're ready to pull down the rest, the download picks up wherever you stopped the first time. Cancel, on the other hand, is the abort button. Click it if you come to the conclusion that downloading this file is a terrible mistake.

   After the download is complete, a little dialog box pops up to gleefully announce the news.

3. **Click OK to make the dialog box go away.**

If something goes horribly wrong (for example, the download gets stuck for some reason), try downloading the file again. If it doesn't work that time either, try once more at a different time of day, particularly early in the morning, just before leaving for work or school.

What if you're *not* on the unlimited time plan and you burn up a bunch of online time for a download that doesn't work? It's no problem — just go to keyword **Credit** and ask for a refund. Fill out the form, complete with the time, date, and minutes lost, and then click Send Request. The America Online credit elves should reply to you within a few days.

After you get the hang of the America Online file libraries, check out the Internet Connection's FTP (file transfer protocol) feature. FTP is your link to millions of files available on the Internet. If instant access to file libraries all over the world already has you salivating, flip to Chapter 16 for details.

How Do You Manage This Many Downloads?

What if you find not one, not two, but 47 fascinating files? Well, you can spend a lot of your copious free time watching the computer draw load-progress bar charts (how exciting!). Or you can use the Download Manager to automate the whole sordid process. The Download Manager's main goal in life is to help you download *tons* of stuff from America Online. Really — that's it.

Using the Download Manager is a two-stage process: You mark the files that you want to download and then you tell the Download Manager to get all of them. The best thing is that you don't need to be there for the second step of the process; your computer gleefully sits and catches all the files you want while you're off doing something *really* fun.

Here's how the process works:

1. **Click the name of a file that you want to download and then click the Download Later button (see Figure 15-8).**

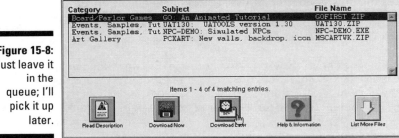

Figure 15-8:
Just leave it in the queue; I'll pick it up later.

The file hops into the Download Manager's queue. By default, the America Online software throws up an annoying little window that *helpfully* explains that you just decided to download this file later (assuming that you mistakenly thought that the *Download Later* button actually washed your car or something).

If you plan to use the Download Later feature a lot, turn off the this-is-what-you-just-did dialog box. To do that, open the Download Manager (that's in step 3 below), then click the Download Preferences button on it. When the Download Preferences window appears, turn off the check box next to Confirm additions to my download list, then click OK. Finally, close the Preferences window and take a moment to smile smugly in the knowledge that you've silenced yet another silly dialog box.

2. **Repeat Step 1 for all the files that you want to download.**

3. **Open the Download Manager by selecting My Files⇨Download Manager from the Toolbar.**

The Download Manager window appears, looking like the one shown in Figure 15-9 (except that your list of files in the middle looks different than mine).

To see the file description one more time, double-click the filename in the Download Manager window. The description appears, just as it did in the file list window.

If you have sudden second thoughts about a file and decide that you don't want to download it, click its name in the Download Manager list and then click Remove Item. Repeat the process as many times as you want.

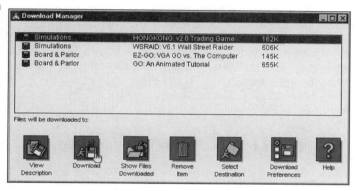

Figure 15-9:
The Download Manager is your digital shopping cart, filled with the goodies you've selected.

4. Click the Download button to put the Download Manager to work.

Two windows appear on-screen, as shown in Figure 15-10. One window shows the overall status of your massive download. The other window displays a progress bar chart for the file that's downloading right now.

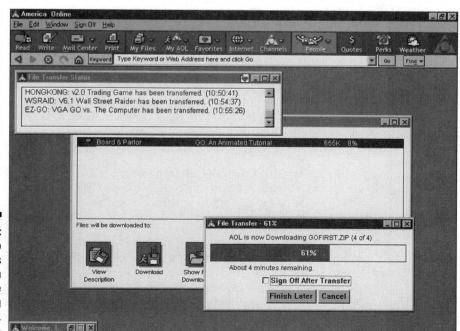

Figure 15-10:
Two windows show you the downloading status.

If you have a *lot* of files to get, click the Sign Off After Transfer check box. That option tells the Download Manager to go ahead and sign you off America Online after the last file arrives. This feature is really handy (and makes sure that you don't waste a lot of online time if the download finishes before you expect it to).

Remember that Automatic AOL sessions work with the Download Manager. You can mark a bunch of files and download them in the middle of the night, when America Online is the least busy. Chapter 6 explains the basics of Automatic AOL, but you need to check the Help menu for details about scheduling the sessions.

The Joys of Stuffing and Zipping

Many files in America Online's various and sundry file libraries end in ZIP, SIT, or ARC. These letters don't mean that they're fast, resting, or that they date from the time of Noah; rather, they indicate that the files were *compressed* so they'd take less time to download (and less space inside America Online's computers). ZIP files come from the PKZip or WinZIP programs, while SIT files are created on the Macintosh by StuffIt. ARC files are an old and rarely used format, but there are still some around.

Before using a compressed file, you have to decompress it. To do that, you either need a copy of the right program (as mentioned above), or you can let the America Online software handle it by itself.

To simplify your life, the America Online access software automatically unpacks compressed files when you sign off the system. (I tell you, those programmers amaze even me sometimes.) To make sure that this setting is on, choose My AOL⇨Preferences. Click the Download button to open the Download Preferences dialog box. Make sure that Xs appear in the two check boxes next to Automatically decompress files at sign-off and Delete ZIP and ARC files after decompression. Then leave the decompressing to America Online.

Installing programs on your computer involves a lot of little niggling details — too many, unfortunately, for me to go into here. I won't leave you high and dry, though (I'd never do that to you!). Take a look at these resources for more about both downloading and installing programs:

> ✔ For a distinctly America Online view of the whole download and install thing, try keyword **Download 101**. This step-by-step tutorial guides you through the whole process in good detail. Pay particular attention to Section 6, Using Downloaded Files, because it covers the toughest part of the download experience.

✔ If the mere thought of folders, directories, and software installation makes you pass out on the floor, put some soft blankets down there to cushion your impending arrival. When they're safely in place, pick up a copy of *Windows 95 For Dummies,* 2nd Edition, or *Windows 3.11 For Dummies,* 3rd Edition (both by Andy Rathbone), or *Macs For Dummies,* 5th Edition, by David Pogue (all from IDG Books Worldwide, Inc.), hit the blankets, and catch up on your reading.

Whether or not you plan to download lots of files and programs, I *highly* recommend downloading and registering a copy of WinZip, a Windows-based archiving program. It's available in versions for both Windows 95 and Windows 3.*x*. This one program knows how to handle almost any type of compressed file thrown at it. That alone makes it worth the minimal registration fee, but all the other tricks it knows (like making a ZIP file on the fly by dragging and dropping files into it from either Windows Explorer or File Manager) make it truly indispensable.

Well, now it's yours — sort of

Three kinds of programs exist in the world: freeware, shareware, and commercial software. If this sounds like horribly dry, technical drivel, you obviously aren't a lawyer (I knew that I liked you). Please bear with me (and stay awake) while I explain further.

Freeware, shareware, and commercial software are the three most common ways in which a program is licensed for use. Freeware costs nothing; the author graciously donated it to the public. Shareware is software that you can download, try, and pay for if you like it. Commercial software is what you buy at the local computer superstore from companies such as Borland, Lotus, Microsoft, and Novell.

Following are a few basic rules regarding the three kinds of software:

✔ **Freeware:** Download it, use it, give a copy to your friends. Isn't freeware great?

✔ **Shareware:** Download it and give it a try. If you don't like the program, don't pay for it.

If you think it's great, get out your checkbook and send in the registration fee. Whatever you do, don't keep using an unregistered shareware program because you don't think that you should have to pay for something you downloaded from America Online. That would be like stealing a book from the library and then saying that it's OK because the library doesn't charge for books anyway. Shareware is often high-quality work and well worth the minimal registration fee.

✔ **Commercial software:** Never, under *any* circumstances, upload or download something that claims to be a commercial program. If you like WordPerfect, that's fine — just don't show your admiration by giving copies of it to your friends. I won't get on my "pirated software" soapbox, I promise. But I will say this: If you like a program, buy your own copy. Okay?

Donating Your Own Efforts

Most file libraries not only offer files for your downloading pleasure but also accept *uploads* — files donated by other America Online members. After all, the library files had to come from *somewhere*, so why not let members chip in things that they like?

To upload a file, you need to know the file's name and location on your computer. You also have to find a potential home for it somewhere in America Online. Look for a place that accepts uploaded files (this step's a must) and that has other files like the one you're sending. If you're sending a game, utility, or other program, use your antivirus software to be extra sure that you're not donating a computer virus, too.

✔ Not every file library accepts uploads. If you're looking at a file list and the Upload button is dimmed, that's a pretty good sign that you're reviewing a read-only library.

✔ Only public domain, freeware, shareware, or items of your own creation can be uploaded to America Online. If you aren't sure about the appropriateness of something that you want to upload, post a message to one of the forum hosts (you can usually find their screen names in a "welcome to this forum" type of document in the forum's main screen). Describe your file and get the host's opinion about your uploading it. Check out the sidebar "Well, now it's yours — sort of" earlier in this chapter for a little more information about the whole freeware, shareware, and commercial software issue.

✔ Don't upload something on your first day in America Online. Wait a little while. Get involved in a forum or two, meet some people, post some messages, and generally get a feel for what goes on before you upload anything to a library.

At this point, you're ready to upload the file. Here's what to do:

1. **Display the file list window of the file library to which you want to upload.**

   Get there through whatever combination of keywords, menus, and mouse-clicks works best for you.

2. **Click the Upload button at the bottom of the file list window.**

   The Upload File dialog box appears.

   If the Upload button is dimmed, this file library doesn't accept uploaded files. Sorry, but that's how life goes sometimes. Also, America Online may tell you that the library is full. In that case, post a message in the forum's discussion boards asking if there's a place for you to upload the file you want to share.

3. **Carefully fill out all the information boxes in the Upload File dialog box.**

   Be as specific as you can. The more that people know about this file, the more likely they'll be to download it.

4. **Click Select File to display the Attach File dialog box; double-click the name of the file that you want to upload; then choose OK to close the dialog box.**

5. **Double-check all the text you typed; after you're happy with it, click Send.**

Don't be surprised if your uploaded file doesn't immediately appear in the file library. Most, if not all, America Online forums check uploaded files for viruses before setting those files free in the library.

Logging Isn't Really Downloading, but It's Close

Sometimes, you want a record of where you were and what you saw. If you didn't, most of the photo film and developing market (as well as a large chunk of camcorder sales) wouldn't exist.

In America Online terminology, what you're looking for is a *session log*: a file that stores the contents of every document that you touched during a particular online period. The session log grabs every e-mail, news story, and bulletin board posting and stuffs them into one long text file.

For all the details on America Online's logging features, flip to Chapter 12.

Part IV
Going Your Own Way

In this part . . .

This part is cool. Each chapter in Part IV looks at America Online from a particular point of view: that of a small-business person, a teacher, or a student, for example. I suggest ways that you can actually *use* America Online to solve problems and get things done in your life.

Pretty radical, huh?

Browse through the chapters and see what you can find. They're designed to draw you in, fill your head with ideas, sweep up a little bit as long as it's in there, and finally send you on your way with a neat, tidy mind. Use your creativity to take my suggestions and find still better ways to do stuff.

Chapter 16
Stuff to Do When You're New

● ●

In This Chapter

▶ Navigating your way to success

▶ Unearthing the online areas meant for you

▶ Finding online help when you need it

▶ Adding to your list of accomplishments

▶ Locating the areas with zing

● ●

*N*othing makes you feel more a part of the online world than jumping in with both feet and carving a niche for yourself. Before you know it, you're a permanent resident! Getting to that point, however, can be a frustrating experience. Not knowing where to go first can be particularly challenging. This chapter attempts to point you in the right directions.

Finding Your Way Around

Where do you turn if you're brand new to computers, or simply new to AOL? AOL Quick Start (keyword **Quick Start**) gives you an introduction to computers in general, a tutorial on the basics of AOL, and a peek at what AOL considers the essentials of the system — e-mail, the Web, and chat.

For a more in-depth look at America Online's features, browse through AOL Member Services (keyword **Help**). As Figure 16-1 shows, the Member Services window offers helpful information on the Internet, e-mail, online safety, and much more. Click one of the question thought bubbles to see a topic's contents; from there, click a subject to see its articles in the item list.

For a peek at what you'll find behind the main channel windows, take a look at *AOL Channels For Dummies* — the gray-edged pages at the back of this book.

Figure 16-1:
AOL
explains
various
online
features.

Tracking Special Interests

I know this will surprise some of you, but there's more to online life than e-mail and the news. America Online abounds with cool forums that discuss everything from music to marsupials (not, thankfully, in the same forum). So how do you find the stuff *you're* interested in? Where do you meet people who have your hobbies and beliefs?

✔ Interest Profiles allow you to tell AOL what you like (keyword **Interest Profiles,** see Figure 16-2). In turn, the system sends you an e-mail suggesting online areas you might enjoy. Find out about Interest Profiles from the articles in the item list, or click Edit to create your own.

✔ Keep current on the news you want to read. News Profiles (keyword **News Profiles**) scours the news services to bring you news tailored to you — and it drops it right into your e-mail box. The Create a Profile button starts you on the path of making your own News Profile. To alter a profile once you've created it, use Manage Your Profiles. This service is a boon for people interested in esoteric topics, such as Victorian costume or solar-powered vehicles.

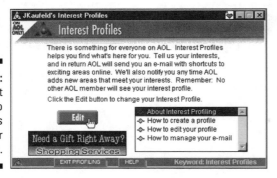

Figure 16-2:
Use Interest
Profiles to
find areas
that fit your
interests.

✔ Search the World Wide Web for your favorite topics with AOL NetFind (keyword **NetFind**). Type your interest or hobby into the Search text field, and then click Find. When the system returns a list of sites, scroll down the list until you find one you like. Double-click the hyperlinked title to visit that Web site.

✔ Locate other members who share your passions through the Member Directory (keyword **Member Directory**). Enter a search word or phrase (such as science fiction or quilting) into the Search entire profile for the following field, press Enter, and see what you find. The system only returns a maximum of 250 profiles, so you may want to narrow your search by using a more restrictive term (such as Asimov instead of science fiction). Highlight any item that looks interesting, and press Enter to open that member's profile.

✔ Use the Random feature (keyword **Random**) to explore all kinds of online areas. Click the roulette wheel and watch it spin. In a few seconds a window appears on-screen. If you like what you see, explore the area. You find this particular area unappealing? Click the wheel again and another window pops on-screen. Spin the wheel several times whenever you find yourself in an adventurous mood, and you'll soon know more about America Online than some members who've had accounts several years!

When you find an area you really like, mark it as a favorite place by clicking the red-heart-on-white-paper icon in the upper right corner of the window.

Getting a Helping Hand

Every now and then you run across something that stumps you, and it would be nice to get some instant (or at least personal) answers. On AOL, you have both worlds when these situations crop up. America Online teems with friendly people and helpful documents just waiting to give that boost you need.

Get help from other members in the Members Helping Members message boards (keyword **MHM**). Post a question of your own, or open the boards to read about e-mail, rural access, and general AOL questions, as well as many other topics. To read a few of the "best" questions and answers, click the Top AOL Questions button. This section includes questions on keywords, billing, e-mail, and downloading.

Here are some other tips to help you find your way:

✔ For answers to your computer questions (not to mention a whole boatload of resources), check out the Help Desk. To learn about the Help Desk and its mission in life, read the Start Here document. To go directly to the answers, open the Frequently Asked Questions folder and select a topic. As Figure 16-3 shows, you'll find all kinds of resources at the Help Desk (keyword **Help Desk**). To find assistance with a specific application or aspect of computing (such as DOS, graphic arts, or games), take a look at the Support Forums list. To see it, click the Support Forums button on the right side of the window.

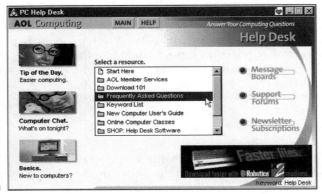

Figure 16-3:
Stop by the
Help Desk
for answers
to your
computer
questions.

✔ Some of the best goodies on America Online are found in the software and file libraries. Games, home budget planners, graphics, electronic texts, and sounds wait patiently for their chance to fill your hard drive. Finding the files online does you little good if you don't know how to download them to your computer. Read the documents in Download 101 (keyword **Download 101**) for the basics, the tricks, and the extras of downloading files from AOL.

Becoming Adept at Online Life

The day soon comes when you're not a newbie anymore. You've spent some time online, whether measured in weeks or months; you know the basics; and you want more. Where do you turn? These areas help you bridge the gap between Online Newcomer status and the I-don't-even-remember-when-I-joined group:

✔ Explore the features and offerings of the Internet with On The Net (keyword **On The Net**). This area supplies both beginners and advanced Net denizens with information, so you're sure to find something you can use — whether you want to design your own Web page, find out about the free Personal Web Space that comes with every AOL account, or learn about gopher, telnet, or mailing lists (look in the Internet Extras folder).

✔ Sharpen your pencil, grab your notebook, and get ready to take notes in the Online Classroom's free computer classes (keyword **Online Classroom**). Click the Class Schedule button to see a rundown of the day's classes, or open any topic folder to check when AOL plans to hold the class you want to take. As Figure 16-4 shows, you can start slowly with a class for beginners, elect to attend a programming class, or brush up on the Web.

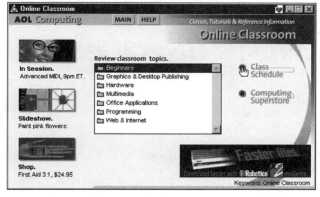

Figure 16-4:
Attend a free computer class!

✔ Create a member profile so that other members know something about you. Select My AOL⇨My Member Profile to open the Edit Your Online Profile window. Enter your information into the fields, and click the Update button. Your profile proudly takes its place among the AOL Member Profiles of the Rich and Famous. Depending on your paranoia level, you may want to include your full name, city, state, and country information, or you may just want to type in your first name or nickname and your area (Pacific Rim, East Coast, or Yukon, for example).

✔ Gain a working chat-room vocabulary with Online Shorthands (keyword **Shorthand**). Learn some of the common smileys (pictures made with keyboard symbols) and shorthand notation that you'll find online. After reading through this area, you'll be able to send a smile :), a hug {}, or appreciate an online joke by Laughing Out Loud (LOL). See Chapter 26 for more new jargon.

✔ Protect your computer investment by spending a few minutes in AOL's Virus areas. Learn about Viruses and Trojan Horses, pick up some tips on keeping your computer safe, and be sure to read through the virus hoax information. If you know which so-called viruses have been thoroughly debunked, you'll know when you don't need to panic (which, actually, is most of the time). Keyword **Virus** takes you to the Virus Information Center, while keyword **Virus Info** opens the AOL Computer Protection Center. Both areas are worth reading. Your surest protection from a virus, however, is never downloading a file from someone you don't know.

✔ Along the same vein, visit the Reach Out Zone (keyword **Reach Out**), AOL's resource for online conduct. Here you'll find some virus information, instructions for notifying AOL if someone violates the Terms of Service agreement, and a heads up to be wary of any online scams or schemes you may run across. The Scams and Schemes section contains several examples of the effort the unscrupulous will expend in the name of getting confidential information. Take the time to read them, so that if you receive anything like them in your mailbox you'll recognize it. Forward the offending message to AOL with keyword **Notify AOL**.

Hearing the Online Heartbeat

Under the windows and menus, AOL thrives with interaction, conversation, and activity. That's all well and good; but if you don't know where to find it, the hubbub continues unnoticed (and unjoined). Here are some ideas of where to look for new friends, activity, and excitement online:

✔ Which celebrity scheduled an upcoming online appearance? Keyword **Live** takes you to AOL Live!, where you can read all the details. Browse through the Coming Attractions or see who's making an appearance today. If you find you missed someone's online event, use the Intermission button to search the Transcripts and Photos.

✔ Did you miss the debut of a new online area? Find out in What's New on AOL (keyword **What's New**). Click any item to open its area on-screen and explore. This window also features some of the most popular areas online.

✔ Drop into the Friendly Face at AOL (keyword **Friendly Face**) and visit various people-oriented places online. Drop into LaPub for a virtual drink and conversation, stop by Playbill On-Line to discuss theater, or stop by the Quantum Que, the message boards for members who love (and hang out) in the People Connection.

✔ Looking for action next door or half a country away? Keyword **Digital City** takes you to Digital City on AOL, where you choose a United States city and explore its news, its people, and community. Interested in virtual travel? Keyword **Digital City UK** takes you to cities in the United Kingdom; use keyword **DC Canada** to visit Digital City Toronto and the Digital Wilderness.

Chapter 17

The Student's Guide to Online Life

*E*ducation is where you find it these days, and you can find a lot of it with America Online. When you're stumped with a problem, digging for facts, or trying to make a perfect (or at least airworthy) kite, you can turn to plenty of online places for help.

This chapter, like the others in this part, provides direction instead of answers. It looks at some highlights to get you started but encourages you to think creatively and come up with your own resources. I know you can do it — now *do it!*

Places to Start

Even in a digital wonderland such as America Online, you still have to start somewhere. A couple of places stand out as excellent jumping-off points:

> ✔ The Princeton Review (keyword **Princeton Review**) offers all kinds of information and services aimed at the high school and college crowd (see Figure 17-1). The gems of the area include insights into the admissions process, a searchable database of school reviews, sample questions with a funny twist in the Dilbert Daily Mental Workout, and descriptions of the SAT, ACT, GRE, and several other acronym-encrusted tests. If you're headed for college, stop here first.

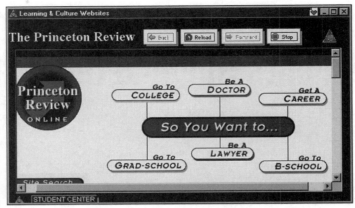

Figure 17-1:
The
Princeton
Review is a
great place
to start your
trip to
college.

✔ Don't just sit there — Do Something! Find out what Do Something, a national nonprofit youth action and training group, is doing in your area. You've always wanted to change the world. Here's your chance! Find out about the Do Something award winners, share your dreams on the message boards, or read about what others are doing. (The keyword, in case you haven't guessed, is **Do Something**.)

✔ What *can't* you find on the Internet these days? This international network of networks is definitely worth a look. America Online offers lots of Internet services through its Internet Connection (keyword **Internet**). See Chapter 14 for all the details.

Getting Help When You Need It

When you're stuck on a homework problem and need some help to get over the hump, fire up the computer and sign on to America Online. Look for your much-needed help in these areas:

✔ When tough homework is on your mind (eww — get it off, get it off!), drop by Ask-A-Teacher (keyword **Ask-A-Teacher**) for help and advice. To reach assistance from the main Ask-A-Teacher window, first choose your grade range (elementary, junior high and high school, or college). Each level's section provides discussion boards and tutoring rooms, plus a database of previously answered questions on nearly any subject. If you need help with a complicated or unusual topic, e-mail a teacher with your question, and in the best of all worlds, a real teacher responds to your query within about 48 hours.

✔ If studying doesn't come naturally, check out the Study Skills Service (keyword **Study Skills**). These folks aren't hawking some elixir that unlocks the Secrets of the Ancient Students. Instead, they have a sound, step-by-step approach you can use to recognize your strengths, identify your weaknesses, and build on both to improve your skills. Although the company has some books available for sale, you can use its method without buying anything.

✔ Need a topic for that research paper? You'll find plenty of ideas in the Research Zone (keyword **Research Zone**). Use the Idea Directory to browse hundreds of research paper topics in art, science, history, business, and society (see Figure 17-2). Who knows, maybe looking over some of these ideas will turn on your enthusiasm for research?

✔ The annual science fair looms before you, and you can't think of a great project to save your life. America Online comes to your rescue once again with Science Fairs (keyword **Science Fair**). Get project ideas, tips for making your project (and its presentation) super, and Web sites where you can begin your research.

✔ Stuck trying to understand the *Aeneid?* Goodness knows I was. Turn to Barron's Booknotes (keyword **Barron's**) for downloadable study guides and plot synopses.

Figure 17-2:
Uncover esoteric research topics with a little help from the Zone.

A Trip to the Virtual Library

Research was never easier than this. Between the online encyclopedia (keyword **Comptons**), the magazines (keyword **Newsstand**), and the whole Research & Learn channel (keyword **Research**), you may not have to look anywhere else.

- Whether you're looking for information on agriculture, economics, or religion and philosophy, somebody somewhere has organized it into *gopher*. Use keyword **Gopher** to bring up the Gopher window and then click Search. Type your search text and click Search. See Chapter 14 for all the details (because I casually left out a few).

- An even broader area of the Internet is the World Wide Web (keyword **WWW**). Start out with the AOL NetFind (keyword **NetFind**), and then try the NetFind's Time Savers Reference Source for links to online encyclopedias, reference desks, and translation dictionaries.

- The Internet newsgroups are another great source of information and discussion. Use keyword **Newsgroups** to get there and then try either Add Newsgroups or Search All Newsgroups to see what tweaks your fancy.

- When you're looking for obscure information about an even more obscure topic, you need a resource worthy of the search. On America Online, this calls for a trip to The Straight Dope (keyword **Straight Dope**). Some of the myriad questions answered in there include Are kosher pickles really kosher? Why does ketchup dissolve aluminum foil? and Where does belly button lint come from? (Okay — a lot of respectable questions are in there too, but I figure that the odds of your giving the place a try are better if it sounds like more fun than a trip to the local Library Reference Desk and Silence Research Facility.)

So many sources, so little time

When you're researching a topic, why not start with America Online? With its forums, magazines, and other resources at your digital fingertips, you'll be done in no time.

Suppose that you have a report on Africa that's due, and you're a little stumped — you don't know where to start. Begin with the continent of Africa (keyword **Africa**), Geography & Maps (keyword **Geography**), the Travel Channel's Where to Go and What to Do section on Africa (keyword **Travel**), and News Search (keyword **News Search**). Browse through Survival World (keyword **Survival World**) for African wildlife facts and downloadable photos. Check Compton's Encyclopedia (keyword **Comptons**) or the Merriam-Webster Dictionary (keyword **Collegiate**) for any terms that are new to you. Wander over to gopher (keyword **Gopher**) and look through the Gopher Directory.

And that's just for starters. Imagine what you can find if you really put your mind to it. (Kinda scary, isn't it?)

Dressing Up Your Reports

When your report is ready to go, why not spice it up with a few well-chosen graphics? Check out the Smithsonian Photo Gallery (keyword **Smithsonian**) for downloadable shots of everything from Egyptian artifacts to the Hope diamond. Another place to see is the ABC Online area (keyword **ABC**), where you can download unmarked maps of the world from the ABC News library. The library also contains flags of the world (updated regularly), clip art icons, video clips, and still more. Look for the flags and maps in Stuff, and then News Stuff. When you see a folder called Digital Warehouse in the item list, you've found it!

Thinking about That Job

If you're over the age of eight, you're probably starting to think about that career at the end of your school years. America Online has some great places that can help you figure out what you want to be when you grow up. (I *still* don't know what I want to be, but I guess I'm not quite grown up yet, so it's okay.)

- Here's one I wished for back in college. The RSP Funding Focus (keyword **RSP**) offers searchable information about scholarships, internships, grants, and more. Check out the Money for Study, Research, Etc. button for more details.

- If you're considering career options, knowing what the job entails is helpful. Read up on hundreds of different careers in the Gonyea Online Career Center's (keyword **Career Center**) Occupational Profiles Database.

- Find out what real people do in a particular industry, and browse resources designed for full-time workers in Professional Forums (keyword **Professional Forums**).

- Researching a particular industry or company? Company Research (keyword **Company Research**) contains stock reports and other financial information for recent years.

As If One School Weren't Enough

If you're one of those people who just wants to *learn, learn, learn,* good for you. I always wanted to order pizza, breadsticks, and salad myself (my college education was merely a by-product of five years in the university dorms). Whether your aspirations are for a degree or for the heck of it, America Online has some educational opportunities for you.

- For computer know-how (particularly in the programming arena), check out the noncredit (and no fee) computer classes in the Computing Online Classroom (keyword **Online Classroom**). Here you'll find classes listed on everything from DOS for Beginners to programming in Visual Basic 5.0.

- The Online Campus (keyword **Online Campus**) offers "personal enrichment" classes on almost any topic for a small fee — usually $20 to $30.

- Earn a Certificate in Computer Graphics online from the Corcoran School of Art (keyword **Corcoran**). These courses are less expensive than traditional classroom instruction, but their costs still fall within the ballpark range of college tuition.

- Register for college credit courses online. Offered by the University of California (keyword **UCAOL**), the course catalog includes classes in the arts and humanities, business, computer science, hazardous materials management, natural sciences, and social sciences. Choose More Courses to jump to the program's Web site, where they also list various high school courses. Fees for high school courses hover around $200 per course; college course fees range from $300 to $500 per course.

Time to Relax and Recharge

Remember to have some fun. All work and no play makes you a financially secure, crotchety old nerd (and California's got enough of them already). Take some time to meet people, play games, and enjoy your online life.

- Three easy options right off the bat are Lifestyles (keyword **Lifestyles**), Interests (keyword **Interests**) and the People Connection (keyword **People**). Browse around and see what's out there — and who.

- The Online Gaming Forum (keyword **OGF**) is home to all kinds of interesting pursuits, from computer gaming to board gaming (and a few other types in between). If you're into improvisational theatre, check out the Free Form Gaming Forums (keyword **FFGF**) as well.

- Teens who love to program computers find a home at Youth Tech (keyword **YT**). Learn the answer to that sticky coding problem in the chat shack, read computer game reviews, or find some top Web sites – whether you're looking for school help or techy news sites.

- If fashion is your thing, curl up with the online edition of *Elle* magazine (keyword **Elle**). Get the scoop on the latest in looking great, feeling good, and emptying your checkbook (sorry — that was a father's perspective).

Chapter 18

Parenting Your Offspring (In Diapers, Online, or In Between the Two)

- -

In This Chapter

▶ Staying about even with the kids

▶ Some wisdom about parental controls

▶ Keeping the kids safe

▶ Remembering what fun's all about

▶ Surviving the work-at-home life

- -

Some days, I think the sole goal of parenting is to make sure that everybody arrives at the dinner table at roughly the same time. On other days, the incredible size of the job looms over me like a monster in a bad '50s horror film. And I don't think that I'm alone in my concerns.

Judging by the resources available to parents through America Online, it looks like parents are finally going to get some help. This chapter points out the best of the resources and gives you a gentle push along the way.

All the resources in the world aren't any good unless you take the time to use them.

Keeping Up with the Kids

We parents have to learn about all this parenting stuff the hard way — by trying something, either getting it right or messing it up, and then trying again. America Online gives parents some unique opportunities to simplify this shoddy arrangement and share information and experiences with one another (and to voice opinions about topics of concern).

✔ The Families channel (keyword **Families**) is a magical doorway to America Online designed especially for parents. It's a gateway to many parent-related forums and areas of the service, so you can quickly find the resources you're looking for.

✔ Take some time to learn about the Internet and what it offers. As a parent, you need to be aware of the wonderful resources out on the Net as well as the potential dangers that lie therein. America Online's Internet Center (keyword **Internet**) is the place to start. If you're completely new to the Internet, take a stroll through Chapter 16 for a bout with the basics. For some interactive help, basic and advanced information, and organized chats, check out On the Net (keyword **On the Net**).

✔ Next on the hit list is The National Parenting Center (keyword **TNPC**). This area contains some great articles and parents' discussion areas. When you don't know where to ask a question or make a comment, try posting a message here.

✔ Education is a leading issue in the country, and America Online has a place to make your voice heard. The National Education Association maintains a public forum (keyword **NEA Public**) with a good discussion area, but it's a little heavy on the propaganda.

✔ If you're a homeschooling family, link up and swap tips with others in the Home Schooling forum (keyword **Homeschooling**), the *Practical Homeschooling* magazine area (keyword **PHS**), and the *Home Education Magazine* Forum (keyword **HEM**).

A Few Thoughts about Control

As you may have noticed, there's a lot to do on America Online. Unfortunately, it's not free. Someone in the family (probably you) pays the bill each month. To keep things from getting completely out of hand, America Online built in some parental controls (keyword **Parental Controls**). Chapter 3 explains them, how they work, and when to use them.

The best parental control is simply working with your kids so they understand that all this fun comes with a price. One parent I know (who uses AOL's hourly pricing option) gives his daughter five free hours each month, but she has to pay for anything beyond that. I'd strongly suggest doing something similar before implementing parental controls (but that's just the kind of guy I am).

Protecting Your Online Kids

This section of the book isn't particularly funny, but it *is* very important. Please take time to read it and then act on what you find.

You already know the bad news: Some sick people are in the online realm, and some of them are trolling for kids. The good news is that you *can* protect your kids — you're not powerless in this frightening mess.

It's important that you, as a concerned parent, *do something* to protect your children, but knee-jerk reactions are *not* the answer. Remember that America Online and the Internet are much like sprawling digital cities. Just as there are parts of your own town that you don't want the kids visiting, you'll also find areas of the online world that are definitely for adults only. Canceling your account or erasing the access software won't protect your kids — doing so just teaches them fear. Instead, you need to interact with your children, help them understand this crazy online world, teach them how to respond appropriately, and take the responsibility that's yours as a parent.

With all this in mind, here are some ideas, tips, and suggestions for keeping your online kids safe. Please take them to heart.

- Educate your kids. Remind them that just because the person they met online sounds like a kid (or even claims to be one) doesn't mean that's necessarily the truth.

- Teach your kids what not to say online. Make sure that they never give out their address or phone number. Never.

- Learn the online system yourself, particularly the offerings available on the Internet (but you're already doing that).

- Observe what your kids do. Ask to join them for an evening online. If they know more about how this stuff works than you do, ask them to teach you. But if you ask, be ready to take notes and really learn — don't merely nod and comment about how amazingly far technology has come. Think of the online system as a hobby that your children enjoy. Your goal is to share that hobby with them.

- Report questionable occurrences. If your child tells you about being approached in a questionable way, get the user ID of the person your child was interacting with and report it to the online service. They'll help you deal with the problem.

- With younger kids, apply parental controls (discussed in the preceding section). These controls block kids from various parts of the service. You choose how much is blocked; they can explore everything else. Look into keyword **Parental Controls** for details.

✔ Encourage your kids' offline activities and friendships. Offer to throw a pizza party, game night, or movie extravaganza for your children and their friends. The cost is minimal, but the rewards are many.

✔ If you're worried, don't simply kill your account or take away your child's computer access. Bad things happen in your city, but you don't pack up and leave every time something goes wrong. Education is the answer, not blind, knee-jerk reactions.

✔ Don't presume that bad things won't happen to your kids. Denial is a marvelous breeding ground for the worst of problems.

✔ Don't automatically assume that everyone your child meets online is a wacko. Lots of real kids are out there.

✔ Don't interrogate your children — be interested, but don't accuse. Show interest, but don't presume guilt. You didn't like it as a child, and neither will they.

Have Some Fun? What's That?

If your kids can have fun on America Online, why shouldn't you? Hmm . . . there's no reason that I can think of.

✔ I love movies (particularly when they're at the dollar cinema). So much happens behind the scenes, so much money is spent to create the masterpiece, so many people with odd job titles — it almost makes you want to take part in the movie biz yourself. Wander over to Movies (keyword **Movies**) and catch some of the excitement. As Figure 18-1 shows, this area is packed with movie and video information. Read about new flicks, join a movie chat, and catch up on the industry buzz from this window.

Figure 18-1:
Come here when you want to know what's new at the movies.

✔ For a more parental twist on movies, check out Parent Soup's movies section. To get there, use keyword **Parent Soup**. After the window appears, click the Fun & Games button, and then open Parents' Movie Picks in the Fun & Games window.

✔ Although movies are wonderful, my top pick for entertainment is still live theatre. To keep up on the latest in Broadway, Off-Broadway, regional, and even international professional theatre, check out Playbill Online (keyword **Playbill**).

✔ If you happen to live in Chicago or Florida, you can order tickets to the theater (or any other events you want tickets to) through Ticketmaster Online (keyword **Ticketmaster**). For the rest of us, there's the Ticketmaster Web site (also available through keyword **Ticketmaster**) with its searchable list of all the events that Ticketmaster covers around the country.

✔ When you're at a loss for something to do, check out Family Life Online (keyword **Family Life**). This area offers projects sure to please family members — for both indoors and outdoors. Find kid-pleasing vacation destinations in the travel section, and read reviews on books, music, software, and videos as you prepare for a quiet night at home.

✔ Few things are more relaxing than a little shopping excursion. Why not wander the online Gifts selection (keyword **Gifts**), Computing Superstore (keyword **CSS**), or any of the other vendors in America Online's Shopping area (keyword **Shopping**)? Heck, I'm getting relaxed just writing about it.

✔ To unwind after a hard day's work, pick up a new hobby or follow an old one in the Interests areas (keyword **Interests**).

✔ If you're a crossword fan, put down that pencil, throw out the newspaper, and give electronic crosswords a try. For a couple of new puzzles every day, try out New York Times Crosswords (keyword **Crossword**). As a special treat, New York Times Crosswords creates an AOL-only puzzle. Be sure to look for it each month. The area also contains the special Across Lite crossword program that you need to work with the puzzles. And it's even available in both Macintosh and Windows versions! (It just doesn't get any better than this.)

✔ Want something a little more interactive? Try the People Connection (keyword **People**), America Online's interactive chat area. Also check out the Online Gaming Forum (keyword **OGF**) for all kinds of online games and game clubs.

Doing the Work-at-Home Thing

More and more families have at least one parent working at home. This exciting lifestyle change has lots of positive aspects, but it also brings some, uh, *challenges* as well.

One of the hard parts of working at home is feeling disconnected from people — missing the impromptu hallway meetings (also known as chats) and unscheduled personal refreshment intervals (or coffee breaks) that often precede them. America Online has some great places to build a group of friends and acquaintances who understand this crazy lifestyle. Here are my top picks (although one is biased, I admit):

- Check out the home business discussions in Your Business (keyword **Your Business**) for freewheeling idea swaps about all aspects of home-work life.

- If you're having a sudden attack of the lonelies, jump into the People Connection (keyword **People**) and see who you can see. The rooms are always hopping, even in the middle of the day and night. Honestly, I don't know what all these people do for work, but whatever it is, it pays their America Online bills.

- Miss the office water cooler conversations? For the online equivalent, grab your coffee mug and amble over to About Work's Work from Home (keyword **About Work**). Link up with other people in your profession, find a Work-from-Home chat to join, and (for those *really* bad days) cast yourself into the helpful hands of a support group. It's all there, just waiting for you! And if you're only beginning your Work from Home adventure, check the Work from Home Resources section for Web sites, free downloads, and sources you can tap for advice.

- Fellow writers, check out a few of the scheduled chats in the Writers Club (keyword **Writers**) and focus on romance, historical, poetry, technical, or the business of writing. Use the keyword to bring up the Writers Club window, and then click the Chat button to bring up the Writers Chat window. Double-click Writers Club Chat Schedule for all the chat and conference information.

- When it's time to refit the home office with some new technology, *Home Office Computing* magazine (keyword **Home Office**) offers feature articles, hardware and software reviews, and buyer's guide comparison articles. While you're there, drop by the Contact Home Office Computing bulletin board for some interesting conversation.

Chapter 19
The Well-Connected Teacher

*C*reating an interesting, involving, and intellectually stimulating classroom environment isn't easy these days. Arguably, it *never* was easy, but when you're dealing with attention spans measured in seconds, I think that cranks up the old challenge meter a few notches.

Whether you teach at a public or private school, or if you're leading a home school, America Online has plenty of resources just waiting for you. This chapter points out the highlights, offers you some ideas to start the creativity gears grinding, and sends you off toward other relevant chapters of this book. Keep your mind open as you read through this chapter — there's a way to use almost *everything* educationally.

The Ultimate Learning Resource Center

As resource centers go, I don't think that you can beat America Online. It's open 24 hours a day, it's stocked with everything from lesson plans to clip art, and it has a friendly face that doesn't yell at you when things go wrong (unlike many resource center keepers I've met in the past).

Here are some ideas to begin your quest for resource material:

✔ Take a look at the Research & Learn channel (keyword **Research**) for online forums, reference material, and Web sites that concentrate on content areas, such as history, science, business, health, geography, reading, and writing. Take a look at Figure 19-1 to see your many options.

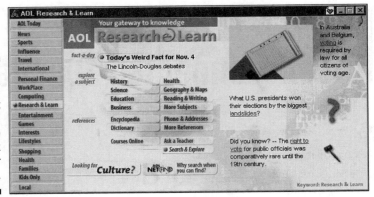

Figure 19-1:
Choose
a subject
and find
gems to
take back
to your
classroom.

✔ Hang out in the Teachers' Lounge (keyword **Teachers' Lounge**) for friendly conversation in the Work Room chat. Look in the item list for ideas, resources, and exams organized by subject — for the work-weary teacher, the Teachers' Lounge is truly one of the best resources online. Also look for ideas and files in The Classroom: Education Forum, part of Chicago's Digital City. You'll find it at keyword **Col Educate**.

✔ When you're looking for children's books, general education titles, or literature, browse through Barnes and Noble @AOL (keyword **Barnes and Noble**) in the Shopping Channel. It's always open — and that means easy access for busy teachers.

✔ Find just the right pictures to accompany your multicultural segments, science projects, and social studies units in Smithsonian Online (keyword **Smithsonian**). Enhance history units and art presentations with Archive Photos (keyword **Archive**) and the Image Exchange (keyword **Image**). The images in here are breathtaking — your students will love them!

✔ And then there's the Internet. Be sure to play with gopher (keyword **Gopher**) and do some poking around in the Internet mailing lists (keyword **Mailing Lists**). See Chapter 14 for more about this stuff.

✔ Speaking of awesome resource materials, how about picking up electronic copies of classic literature? They're available for downloading from the Palmtop Paperbacks forum (see Figure 19-2) at keyword **Etext**. Because Etexts are plain-text files, you can use any word processor to work with them. And they're free. If this area piques your interest, look for even more Etexts on the Internet. For starters, try the Etext Archives (choose Favorites⇨Go to Keyword, and then type **http://www.etext.org**) and the Online Book Initiative (choose Favorites⇨Go to Keyword, and then type **ftp://ftp.std.com/obi**).

Figure 19-2:
Download
a whole
disk drive
full of
books.

✔ The White House Forum area (keyword **White House**) includes releases and speeches direct from the White House, plus presidential proclamations, vice presidential statements, and an opportunity to e-mail the White House.

✔ One of your students wants to be a physicist? Use the Career Profiles in the Gonyea Online Career Center (keyword **Career Center**) to search for information on specific job titles. Entering a generic title, such as physicist, returns a list of occupations that utilize a physicist's skills. Double-click any entry to read all about it.

✔ Covering weather in science this year? Be sure to check out the Weather Classroom portion of Today's Weather, at keyword **Weather**. Here you'll find explanations of hurricanes, tornadoes, and a collection of weather Web sites. Also at Today's Weather, you'll find a set of current national weather maps that print beautifully on a color ink-jet printer.

✔ If biotechnology tweaks your genes, check out Genentech's Access Excellence (keyword **Excellence**) for information and discussion from the front lines of genetic science. Although the site moved from America Online to the Web, the keyword still takes you there.

✔ Speaking of the Web, don't forget about the mind-boggling sites waiting for you there. For starters, use AOL NetFind (keyword **NetFind**) and try a search on Education — or any other field of specialty, such as Science or Special Education. When NetFind returns a list of sites, find one that sounds appealing and click it to go there.

✔ Use the Educational Resources Information Center (fondly known nationwide as ERIC) to locate resources for virtually any subject on the Web. Available at keyword **AFT**, click the AskERIC Online button and then double-click Eric in Cyberspace. If you're looking for a subject not listed in the Eric Internet Sites window that appears, double-click AskERIC — WEB to visit the ERIC Web site.

✔ For history, science, and technology, take a trip to keyword **Discovery Online**. From the main Discovery Online Web site, you can navigate to Discovery Channel content, The Learning Channel's site, Animal Planet, the Civilization Network, and the Science Network. Click the School link to visit an area designed just for you. Sign up for the Educator Guide, take a peek at the Discovery video curriculum, and pick up a new classroom activity or two.

Bringing School Home to Meet the Kids

Who says that you have to leave the house to get a good education? You don't need to leave for entertainment — and there's no reason to take off in the name of learning stuff. Homeschooling is growing fast all over the country as parents look for quality alternatives to the Education Theory of the Month Club masquerading as the local public school.

America Online offers lots of resources to support and connect homeschoolers. Here are some to get you started:

✔ A good general place to start is the Homeschooling Forum (keyword **Homeschooling**), but you probably found this one on your own. The area features regularly scheduled chats, a wide variety of lively discussions, and links to education-related areas within America Online (like the Lesson Plan Library and the Academic Assistance Center).

✔ Practical Homeschooling (keyword **PHS**) is the online extension of the magazine by the same name. Look for articles from recent issues of the magazine, a *really* strong file library, lots of discussion topics, and regularly scheduled chats. Don't forget the PHS Projects folder, either.

✔ *Home Education Magazine* (keyword **HEM**) covers most homeschooling philosophies but tends to concentrate on the John Holt "unschooling" crowd. The area features many worthwhile things, but one item that's a *must see* is the Homeschooling Resources folder.

It's an Online Louvre

When you're looking for the perfect addition to a bulletin board, worksheet, or professional presentation, check out these resources and prepare to say "Whoa!"

✔ Download U.S. and world maps from ABCNEWS (keyword **ABC**). Click the Stuff button in the ABC Online window. Next, click the News Stuff button, and then double-click the Digital Warehouse option in the Item list. When the Digital Warehouse window appears, you're ready to do the download thing. In addition to the maps, also check out the world flags, video clips, photographs, and clip art libraries. These same images are used in nightly television newscasts, so your students are sure to recognize them.

✔ For pictures of the kids' favorite TV stars, check out ABC (keyword **ABC**), the Warner Brothers kids area (keyword **KidsWB**), the Cartoon Network (keyword **Cartoon Network**), and other media resources.

✔ Of course, no discussion of clip art would possibly be complete without a nod to the Desktop Publishing forum (keyword **Desktop Publishing**). You can also pick up new fonts here to accompany the clip art.

Taking Your Classroom to See the World

If you have a computer in the classroom and access to a phone line, your students' world doesn't end at the walls of the room. Consider the following ideas for field trips without even leaving the school:

✔ Check out Today's News (keyword **News**) before class and at lunch. Discuss a current story and follow its development by making "today in the news" a part of your students' day. This idea works well for a unit study (that is, the study of several school subjects around a single item, such as news) because you can concentrate on whatever kind of news you want — sports, business, world, U.S., and so on.

✔ Highlight social studies with information from the Travel area (keyword **Travel**). Students can plan an entire trip with information about airline and train fares, where to eat, weather predictions, and more.

✔ America Online's new international expansions put a wealth of foreign language material at your disposal. Whether you're looking for texts or live interaction with native speakers, it's all waiting for you behind keyword **International**. Flip back to the International channel information in *AOL Channels For Dummies* — the book-within-a-book that's way at the back of this book — for all the details, or to try it right now, sign on and visit the Bistro (keyword **Bistro**).

✔ Combine listening and research skills with supplementary materials in the National Public Radio Outreach (keyword **NPR**).

✔ Study the ins and outs of the federal government through the Congressional Quarterly Online area (keyword **CQ**). Track the latest bills, read the actual text of floor speeches and press announcements, and look up the e-mail addresses and fax numbers for your representatives. It's all here!

✔ For the best in cool Internet stuff for kids, have a look at the Kids Only Top Internet Sites (keyword **Kids Only**, and then click the Web button). The Random Surf button takes you to several really cool places.

✔ Take advantage of live conferences on America Online. Business leaders, writers (yes, even people like me), media favorites, and all kinds of other people appear in the large conference areas to discuss their areas of expertise and answer questions. What an opportunity for your class! Check out AOL Live! (keyword **Live**) for upcoming events. Figure 19-3 shows the AOL Live! Main Screen, where the box office is open 24 hours.

Figure 19-3: Welcome to AOL Live!

✔ Find your own experts in any field and introduce them to the class. Locate a chef through the electronic Gourmet Guide forum (keyword **eGG**), a computer technical wizard through any of the computer forums (keyword **Computing**), and perhaps even a vet through the Pet Care forum (keyword **Pet Care**). You then can schedule an online chat in a private People Connection room. The possibilities are endless. Look in Chapter 7 for details on the People Connection.

✔ Make history come alive with discussions in SeniorNet Online's Generation to Generation board (keyword **SeniorNet**). This discussion board is specially designed so that seniors and students can learn from and about each other. Classes can post questions and get real-life experience in response.

The Involved Teacher

There's never enough time for you, the teacher. To make the most of the time you *do* have, check out some of these professional resources:

✔ The National Education Association (NEA) maintains a large forum in America Online that offers discussion and services to NEA members and whoever else wanders in. Use keyword **NEA Public** to find the details.

✔ Turn to the American Federation of Teachers (AFT) for AFT News, periodicals, and resources. Many of the forum sections are available to AFT members only; keyword **AFT** tells you all about it.

✔ The Internet newsgroups have an entire section of groups called the *K12 hierarchy*. These groups cover all aspects of the kindergarten through 12th grade experience, from the points of view of both the teacher and the student. To find these groups, use keyword **Newsgroups** and then click Search All Newsgroups. Search for the title **K12**. All the newsgroups in that heading (and perhaps a few more) appear in a search results window. Check out Chapter 15 for more details on where to go from there.

✔ If you need grant money to support a special project, check out the RSP Funding Focus (keyword **RSP**). This service, sponsored by Reference Service Press, tracks money for teachers, students, and noneducators and includes the contact information, requirements, and so on.

Peering into the Future

To keep up on innovations in the classroom, check out the Electronic Schoolhouse (keyword **ESH**). For a peek at how the Internet is already changing education, browse through the Internet Public Library. To get there, click the browser bar's text field and then type `http://www.ipl.org/ref/RR/static/edu0000.html`. Click Go to launch the browser.

Chapter 20
Big Help for Small Business

. . . .

In This Chapter

▶ Starting with the small business resource

▶ Collecting news of the business world

▶ Promoting and building your business online

▶ Keeping the computer happy

▶ Hopping onto the highway

. . . .

*T*hanks to the wonders of computer technology, your small business can be as "big" as you want. Want inexpensive global e-mail? No problem. How about access to U.S. government contract information? It's a cinch. Sniffing around for product and service ideas? Get ready to find them. This chapter introduces you to the America Online and Internet resources available to build, mold, expand, and promote your small business.

Starting at the Source

The Your Business area (keyword **Your Business**) is America Online's official small business resource. It's home to everything related to small business — and I do mean everything! Figure 20-1 displays your ticket to the best in business seminars, information, magazines, discussion boards, and more. The area is also filled with links to other business-related America Online areas, like Inc. Magazine (keyword **Inc**), the Small Business Administration (keyword **SBA**), and frequent flyer updates from Inside Flyer Online (keyword **Inside Flyer**).

I highly recommend signing up for the *free* Your Business electronic newsletter. This weekly report is definitely the best way to keep up with what's new and useful in the burgeoning small business resource area. To sign up, use keyword **StartUp** and double-click the Free Channel Newsletter option in the item list.

Your Business

AOL WorkPlace   MAIN   HELP

Your Business
The entrepreneur & business owner's resource

Smart Assets:
Getting the banks
to say yes.

SALES & MARKETING
Selling to angry customers?
Change your perspective.

Getting Started
Finance Center
Sales & Marketing
Doing Business Online
Business Travel
Tools & Reference
Business Classifieds

Professional Forums
Chats & Messages
Regional Resources
Products & Services

Daily Business Solutions for You!

Keyword: Your Business

Figure 20-1:
The small
business
resource.

Taking the Pulse of Business News

Being in business means staying on top of what's happening in the business world. Information *is* power in business. With America Online, you have access to far more information than your offline competitors do.

✔ For general business news and corporate press releases, look to the business section of Today's News (keyword **Business News**). The window begins with a display of the top news stories, but a quick click brings up several other options (see Figure 20-2). I particularly like the Industry section, because it narrows your focus to a particular vein of business. If you choose Industry, be sure to use the elevator button in the item list, because the window shows only the first half of the industries it actually covers.

✔ If you're looking for stories about a particular company in the Business News section, try the Company Search button. It scours all the news resources (even recent archives) by the company's ticker symbol.

✔ Regional business highlights are in the *New York Times* on America Online (keyword **Times**), the *Chicago Tribune* (keyword **Chicago Tribune**), *Crain's Chicago Business* (keyword **Crains**), the *Arizona Business Gazette* (keyword **Arizona Central**), and the *Orlando Sentinel* Online (keyword **OSO**).

✔ In small business, you often don't have time to sift through tons of news to find that all-important informational nugget. America Online's News Profiles service (keyword **News Profiles**) solves this problem for you by delivering the latest stories about topics you choose directly to your mailbox. This service comes at no extra charge, so it's definitely worth a look. One word of caution, though: If you're tracking a popular topic, your mailbox may quickly fill up.

Figure 20-2:
Use the
Departments
buttons to
locate the
Business
News you
need.

> ✔ Newspapers aren't the only source of business information about America Online. Look for the nation's top magazines as well, like *Business Week* (keyword **BW**), *Investors Business Daily* (keyword **IBD**), and *Crain's Small Business* (keyword **Crains Small Biz**).
>
> ✔ Keep up with the computer industry and the online world through the particularly strong Internet Newsstand (keyword **NetNews**).
>
> ✔ If you track government Requests for Proposal (RFPs), be sure to put the *Commerce Business Daily* (keyword **CBD**) on your regular reading list.

Resources to Relish

When do you sit back, rest on your laurels, and say "Whew! I've done enough! No more working this month (or year)"? If you're a small business owner, the answer is — never! Just as you never stop thinking, planning, or advancing your business, you also can never have enough business resources at your disposal. Who knows what you'll need next? In addition to the areas listed above, you may utilize some of the following resource areas online.

> ✔ About Work, an online area devoted to those of us who work for a living, contains excellent small business resources (look under the light bulb icon). There you can find a Business Starter Kit that discusses business plans, taxes, and whether you should jump into this adventure at all. If your small business happens to run out of your home, you'll also appreciate About Work's home-based business section, hiding under the house icon. Look for it all at keyword **About Work**.

- ✔ For reference-oriented material, take a look at the Business section of the Research & Learn channel (keyword **Research**).

- ✔ Find toll-free numbers, a business directory, and personal phone numbers at the Switchboard (keyword **Switchboard**).

- ✔ Research demographics by zip code when you search Neighborhoods, USA (keyword **Neighborhoods**).

- ✔ Relax a few minutes with daily Dilbert cartoons (keyword **Dilbert**). Everybody needs a good laugh to keep the doctor away.

Blowing Your Online Bassoon

Now that you and your business are online, advertise your arrival! Be careful though, because promoting your business online isn't as easy as it sounds. Sure, lots of prospective customers are out there, but you have to approach them appropriately. *Slow* and *subtle* are the keys to your success.

For starters, let your customers know you're online by printing your company's America Online screen name on business cards and brochures. Depending on how familiar your clientele is with online services and the Internet, you may want to list your address twice. First, identify it as an America Online screen name for your customers who subscribe to America Online. Next, format it as an Internet mailing address by taking out any spaces in your screen name, and then adding **@aol.com** to the end of it. For example, my America Online screen name is JKaufeld, so my Internet address is jkaufeld@aol.com. Notice that the Internet version is all lowercase — it's a subtle thing, but it shows that you know about the Net.

Here are some other tips to keep you ahead of the game:

- ✔ Obey the rules of the digital road. Inside America Online, sending unsolicited (read that as "junk") e-mail messages is a violation of the Terms of Service agreement. Likewise, some discussion areas on the Internet don't appreciate blatant advertising.

- ✔ When posting a message in a newsgroup or online discussion, pick an area that's relevant to your business. If you're promoting financial planning services, don't post an ad in a cancer support discussion because you reasoned that terminally ill people need lots of financial planning help. If you have to make excuses about why you're posting in a particular area, it's probably not the right place for your message.

Discussion Builds Business

How can your small business even hope to compete with companies that can afford such "luxuries" as extensive market research, product development staff, and customer focus groups? By leveraging your business acumen with the power of America Online, that's how. Here are some ideas to get you started:

- ✔ Want to know what's on your customers' minds? Find the forums they frequent and monitor the discussions.

- ✔ If children are part of your market segment, don't forget about the discussion boards in the Kids Only area. Let the kids themselves keep you abreast of new trends and interests.

- ✔ Discover new product lines by listening to the complaints and discussions of your customers. No better product idea exists than a customer's hopeful prayer of "Wouldn't it be great if . . ."

- ✔ Conduct live, online meetings in the People Connection. Use them for brainstorming sessions with other business people from the small business center, online meetings among your outside sales staff, customer focus groups, or anything else you can imagine.

Self-Help for the Computer

Small businesses, particularly small home-based businesses, often rely heavily on a computer but lack the support resources to haul themselves out of trouble when problems strike.

Take a peek into the Computing channel (keyword **Computing**) for some great places to find the computer help you need. Also check out *Home Office Computing Magazine* (keyword **Home Office**) for equipment reviews, the ever-popular buyer's guide, and a good discussion area filled with ideas on getting the most from your sometimes-reluctant hardware and software.

Joining the Information Superhighway

If the '90s has a certified hot topic, it's the Internet. For a small business person, the Internet represents an information source that you can't afford to pass up. America Online's links to the Internet are quite good. Chapter 14 explores the Internet and explains all those crazy terms like FTP, WWW, and Gopher. Here are some other small business helps to try on the Internet:

✔ Join some Internet mailing lists. Use keyword **Mailing Lists** to open the Internet Mailing Lists dialog box and then click Browse the Directory. Use the Search option and enter a word or phrase about your business, your customers, or whatever else interests you.

✔ Internet newsgroups are a great place to hear your customers. With well over 10,000 newsgroups out there (and more being added every day), monitoring a few well-chosen newsgroups is almost like target marketing. Look through Chapter 14 for more details.

✔ Put your business in front of millions of potential customers by building a site on the World Wide Web. Many businesses offer their services on the Internet with this graphical, point-and-click system. You're halfway there already because your America Online account includes storage space for a Web site! To learn more about the Web and how to use it in your business, check out On The Net (keyword **On The Net**). You can find information about My Place, your personal Web storage space (keyword **My Place**); Personal Publisher and AOLPress, Web design tools; and free online classes that help you put it all together.

✔ Do you have a great idea for a new service within America Online? There's always room for more, and America Online knows it. To help grow ideas for new online content, the company created its unique Greenhouse program (keyword **Greenhouse**). Areas like NetNoir Online (keyword **NetNoir**), the electronic Gourmet Guide (keyword **eGG**), The Motley Fool (keyword **Fool**), and Real Fans Sports Network (keyword **Fans**) all got their start through the Greenhouse program.

Trading on an International Scale

If you never envisioned your business moving in the realm of international trade, it may be time to think again. World trade is the order of the day, and the Internet can help you join the club. Start with a quick search of the Internet Mailing List database for the International Trade List (see the first bullet in the preceding section to find out how). Subscribe to this list, read it a while, and get ready to go international.

Part V
Secret Tricks of the AOL Gurus

The 5th Wave   By Rich Tennant

"Now, that would show how important it is to distinguish `fertilizing practices` from `fertility practices` when typing in keywords."

In this part . . .

In addition to its great content areas, strong Internet links, and dandy little triangular logo, America Online harbors secret powers known only to a select few. In the past, only the Acolytes of the Great Circle–Triangle–Thingie knew the twists and turns of the system's hidden paths — only they were admitted to the powerful inner sanctum of America Online, where customized profiles, Internet software tricks, and personalized menus are part of everyday life.

The chapters in this part tear away this veil of secrecy, exposing the steps that bring these extraordinarily cool extras into your online life, too. With these powerful techniques in hand, you too are ready to join the ranks of the initiated — the ranks of the AOL Gurus.

Chapter 21
Making a Truly Cool Profile

In This Chapter

▶ Unlocking the secrets of the custom profile

▶ Making your profile a thing of personalized beauty

After joining the digital world of America Online, one of your first meet-the-neighbors tasks is filling out your member profile at keyword **Profile**. It tells people who you are and what you do when you're not online (you know — in that *other* world), and generally gives them a little peek into your cyber-psyche.

Unfortunately, the basic member profile offers very little flexibility. It's so, well, *basic* — state your name, birthday, occupation, marital status, blah, blah, blah — I feel like I'm filling out a tax form.

To avoid that federal form feeling, spice up your profile with some custom categories and simple formatting. Thanks to careful research and lengthy undercover investigation (okay, so I accidentally bumped into someone in a chat room and he willingly shared the secret), this chapter reveals the details of the once-clandestine steps to making a perfectly cool profile.

It's All in the Wrists (And the Tabs and Colons)

Customizing your profile involves fooling America Online into doing what you want. (Yes, you're playing tricks on the software — isn't that a wonderful feeling?) When you build a normal profile, it's a fill-in-the-blanks experience. You type some clever thoughts, click Update, and then America Online does the rest.

Behind the scenes, though, America Online adds some extra control characters to your words. When the system displays your profile, it automatically looks for these special characters and uses them to figure out how to display your information.

Those special characters are the key to the whole customization process. By typing them into the profile yourself, you can add new categories and generally make your member profile look awesome.

The characters in question are Ctrl+Backspace and Tab. For reasons beyond comprehension (and, frankly, beyond our interest) the America Online programmers chose Ctrl+Backspace to mark the start of a new category and Tab to mark the break between a category heading and its associated text.

Profile Remodeling for the Do-It-Yourselfer

Enough of this dreadful theory — it's time to haul out the implements of destruction and make a cool, custom profile. Best of all, unlike the folks on those "Let's remodel the house in 30 minutes" TV shows, you don't need any special equipment, extra software, or even a witty sidekick to accomplish the job. What a deal!

Before signing on to the system and starting profile surgery, take a few minutes to jot down your profile ideas on a handy piece of paper. Just as good blueprints keep a building project on track, knowing precisely what headings and information you want to put in the new profile makes creating it a lot easier.

A personal Web page is the ultimate profile

Even though you can add new categories to your member profile, the whole process still suffers from some frustrating limitations. To escape those restrictions and discover a whole new world of possibilities, check out America Online's *Personal Publisher* system (keyword **Personal Publisher**) and build your own World Wide Web page.

Want to change fonts? No problem. How about adding a picture, too? It's a snap. You don't need to know a lot of technical mumbo-jumbo to make it work, either. Personal Publisher puts you in the creativity driver's seat while *it* handles the digital details.

With your paper-based sample in hand, get ready to join the ranks of Those With Cool Profiles. Here's what to do:

1. **Sign on to America Online and head into the People Connection.**

   For what I have in mind, any chat room will be fine. (Yes, this *does* lead to customizing your profile — trust me.)

2. **Carefully highlight the space between the colon next to someone's name and the beginning of the person's chat room comment (see Figure 21-1).**

   That space is really a *Tab* character, just like the ones you get in a word processor by pressing the Tab key. Because hitting Tab in the Edit Your Profile window moves the cursor from one field to another, we have to cheat and find another way to insert a Tab character — and *that* is what you're about to do.

Figure 21-1:
That's the
spot —
right there!

3. **Select Edit⇨Copy from the menu bar or press Ctrl+C, then close the chat room window.**

   This copies the Tab character into the Windows Clipboard. With the Tab character in hand (or, more specifically, *in clipboard*), you're ready to create a masterpiece.

4. **Take a deep breath in heady expectation, then select My AOL⇨My Member Profile from the Toolbar.**

   A screen containing your existing profile pops into view.

5. **Pick one of the current entries (Your Name, Hobbies, or one of the others) and click in its text area. When the flashing toothpick cursor appears, press End.**

   The little toothpick cursor moves to the end of the entry.

6. **Press Ctrl+Backspace, then type the name of a new category for your profile. Put a colon (:) after the category name just to make everything official-looking.**

   If the process worked right, your entry now contains a box (from the Ctrl+Backspace key combo), the category name, and a colon. In fact, it should look much like Figure 21-2.

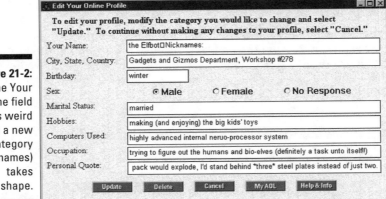

Figure 21-2: The Your Name field looks weird as a new category (Nicknames) takes shape.

Edit Your Online Profile

To edit your profile, modify the category you would like to change and select "Update." To continue without making any changes to your profile, select "Cancel."

Your Name:	the Elfbot☐Nicknames:
City, State, Country:	Gadgets and Gizmos Department, Workshop #278
Birthday:	winter
Sex:	● Male ○ Female ○ No Response
Marital Status:	married
Hobbies:	making (and enjoying) the big kids' toys
Computers Used:	highly advanced internal neruo-processor system
Occupation:	trying to figure out the humans and bio-elves (definitely a task unto itself!)
Personal Quote:	pack would explode, I'd stand behind "three" steel plates instead of just two.

Update   Delete   Cancel   My AOL   Help & Info

To make a new line without a category heading (it makes really long entries look good), put in the Ctrl+Backspace character, but leave out category and colon. Instead, skip straight to the next step.

7. **With the new category in place, press Ctrl+V or select Edit⇨Paste from the main menu.**

   Another box appears, but this time it's the Tab character that you borrowed from the chat room window. Despite the screen's increasingly odd look, you're doing just fine.

8. **Type the text that goes with your new category.**

   This works just like it always did — no surprises here.

9. **Repeat Steps 5 through 8 to keep adding new categories and entries.**

   Feel free to keep adding new categories and information to your profile, just like Figure 21-3.

   There *is* a limit to the number of characters each profile entry holds (see Table 21-1 for the details), but that's not a big problem. When you run out of room in one entry, just go on to the next one!

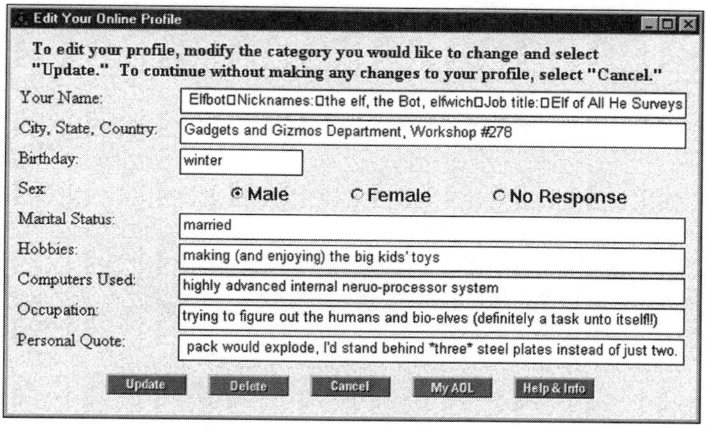

Figure 21-3:
Stack new
categories
and
information
one after
the other
until you fill
up the
entry, then
go on to the
next one.

> **Edit Your Online Profile**
>
> To edit your profile, modify the category you would like to change and select "Update." To continue without making any changes to your profile, select "Cancel."
>
> Your Name: `Elfbot☐Nicknames:☐the elf, the Bot, elfwich☐Job title:☐Elf of All He Surveys`
>
> City, State, Country: `Gadgets and Gizmos Department, Workshop #278`
>
> Birthday: `winter`
>
> Sex: ⦿ Male ○ Female ○ No Response
>
> Marital Status: `married`
>
> Hobbies: `making (and enjoying) the big kids' toys`
>
> Computers Used: `highly advanced internal neuro-processor system`
>
> Occupation: `trying to figure out the humans and bio-elves (definitely a task unto itself!)`
>
> Personal Quote: `pack would explode, I'd stand behind *three* steel plates instead of just two.`
>
> [Update]   [Delete]   [Cancel]   [My AOL]   [Help & Info]

10. When you're done, cross your fingers (this is *very* important) and click Update.

After a moment, America Online acknowledges your request and updates your profile.

Table 21-1	**Category Sizes**
This Category	*Holds This Many Characters*
Your Name	128
City, State, Country	255
Birthday	32
Marital Status	32
Hobbies	255
Computers Used	128
Occupation	128
Personal Quote	255

Check the finished profile to make sure it came out just as you envisioned. Do that by pressing Ctrl+G and putting your screen name in the dialog box.

Chapter 22

Dressing up Your Software with Fresh Buttons and a New Menu

. . . .

In This Chapter

▶ Building a better Toolbar

▶ Creating a menu one item at a time

. . . .

*C*ustomizing means extraordinarily different things to different people. To one, it means adding a pinstriped dash of color to the exterior of a car, while to another it involves some light-hearted reorganization of the vehicle's body parts with the help of a handy acetylene torch. (Okay, maybe that's *art* instead of customization, but you get the point.)

In the world of software, customer customizable features started out small ("You want to change the color of your screen? You got it!") and gradually grew to the point we're at today. With many applications on the market, you can adjust almost anything at all — including the menus.

The America Online 4.0 software rides this trend by including two big customization features. You, the nonprogramming America Online member, can add new buttons to the Toolbar and create your own navigational menu system (complete with hot keys, too). This chapter explores the ins and outs of these two great customizing features. First, it tackles the Toolbar, then it illuminates the My Shortcuts menu, making both of these great tools easy to understand and use.

Although it's not very hard to build your own Toolbar buttons and menus, it's a lot easier if you know about the Favorite Places heart-on-the-paper icon, and also understand how keywords work inside America Online. To find out about them both in one easy step, flip to Chapter 5.

Dancing the Toolbar Tango (Or Is That the New Button Bop?)

Up to now, the Toolbar just sorta hung out at the top of the screen and stared at you a lot. Granted, it's very useful (and colorful as well), but it wasn't terribly interactive. The America Online programmers put a lot of thought into precisely which buttons should appear on the Toolbar and they carefully put them there. If you didn't like one or another of them (my personal nemesis was the Quotes button — the stock market and I just don't mix), there wasn't anything you could do about it.

With the America Online 4.0 software, the programmers discovered customization, and now the Toolbar (or at least a little corner of it) is your personal navigation playground. Although most of the Toolbar is still locked in place — it *has* to be, because most of the new menu items migrated from the pull-down menus under the Toolbar — the plum-color area on the far right end of the Toolbar (shown in Figure 22-1) belongs to you. Fill it with up to three buttons pointing to your favorite America Online areas, chat rooms, or Web sites.

Figure 22-1:
The three custom-izable Toolbar buttons live on the far right end.

Buttons that you're stuck with   Customizable buttons

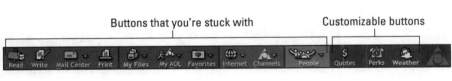

Read Write Mail Center Print My Files My AOL Favorites Internet Channels People Quotes Perks Weather

If the online area that you want to create a Toolbar for has a Favorite Places icon on its window, then you're as good as done with the whole process. Just look at the steps below for all the details. If the window *doesn't* have a Favorite Places icon on it, though, you can't create a Toolbar button for the area. Sorry, but that's how it goes. (Even in flexibility, there are limits.)

To put a button of your own on the Toolbar (or to replace an existing button with a new one), follow these steps:

1. **Decide which of the customizable buttons you don't need any more.**

   If you have an open space in the Toolbar's customizable section, then skip ahead to Step 4.

No, it doesn't seem fair that you need to lose a button to gain one, but unless there's open space in the customizable section of your Toolbar, that's how things go.

2. **Right-click the button you don't want any more.**

   A short pop-up menu (if a menu with only one item can actually be called a menu) appears next to your cursor.

3. **Click the Remove from Toolbar option on the pop-up menu (it's the only one, as you can see in Figure 22-2), then click Yes in the Are you sure? dialog box.**

   Quick as a wink, the Toolbar button vanishes, leaving an open space for your button.

4. **Through whatever way you usually do it (keyword, Favorite Place entry, menu browsing, and so on), view the online area destined for its own Toolbar button.**

   Just as it always does, the online area of your heart hops onto the screen.

5. **Drag-and-drop the little heart-on-a-page icon anywhere onto the customizable Toolbar area (see Figure 22-3).**

   When you let go of the cursor, the Icon Selector dialog box hops onto the screen.

   It doesn't matter where in the customizable section you actually drop the Favorite Places icon. The America Online software always adds the new button in the last position on the far right side of the Toolbar.

6. **Scroll through the collection of pictures until you find one that looks vaguely like what you want, then click it.**

   The picture in the icon list highlights with pride.

   By the way, you can't add your own pictures to the icon list. For now, you simply enjoy the opportunity to use the artwork graciously provided by the America Online developers.

Figure 22-2:
Just one click and the Toolbar button is history.

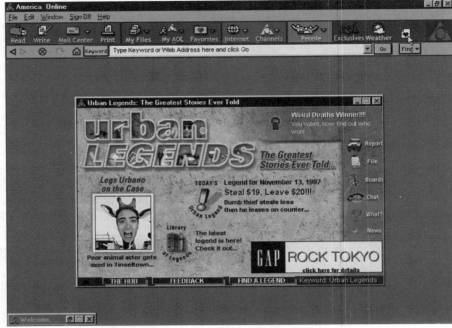

Figure 22-3:
Drop the icon anywhere on this end of the Toolbar to make a new button.

7. **Click in the Label box, then type a 1-to-8-letter label to go under your new Toolbar button. When you're done, click OK.**

   The button proudly takes its place on the Toolbar, looking something like Figure 22-4.

Figure 22-4:
The shiny new Toolbar button.

Each screen name gets its own custom Toolbar buttons, so don't be surprised when your new button vanishes the moment you switch to a different screen name. When you change back to the original screen name, the custom button comes back as well.

To use the button with other screen names on your account, sign on with each of the other names and go through the whole make-a-button process above for each one. If you have multiple copies of the America Online software (one on your home computer and one at work, for instance), you need to add the buttons in both places. Custom Toolbar buttons aren't stored in the America Online computers; they're stored on your computer.

Also, you can't create custom Toolbar buttons when signed on with the Guest option — it only works on your very own copy of America Online.

A Menu to Call Your Own

My Shortcuts is your very own customizable menu space. Load it with up to ten of your favorite online destinations. This menu comes preloaded with entries for seven popular parts of America Online (or at least parts America Online *wants* to be popular, like Sign on a Friend), but you can easily change those entries to things *you're* interested in.

✔ Why go to the trouble of putting something into My Shortcuts when it's so easy to add things to your Favorite Places list? Good question — I'm glad you asked. In addition to appearing in My Shortcuts, every item in this special menu gets a *hot key* assigned to it — something that Favorite Places can't do. Instead of working your way through the menu or manually typing the area's keyword, you can press a Ctrl key combination (Ctrl+1 through Ctrl+0, depending on which position the item holds in My Shortcuts) and go there immediately.

✔ You just need to keep one rule in mind: Only services and forums with a keyword can be in the special My Shortcuts menu. If you can't get there with a keyword, you can't get there with the My Shortcuts menu, either.

✔ I probably shouldn't tell you this, but it *is* possible to bend the "only keyword areas go here" rule just a bit. In addition to keywords, you can include Internet locations as well, such as Web sites or gophers. Type the address *exactly* as you do when using your Web browser to get there. That means using what the techies call *URL format,* including the http:// part in front of the site's address.

✔ Some of my picks for a starter My Shortcuts menu include *Business Week* magazine (keyword **BW**), the New York Public Library Online Reference Books (keyword **Desk Reference**), the Space Wars simulation area (keyword **Space Wars**), and the multiplayer word game Strike-A-Match (keyword **StrikeAMatch**). If you're a fellow fan of "Pinky and the Brain," save a spot on your menu for the Warner Brothers kids area (keyword **KidsWB**).

Here's how to customize the My Shortcuts menu with *your* Favorite Places:

1. **Find something that you want to add to the menu, and get its keyword or Internet URL and name.**

   Make sure that the keyword is correct; otherwise, the menu option won't work (and the programmers of the world don't need *any* help in developing software that doesn't work).

2. **Choose Favorites⇨My Shortcuts⇨Edit Shortcuts.**

   This displays the Edit Shortcut Keys dialog box.

3. **Decide which key you want to use for the new item, and click the Shortcut Title box for that key.**

   If the box already has an entry, press Backspace or Delete to remove it (see Figure 22-5).

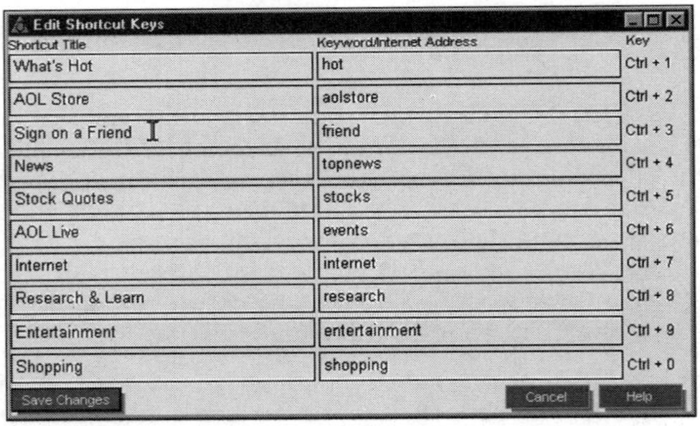

Figure 22-5: Take out the current entry to make room for your new one.

4. **Type the name of the item in the Menu Entry box.**

   Whatever you type appears in the My Shortcuts menu, so keep it kinda short — one to four words at most.

5. **Press Tab to move to the Keyword/Internet Address box.**

   If you're replacing an existing entry, press Backspace or Delete to remove it.

6. **Type the keyword or Internet address for your new menu item in the Keyword/Internet Address box (see Figure 22-6).**

   Double-check your typing to make sure that the keyword is correct. If you entered a Web site address, make sure you included the `http://` part at the beginning!

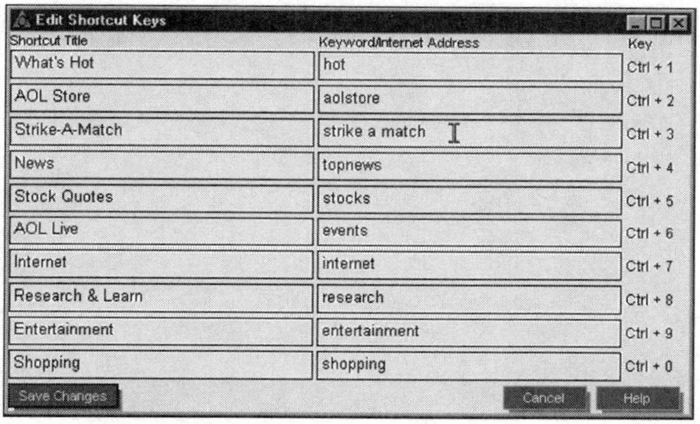
Edit Shortcut Keys
Shortcut Title
Keyword/Internet Address
Key
What's Hot
hot
Ctrl + 1
AOL Store
aolstore
Ctrl + 2
Strike-A-Match
strike a match
Ctrl + 3
News
topnews
Ctrl + 4
Stock Quotes
stocks
Ctrl + 5
AOL Live
events
Ctrl + 6
Internet
internet
Ctrl + 7
Research & Learn
research
Ctrl + 8
Entertainment
entertainment
Ctrl + 9
Shopping
shopping
Ctrl + 0
Save Changes
Cancel
Help

Figure 22-6: Watch your spelling (after all, nobody else will).

7. **Click the Save Changes button to make the new entry part of your My Shortcuts menu.**

   Your new menu item is ready to test!

   If you have a sudden desire to forget that you ever considered changing the menu, click Cancel in Windows or close the window on a Macintosh.

8. **Select My AOL⇨My Shortcuts and choose your new item from the Favorite Places section (see Figure 22-7).**

   If something that looks like the dialog box shown in Figure 22-8 pops up after you try your new menu item, go back to Step 6 and check the entry in the Keyword/Internet Address area. The odds are high that it's a little spelling-challenged.

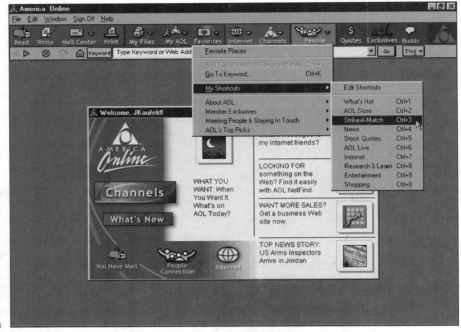

Figure 22-7:
Your new entry looks great strutting on the My Shortcuts menu.

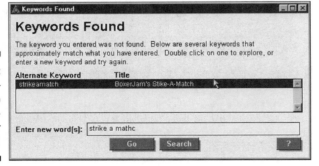

Figure 22-8:
Whoops — time to double-check your spelling!

Part VI
The Part of Tens

In this part . . .

As expected, the book closes with The Part of Tens, IDG Books Worldwide's answer to all the silly things you had to memorize as a child in school. Don't memorize these — don't even try. Instead, read them, laugh with them, and put them to work for you.

Chapter 23

Ten Things Everyone Looks for Online

*D*epending on who you ask, the online world and the Internet are either chock-full of the latest information about every topic under the sun, or they're factual mirages that look promising from a distance, but disappear as you arrive. Why do people hold such radically different views on the subject? Because the first person *found* what he or she looked for, while the second one didn't.

The key to finding stuff, of course, is knowing where to look. In the online world, that's quite a challenge, because there are so many places to look. This chapter provides you with some starting locations as you search for fun people, nifty places, and various online features.

Always be on the lookout for new resources — you never know when you may find one. Feel free to jot down the area's keyword or address here in your book, too, so it doesn't get accidentally lost in the shuffle.

Scoping for a Particular Chat Room

The People Connection ranks as one of America Online's top destinations. Finding the room that's right for you may take some time, particularly because the area contains hundreds if not thousands of active chats all the time.

To simplify your chatting life (and find your favorite chat room quickly), use the People Connection's Find by Name feature. Here's what to do:

1. **If you aren't already there, get into the People Connection through keyword** People Connection **or by clicking the People toolbar button and selecting Chat Now from the drop-down list.**

2. **In the chat room window, click List Chats (along the bottom right of the window).**

3. **When the chat room list appears, click Find by Name.**

4. **Type the name of the room you're looking for, then press Enter. Type it carefully — spelling counts!**

5. **If there's a room with that name, America Online displays a dialog box showing you the room's category (Town Square, Life, Places, and such) and the number of people currently chatting there.**

6. **To hop directly into the room, double-click the chat room's name. If there's space for you (remember that each chat room only holds 23 people), you immediate pop into the room. If the room is full, the software lets you know.**

Once you get into the room, you can also add it to your Favorite Places list by clicking the little heart-on-a-page icon in the chat room's upper-right corner. For more about Favorite Places, see Chapter 5. To delve the depths of chatting, see Chapter 7.

Finding People Like You

Regardless of your hobbies, interests, or particular spin on life, somewhere among America Online's 8 million members there's a person much like you. (And you thought the world was safe, didn't you?) To find that particular someone, try the Member Directory search system at keyword **Member Directory**. The directory cross-references all the entries in every member's online profile. Just type the term you want to find (like **model railroad**, **ham radio**, or **kite**) and the system displays a list of the people who have included that word or phrase in their profile. Browse through the list until you find someone that looks like a match, and then send that person a friendly e-mail to introduce yourself.

Because the search system relies on the member profile, though, it only finds people who created a profile. If you want to exclude yourself from the Member Directory, then leave the profile fields blank (America Online won't fill them in for you). For details on profiles, flip back to Chapter 4. To make an incredibly cool profile — and I do mean cool — try Chapter 21 instead.

Tripping through the Coolest Online Areas

After spending some time on America Online, it's easy to fall into a rut. You find a few areas that match your interests, visit them regularly, and get to know the members there. But after a while, you may long for something new — a change of pace and scenery, perhaps.

When the urge strikes, answer it with a quick trip to the Find system (keyword **Find**), the What's Hot list (keyword **Hot**), or the Member's Choice selections (keyword **Members Choice**). Each of these resources presents you with links to both new and popular online areas. It's a never-ending supply of great places to go.

Sifting through Sites on the Internet

America Online offers a ton of useful and entertaining information, but sometimes you need something, well, a little different. When that urge strikes, you know there's only one place to go — that home of the odd and esoteric, the last bastion of the strange, mundane, and darned peculiar — yes, I'm talking about the World Wide Web.

The Web's huge size makes it a potential gold mine of information, but its total lack of organization often hides the best areas from view. To get the most from the Web, try using several different search systems. Start with America Online's NetFind (keyword **NetFind**), then take a spin over to Yahoo! (http://www.yahoo.com). If you still can't find what you want, try The Mining Company (http://www.miningco.com) and see if one of their Net Guides has any suggestions.

Seeing Your Favorite Celebrities

Sure, the stars come out at night — but at AOL Live!, they shine the rest of the day, too. Some people appear regularly on their own shows (like my *America Online For Dummies* chat at 10 p.m. Eastern Time on the third Thursday of every month), while others drop in for a one-shot event.

To check the schedule for upcoming AOL Live! appearances by your favorite entertainment, sports, political, and business personalities, use keyword **Search AOL Live**. When the Search window appears, click Search for Live Events, then enter your luminary's name. If they have an event coming up, a dialog box containing all the details appears on-screen.

To search for transcripts of previous events, click Search Transcripts in the Search window instead of the Search for Live Events button.

Downloading the Best Software

There's nothing like a huge, free collection of programs to bring out the computer person in anyone (it always works for me, but then again, I may not be the best sample population). Let your inner nerd run free in America Online's DOS, Macintosh, and Windows software libraries. Download some business programs, home management tools, or even a few games — everything is yours for the taking.

To search the libraries from Windows or DOS, use keyword **Filesearch**, then click the Search button and follow the prompts. On the Macintosh, try keyword **Mac Software**, then click File Search to get into the search screen; finally, click the Search button to enter the Mac's very own file-finding system.

For more about downloading and its perils and pleasures, see Chapter 15.

Finding Obscure Online Areas

Every area inside of America Online (plus more than a few sites on the World Wide Web) is blessed with a keyword for quick access. Once you know the keyword, navigating through the wilds of America Online only takes a few moments.

Although most keywords explain themselves (like **Newsweek**, **MTV**, and **Dilbert**), some keep you guessing. To make your quest for neat online areas a little easier, America Online created the Find system (keyword **Find**). Give the Find system a word like *cards*, *cats*, or *carnival*, and it scans through a huge database of online areas, looking for spots that include your topic of interest. It tells you a little about the areas, and offers to take you there so you can see things for yourself.

To use Find, open up the Find dialog box with keyword **Find**, then think of a few words that describe what you want to see. Feed the terms to the AOL Find dialog box and click Search. When AOL displays what it found, double-click something that looks interesting. If the system didn't find anything, try another search, but use a different word this time.

Locating Your Online Buddies

Playing in the online world is fun, but it's even more fun when you do it with friends. After just a few days online (or a few hours, if you're particularly outgoing), your digital friend list may grow too large to handle. At that point, it's time to build a Buddy List (keyword **Buddy List**). Organize people by shared interests or where you met, then let the Buddy system tell you when they sign on to America Online. It's fast and easy, but best of all, it's free.

To manually find out if someone is online, use the Locate command (Ctrl+L in Windows, ⌘+L on the Macintosh).

Ferreting Out Your Long-Lost Friends, Wherever They May Be

Want to find your old flame from high school? Interested in seeing your college roommate again? (Maybe he finally has the rent money he still owes you!) Regardless of the purpose, America Online has the people-search tools you need.

Finding a person's e-mail address, street address, and phone number can't get much easier than it is with Switchboard (keyword **Switchboard**) and Four11 (keyword **Four11**). Both systems include directories of individuals and businesses, making them a smorgasbord of searching.

Tracking Packages throughout the World

Depending on what you do for a living, following the progress of little boxes as they wing around the world may (or may not) be of particular importance to you. If you ship a lot of things, though, or if you work from home, then knowing the current location of a much-needed carton or document envelope often makes or breaks your whole day.

Thanks to the Internet, package tracking information is only moments away. Sign on to America Online, then bring up the Keyword dialog box (press Ctrl+K in Windows, ⌘+K on the Mac), then type in the appropriate shipping company address from the list below:

Airborne Express	`http://www.airborne-express.com`
Federal Express	`http://www.fedex.com`
United Parcel Service	`http://www.ups.com`

America Online automatically launches your World Wide Web browser and opens the page. Carefully follow the on-screen instructions to find the package you desire.

Collecting Free Stuff from the Government

I just couldn't resist including this one. You know them from late-night TV and those little ads in the back of your favorite magazines, but now those zany folks from Pueblo, Colorado, are on the Web! Behold: It's the electronic version of the *Consumer Information Catalog.*

Their Web site (`http://www.pueblo.gsa.gov`) offers hundreds of federal publications for free. Search the site for anything from gardening tips to business loan advice, then either read the documents online or save a copy to peruse later. (I *still* can't believe it's all free — this is just too cool!)

Chapter 24

Ten Common Things That Go Wrong (And How to Fix Them)

I often think that computers and software were invented by a cabal of psychiatrists and psychologists as a long-term project to ensure that Western civilization would have trouble coping in the 20th century — and therefore would need their services for many years to come. With that meaningful observation off my chest, it's time to consider the problem at hand — namely, the one that you're having right now. Look for your problem in the following sections. If you find it (or one a lot like it), read the information in that section and try the solution I suggest.

If you can't find your problem here, try the Doctor Tapedbridge Miracle Elixir: When things start failing for no apparent reason, quit the program, restart your computer, and try again.

America Online Won't Answer the Phone

Ring. Ring. Ring. (Or beep. Beep. Beep.) It's bad enough when computer companies don't answer the phone, but being ignored by the computer itself really hits a new low. Don't fret too much, though. This rejection isn't the first strike of some technological vendetta against you. You merely wandered across a modem that's sleeping on the job.

When this happens, wait a minute or two, and then try signing on again. If you still don't get an answer, wait a little while longer and give the modem another chance. If the modem doesn't answer this time, call America Online's support department (800-827-3338) and enlist their help.

The Computer Almost Signs On

Your password is in, the modem is singing, and all is good with the world. At least it *was* until you couldn't complete the connection to America Online.

Usually, this happens at Step 6 of the connection process — the one that says `Connecting to America Online`. This problem isn't your fault; the fault belongs to America Online itself. For some reason, America Online's computers didn't acknowledge your existence. Perhaps the computers have so much going on that they can't spare a moment from their busy schedule for you. Perhaps the computers aren't running at all. Whatever the reason, wait awhile (15 to 20 minutes) and then try again. If this behavior keeps up for more than an hour, call the America Online support number (800-827-3338) and find out what's happening.

The Host Isn't Responding to You

This is nerd lingo for "the computer didn't answer your request," usually expressed in human terms as "Huh? What? Were you talking to me?" You wanted to do something simple (like display the Channels window), and the big computers at America Online weren't paying attention. Isn't that just like computers? Give them a little power, and they walk all over you.

Stuff like this happens when a lot of people are using America Online at the same time. Don't be surprised if you get these errors in the evening, because that's when *everybody* is usually signed on. When this happens to you (and if it hasn't yet, don't feel left out; it will eventually), the first thing to do is try again. This time, it should work. If you're still having problems, sign off, sign on, and try again. Beyond that, throw up your hands in defeat and go have some ice cream.

The System Rudely Kicks You Off

You're minding your own business, wandering online through this and that, when WHAM! — Dorothy, you're not in Virginia anymore. The technical term for this is being *punted,* as in "Rats, I was punted."

There's no particular reason why this happens. It could be noise in the phone line; it may be your call-waiting feature kicking in; perhaps the digital gremlins are at work. Whatever the cause, sign on again and continue your pleasurable labors. If this happens a lot (more than, say, ten times a week), call the phone company, tell them that you're having a lot of lost connections with your modem, and ask them to check your line for interference.

America Online Doesn't Talk to You

Your friends said that America Online would talk to you. They even demonstrated it to really sell you on the point. So you went to the local computer store and spent big bucks on a sound card and speaker system. For that much money, America Online should say "Welcome" or "You've got mail" once in a while, if not perform entire Wagner operas. Instead, the service is mute — nothing has changed. This situation bothers you (as well it should).

First, make sure that your sound system works with other programs. If your favorite game or multimedia program brings forth glorious melodies, the sound card is working just fine. If those programs can't make a peep either, double-check your new sound card to make sure that it's working.

When you know the sound card is okay, make sure that the America Online access software knows that it's supposed to use sounds. Sign on and choose My AOL⇨Preferences, then click the General button in the Preferences dialog box. Click the Enable event sounds and Enable chat room sounds check boxes. Sign off, and then sign back on. You should be greeted by a friendly "Welcome" just before the Welcome window appears. If the sound still isn't working, look for assistance in the Member Services area (keyword **Help**).

Your Computer Locks Up While Downloading Files or Using Automatic AOL

You started with a simple goal to save some time. You invested in a 28,800 bits per second modem, one of the fastest that America Online supports. You used Automatic AOL to minimize your online time for e-mail. It's a great plan — except for one tiny little detail: Your computer locks up almost every time you try to download a file or run an Automatic AOL session. Whoops.

Don't worry — you're not the target of an electronic conspiracy. Believe it or not, the odds are good that this problem belongs to your modem.

Many low-cost 28,800 bits per second modems contain a set of control chips known in nerd lingo as *RPI* (it's an acronym, but not one that you need to worry about). This isn't the brand name on the front of your modem; it's part of the device's genetic code. RPI modems are usually very inexpensive, like under $100. Unfortunately, you get what you pay for. RPI modems don't know anything about error correction and data compression, which are supposed to be second nature to all 28,800 bits per second modems. Because they're clueless on these topics, RPI modems don't work correctly with America Online during Automatic AOL sessions and file downloads. But don't throw the modem out yet — read on for the solution!

Luckily, the America Online programmers found out about the problem and devised a clever solution. All you need to do is tell the America Online software that you have an RPI modem. To accomplish that, click Setup in the Sign-on window, and then click the Connection Devices tab in the Connection Setup dialog box. Along the bottom of the box are a series of buttons. Click Expert Add, then wait for the AOL Setup dialog to appear. Make sure the Type entry says Modem, then click Next.

After noting the current modem setting, scroll through the modem list to the WinRPI Modem entry and click it. There are two other WinRPI entries too, but don't worry about them for now. Click OK, then click Close to get back to Setup & Sign On. Finally, when you're good and ready, try an Automatic AOL session. If the computer still locks up, go back and choose the WinRPI+ Modem option and try again. If it still doesn't work, something else is wrong with the system. In that case, call the technical folks at America Online and seek their help.

File Downloads Take Too Long

When you look at a file description, it displays a statistic labeled DL time, which is the approximate time that the file will take to download in a perfect world with whatever speed of modem you're using right now. The most important words in that sentence are *approximate time* and *in a perfect world*. You see, approximations are rarely correct, and the world is most certainly not perfect. Don't computers make stupid assumptions about real life?

Here's the reality of this download-time thing: The actual time that it takes to download something depends on how busy America Online is, how noisy the phone line is, and the current phase of the moon. If your download is *really* big (like multiple megabytes in size), the AOL software may not even try to make an estimate, but instead presents you with an approximate download time that it picked out of thin air. (No, I'm not making this up.)

If a download seems to take forever, first be patient. If it looks as though the download really *is* going to take forever, cancel it; then try again, or use the Download Manager and an Automatic AOL session to resume the download at a less busy time. See Chapter 15 for more information about that.

Automatic AOL Mail Goes Undercover

Automatic AOL sessions are great things that save you time, money, and effort. Of course, they also kind of hide your incoming mail from you.

Your mail really isn't hidden; you just have to access it through a new menu item (new to those of you who use Windows). To find your "lost" missives, choose <u>M</u>ailCenter⇨Rea<u>d</u> Offline Mail⇨Incoming/Saved Mail.

Your Internet Mail Is Undeliverable

The America Online Internet mail gateway is great if you have friends or business associates on the Internet. Unfortunately, the Internet is a techno-logically wild place. Mail messages that are misaddressed in even the smallest way come screaming back into your mailbox, sent by angry computers with names like MAILER-DAEMON@mail02.mail.aol.com (which sounds like a character from *Tron Meets the Exorcist*). The nice thing — if you can really say that about returned mail — is the fact that these computers usually tell you what's wrong with the message.

If your friend's Internet mail address is `minstrel@whimsey.com`, `minstrel` is the *user* part of the address (the person's screen name on that system), and `whimsey.com` is the name of the computer, just as `aol.com` is the system name for America Online. This technical drivel is necessary for understanding the two most common mail errors: User unknown and Host unknown. Both messages mean that the address you entered has a slight problem. A User unknown message means that the problem is with something to the left of the @ symbol in the address; Host unknown means that the problem is to the right of the @ symbol. The error code itself appears in the subject area of the returned e-mail message.

Whatever is wrong, check and double-check the address to which you're sending mail. Be particularly alert for the difference between the number one (1) and the lowercase letter *L* (l), as well as the difference between the number zero (0) and the uppercase letter *O*. Computers get all hung up about this stuff.

If the address seems okay but the message still won't go through, try having the other person send a message to you. After you get that message, click the Reply button to insert the sender's address automatically. Copy the address (by highlighting it and then choosing Edit⇨Copy) and paste it into the Address Book. Now you know that the address is correct.

The New Item in Your Go To Menu Goes to the Wrong Place

In Chapter 22, you flirted with the frightening realm of nerddom and create your own items on the Favorites⇨My Shortcuts menu. Now, however, the item is there in the menu, but it doesn't quite work. Don't let this little setback worry you. It usually takes a professional to make a menu item that doesn't work; you managed to do it with little or no training!

This glitch is relatively easy to fix. The problem is the keyword that you entered in the Edit Shortcut Keys box — the odds are high that it suffers from a slight spelling problem. Select Favorites⇨My Shortcuts⇨Edit Shortcuts from the Toolbar, and look at the keyword that you entered for the nonworking menu item. You will probably discover that the keyword is just the tiniest bit misspelled.

Use the menus to get back to this favorite of your online places and note the keyword when you arrive. Then go back to the Edit Favorite Places dialog box and type that keyword *very carefully*. Save your changes by clicking Save Changes. Then try your new item. Isn't programming fun?

Chapter 25

Ten Internet Resources Worth Checking Out

- -

In This Chapter

▶ Checking out the coolest newsgroups and mailing lists
▶ Finding fun-filled Gopher, Web, and FTP sites

- -

*T*he Internet is a most amazing place. With connections to most of the countries in the world, and with a truly daunting array of services and information, the Internet is like a giant library, discussion group, and digital Wal-Mart all rolled into one. As I said, it's a most amazing place.

This chapter gives you the expected ten interesting things to try on the Internet, plus a couple of bonus items. The goal is to pique your interest in the Internet and give you a sample of the incredible range of stuff out there.

To use these Internet services, go to the Internet Connection and click the appropriate service button (World Wide Web, Gopher, Newsgroups, and so on). If you need some help with the Internet Connection itself, refer to Chapter 14.

alt.folklore.urban (Newsgroup)

Heard the one about the beached whale that the Oregon Department of Transportation blew up with dynamite? Or about the Procter & Gamble logo being linked to "forces of evil"? These are *urban legends* — stories that get told and retold until they take on a life of their own. And they have a home on the Internet.

If you like this kind of thing (or if you've heard a legend and want to know if it's true), check out the alt.folklore.urban newsgroup. Here, you find discussion and commentary on all things odd, improbable, and larger than life. Sign up at keyword **Newsgroups**. In the Newsgroups window, click Expert Add, type **alt.folklore.urban**, and then click Add. When the system asks if you *really* want to subscribe to the newsgroup, click OK.

In case you're wondering, the Procter & Gamble logo is just that — a logo — and nothing more. And yes, the Oregon Department of Transportation really blew up a beached whale with dynamite back in 1970. (Don't worry; the whale was already dead before being scattered over the landscape.)

rec.food.veg (Newsgroup)

For those of you with an eye for the greener things in food (or you carnivores who'd like to try something a little different for a change), subscribe to the rec.food.veg newsgroup. This newsgroup covers the best in vegetarian food and lifestyles. For help subscribing, see the preceding section about alt.folklore.urban.

If you're looking for recipes, try rec.food.veg.cooking — some truly delicious recipes are in there!

The OCF Online Library (Gopher)

A delicate balance keeps the world in order. I don't mean the balance of military power — I'm talking about the Balance of Normality. Some places on earth (like Britain and the Great Plains states) are particularly level-headed. Others, like Berkeley, California, aren't.

So what happens when you give those zanies at Berkeley a bunch of networked computers? They come up with the OCF Online Library, that's what. Who else could (or even would) compile a collection that includes the Declaration of Independence, the CIA World Fact Book, a parody of Edgar Allan Poe's *The Raven* ("Once before a console dreary, while I programmed, weak and weary . . . "), and a wonderful set of transcripts from Monty Python movies and TV shows?

To check this place out for yourself, click in the Navigation bar Address box, and then type **gopher://gopher.ocf.berkeley.edu/11/Library** and click GO. By the way, capitalization does count, so be sure to type *Library* with a capital L.

The Mother of All Gophers (Gopher)

This is the "Big Gophuna" — your link to the Gopher world. With one connection to this service, you can reach almost every single Gopher in the whole world. (No, I'm not kidding.) And it's available right from America Online.

To get there, type **gopher://gopher.tc.umn.edu** into the Address box on the Navigation bar and press Enter (or Return).

InterText Magazine (Mailing List)

If you like to read, the Internet has plenty to offer — and it comes right to you. If fiction is your interest, subscribe to the InterText online magazine, and, every two months, it appears in your America Online mailbox. InterText is a moderated collection of subscriber-submitted fiction, which means that they won't necessarily include your story just because you send it to them.

Subscribe by e-mailing a request to subscriptions@intertext.com. In the Subject line, put either ASCII (to show that you want the magazine e-mailed to you) or NOTIFY (you receive an e-mail when a new issue comes out, but you must go to the Web site and pick up a copy on your own). Your subscription starts when the next issue comes out.

NETHUMOR (Mailing List)

The NETHUMOR mailing list offers a daily dose of humorous Web sites, mailing lists, and other Net resources. It includes the site address, general information, and a brief sample of the site's humor. The listing also notes whether the site offers any (ahem) mature jokes that aren't fit for kids (and some accountants).

To add some fun to your life, send an e-mail to majordomo@bapp.com. The subject can be anything, but in the body of the message, type **SUBSCRIBE NETHUMOR** and then your Internet e-mail address (that's your America Online screen name with **@aol.com** after it). Because my screen name is JKaufeld, my subscription request was SUBSCRIBE NETHUMOR jkaufeld@aol.com.

Trojan Room Coffee Machine (World Wide Web)

This entry falls under the heading "Technology Run Amok." A bunch of computer people at Cambridge University decided that walking down several flights of stairs for a cup of coffee, only to find out that the pot was empty, was too much trouble. So they devised a clever solution worthy of their time and talents: They put their coffee pot on the Internet.

Yes, from anywhere in the world, you can see a digitized video image of their coffee pot and find out whether they're low on java. The address to use is `www.cl.cam.ac.uk/coffee/coffee.html`.

World Wide Web Site Indexes

After you use the World Wide Web a few times, you start wanting more. It's addictive — just like those little candy bars you get at Halloween. Luckily, some highly technical people got themselves addicted to the Web as well and created an index of Web sites all over the Internet.

To get more of the Web than any rational person would want, check out these indexes:

AltaVista	`http://altavista.digital.com`
Excite Netdirectory	`http://www.excite.com`
InfoSeek Guide	`http://www.infoseek.com`
NetFind	Keyword **NetFind**
Yahoo!	`http://www.yahoo.com`

MS-DOS, Macintosh, and Windows Software Archives (FTP)

These last three entries are software libraries (or *FTP sites*) out there on the Internet. Each library has a *lot* of software: business programs, utilities, virus detectors, and (of course) games. Each site specializes in programs for a different platform, so be sure to hook up to the right one for your computer.

MS-DOS	`oak.oakland.edu`
Macintosh	`sumex-aim.stanford.edu`
Windows	`ftp.winsite.com`

These are only a few of the most popular FTP sites — you can find plenty more where these came from. Look in the Internet Connection Message Board to learn about other sites.

Chapter 26

Ten Terms for the Chat Room–Challenged

- -

In This Chapter

▶ Telling people when you leave, come back, or feel tickled pink

▶ Expressing what's in your heart in four letters or less

- -

*N*o matter where you go in the People Connection (or any of America Online's other chatting areas), odd abbreviations and wacky terms wait to prey upon you. This chapter unmasks ten (or so) of the most common abbreviations and terms skulking around out there. Read them, learn them, and use them — it's for your own safety (and to keep you from ::blushing:: too much in the chats).

Away from the Keyboard (AFK)

You're chatting the night away in the People Connection and suddenly hear the call of nature — or, as so often happens to me, you're assailed by the Call of the Small-Bladdered Dog Who Needs to Go Outside Right Away. It takes too long to type "I have to go let the dog out before she detonates all over the kitchen floor like she did last week when I was in a chat room and ignored her because I was having too good a time" (besides, nobody really wants to know that much about it). It's rude to just pop out of the room without saying good-bye to everyone (besides, you're having too much fun to leave now). But the dog's timer is ticking, and the linoleum's looking scared. What to do, oh what to do?

Here's your solution: Type **AFK,** press Enter (or Return), and then put the pupster on a trajectory for the backyard. AFK is the universal chat room notation for Away from the Keyboard — online shorthand for "I'll be right back." Just remember to let everyone know you're BAK (covered in the next section) when you return!

If someone you're chatting with types in a quick AFK, you should reply **K** (short for "okay") so the person knows that you understand and that you are waiting for him or her to return. Kinda scary that something as wild and frolicsome as a chat room is so darn organized, isn't it?

Back at the Keyboard (BAK)

Telling folks that you're AFK is common courtesy, but it's equally important to let them know when you return from your task, suffused with the glow of a Job Well Done (or a Dog Well Launched, as the case may be). A quick **BAK** is all it takes to announce your re-entry into the conversation.

Drinks and Glassware

Nothing soothes the soul (or makes friends faster) than a couple of digital drinks in your favorite chat room. If bartending duties fall to you, be sure your bar stocks all the best in online glassware. After all, serving coffee in a martini glass certainly won't win you any friends!

c(_)	Coffee cup
c|_|	Beer mug
_/	Double old-fashioned or generic bar glass
|_|	Water or generic kitchen glass
Y	Martini or stemmed wine glass (yes, it takes some imagination)

As you see other cool glasses wander by online, jot them down here or on the Cheat Sheet. You don't want to drop a good glass!

Emoticons

Sometimes you need to say more than mere words can convey (which explains why we have comic books). But how do you include a picture in a typewritten message? Easy — with *emoticons,* emotion icons.

Feel free to use these symbols in your e-mail messages, bulletin board postings, and everyday conversation. Emoticons make up for the facial expressions and other kinds of body language that are missing from electronic communication. And they're kinda fun to type, too.

:-)	Smile
;-)	Wink
:-/	Befuddled
:-(	Frown
:-p	Bronx cheer
8-)	I drew a figure eight on my face (actually it means that you wear glasses)

For a more complete list of the best emoticons that typing can make, check out keyword **Shorthand.**

Emotion and Action — ::Smiles and Waves::

If you hang out in the People Connection too long or accidentally wander into one of the online simulations (keyword **Sim**), someone may enter the chat room and ::wave to all:: or ::looks bewildered, walks into a wall::. These folks don't love colons that much (only a doctor can muster that much affection for a simple organ). No, they're *doing something* in the chat room. Items encased in double colons usually indicate action (::swinging on the chandelier::) or a facial expression (::looking completely puzzled::). Sometimes double colons disclose thoughts (::wondering if I should even answer that question::), but that's the exception, not the rule.

Hugs {} and Kisses*

Have a friend who's feeling glum? There's nothing like a hug or two to keep someone going. You can give someone a little hug {}, lots of little hugs {}{}{}{}, or a great big hug {{{{{{}}}}}} — the choice is entirely yours.

These days, the online kiss (*) is one of the best ways to show affection. The kiss can be quick (or long — *really* long if need be) and safe, and it doesn't lead to anything, except perhaps an online hug ({ }).

Laughing out Loud (LOL)

Although *LOL* isn't a computer acronym, the only place you'll probably ever see it is in the People Connection or the message boards. LOL is America Online shorthand for "I'm laughing out loud!" A variation on this theme is LOLOLOL, which means "That's really, really funny" or "I particularly like consonant-vowel combinations tonight and wanted to share one with you."

Lofting

Conversations flow wild and free in a busy chat room, but sometimes you want to share a private thought with that special someone. Or course, one thought quickly turns to many, and before you know it, the chat room banter leaves you far behind. Focusing on a private, Instant Message–based conversation while in a chat room is called *lofting*. Often someone types a message like Greetings from the loft! to show that he or she is still around, but not really listening to the chat room right then.

Rolling on the Floor Laughing (ROFL)

Use this abbreviation when someone *seriously* tickles your funny bone. Like its little brother LOL, ROFL is a communication shortcut that most everybody on America Online understands. Expect to find it in the People Connection and on various message boards.

Swatting IMsects

Instant Messages are wonderful things — at least until you get inundated with them, that is. If a swarm of IMs distracts you from the chat room, let everybody know by dropping in a quick comment like Sorry I'm not paying attention — I'm busy swatting IMsects! It's a small thing, but it assures your chat room buddies that you aren't ignoring them (at least not completely).

AOL CHANNELS FOR DUMMIES®

by John Kaufeld

IDG Books Worldwide, Inc.
An International Data Group Company

Foster City, CA ♦ Chicago, IL ♦ Indianapolis, IN ♦ Southlake, TX

Table of Contents

Chapter 1

Getting Started with AOL Channels

• •

Some days, nothing feels as good as camping in your favorite chair, sucking down a cold soda pop, and channel-surfing the moments away. After all, with the hundreds of channels available on TV, you're bound to find something that tickles your fancy (even if it's just the relaxing sight of the different channels flipping by).

Even though the channels themselves provide some small amount of entertainment value, their main purpose in life is to organize the TV programs so that consistently finding reruns of "The Man from U.N.C.L.E." doesn't completely whack our brains. Combined with a good printed reference, the various TV channels make viewing less of a chore and more of a time-consuming obsession.

The 19 channels on America Online do the same thing — organize information, that is, not turn our online time into an obsession. (If you're like me, you're quite capable of doing the online obsession thing on your own, thank you very much.) The channels give you a ready to use, subject-oriented guide to all the content in America Online. Just pick the channel that sounds like it matches your interests and start browsing. You never know what you may find!

If you want a truly wild trip through America Online's content areas, try keyword **Random**. This sends you to a randomly selected online area somewhere in the wilds of the system. You never know quite where you'll end up, but that's what makes it fun!

Searching for Haystacks, Needles, and Whatever Else Strikes Your Fancy

When the folks at America Online redesigned the system's channel lineup, they moved things around, pushed the content areas into different cubbyholes, and generally gave the system a clean, freshly painted look. They also added a new tool to your arsenal of goodies: a vastly improved channel search system.

The new search system includes cool features like content limits that control where you want to find information and a filter to adjust how narrowly or broadly you want to search. All in all, the search system is a big improvement over the old way of searching the channels, even if it does mean that you need to invest a few minutes in figuring out the details of how to make it work.

To simplify that task, I present you with the following steps. They guide you through the channel search process in an utterly painless way. (If your personal pain quotient is low today, feel free to slam your head into the wall between steps.) Here's what to do:

1. **Get into whichever channel you want to search by clicking _C_hannels on the Toolbar, and then selecting the appropriate channel from the drop-down list.**

   The Channels window appears. After a second or two, the actual channel you select fills out the window.

2. **Click the Search & Explore department option for that channel.**

   After a moment of deep thought, a window much like the one shown in Figure 1-1 appears.

3. **Carefully type the term or terms you want to find into the Enter search word(s) box.**

   Gud speeling iz a must-hav sorta item here, sew pulhezzee be kareful.

4. **Click the down arrow next to the danglingly named Find articles within the last and select a time frame for the search system to explore.**

   For most searches, leave this item set to All articles.

Figure 1-1:
Thanks to
the Search
& Explore
system, you
can find
almost
anything
within the
America
Online
channels.

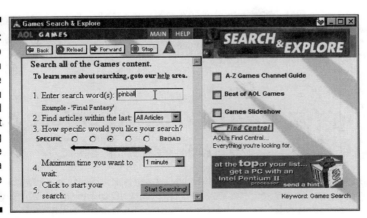

5. Choose how specific you want the search to be by clicking the appropriate radio button (the ones marked A through F).

By default, the system uses a simple *AND* approach, so if you search for *John Adams,* the search engine returns any document with the words *John* and *Adams* anywhere in it. To make it search for the exact phrase that you type, click the radio button next to Specific. To loosen the search and turn it into a fuzzy, I-want-this-and-things-like-it search, click the button next to Broad.

To figure out all of the nuances of manually adjusting your search, click the Help link at the top of the search window.

6. If you feel impatient today, adjust the Maximum time you want to wait setting and impose a deadline on the search system.

Unless you harbor a really good reason, don't change this setting — it's just not worth it.

7. Click the Start Searching button to do the dirty deed.

After chugging away for a few moments, the results window appears, looking something like Figure 1-2.

8. Scroll through the search results list and click whatever looks interesting to see it.

To start another search, click the Back button at the top of the window.

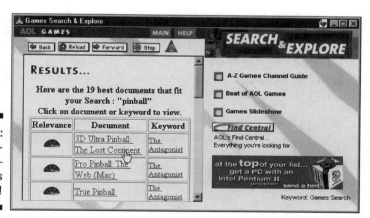

Figure 1-2: Congratulations — the results are in!

Chapter 2

AOL Today Channel (Keyword AOL Today)

Sliced bread was a pretty nifty invention. If it hadn't been, people wouldn't still be using it as a measure of time (as I'm about to do). Precisely *why* people honor innovations by marking their usefulness in since-sliced-bread years, I leave to people with more pages at their disposal (and more time on their hands) than I have with this book.

The AOL Today channel ranks right up there as one of the world's best inventions since the concept of evenly apportioned bakery goods. AOL Today is a little bit of everything rolled into one spot, presented to you on a quick-to-peruse digital platter. Better still, it marks the passing of time by adjusting itself and its offerings, truly making AOL Today the best place to start your online adventures.

Figure 2-1 shows the AOL Today channel looking sunrise-yellow and almost too darn chipper, fresh from its morning pot of whatever bleary-eyed content windows consume to help them wake up in the early hours of the day. As you can see, this channel is packed with the things your morning moments crave, like news, weather, and David Letterman's Top 10 list (in case you just couldn't stay awake for it last night).

Figure 2-1: Your morning wake-up call, your afternoon companion, and your evening guide — it's all in AOL Today.

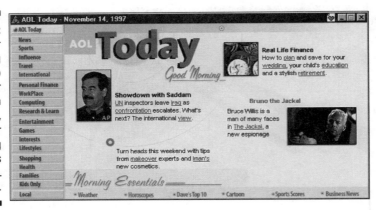

As the day goes on, the channel's cheery Good morning! motif segues into a more businesslike (and, more important, significantly less yellow) Midday look. The window's content options shift as well, offering more business and entertainment news, discussion links, helpful items for busy families, computer tips, and so on. You can even find a dedicated link to the airline reservation area to assist the frantic, work-at-home businessmom.

When afternoon turns into early evening, AOL Today shifts gears again into Prime Time. The content lists change as well, focusing on important issues like what's new in world news, what happened in the business scene, and what's coming up on TV. (The answer to that last one is easy: Nothing — so hop on America Online instead.)

The last stop of the day is AOL Today's Late Night look, when entertainment and relaxation are the orders of the moment. Look for sports scores, the classifieds, plus links to all kinds of AOL Live! presentations and People Connection chat areas. The work day is done, so relax with AOL Live!'s answer to the end-of-the-day wind-down time.

Chapter 3

Computing Channel (Keyword Computing)

*W*hen computers made their first appearance in the '40s, they were an incomprehensible morass of wires, tubes, huge boxes, and cooling fans. Thanks to the wonders of modern technology, the computer of the '90s bears little resemblance to its long-antiquated counterpart. Today, computers are an incomprehensible morass of boards, chips, little boxes, and cooling fans. Fills you with hope for the future, doesn't it?

Whether or not you comprehend the morass, you still need a place to go with your questions, concerns, and general complaints. In America Online, look no further than the Computing channel, shown in Figure 3-1. It covers all your computer woes from hardware to software, from laptops to palmtops. Gather up all those computer questions you have lying around, wade into the Computing channel, and demand answers.

Features   Department buttons   Spotlight areas

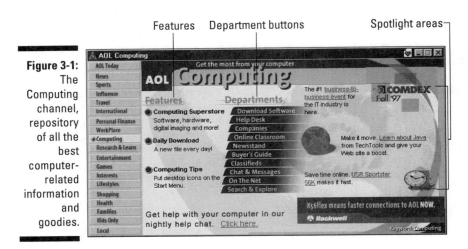

Figure 3-1:
The
Computing
channel,
repository
of all the
best
computer-
related
information
and
goodies.

The channel window itself breaks into three main sections. Starting on the left, you find the features area, a set of buttons leading to popular Computing-related areas. In the middle of the window, you find the department buttons. These buttons lead to the true informational depth of the Computing channel. What you find in each one is detailed in the coming sections. Finally, on the right side of the window, are the spotlight areas. Sometimes fun, sometimes educational, but *always* useful, these buttons change frequently, highlighting all kinds of timely content in the Computing channel.

Download Software Department (Keyword Download Software)

When you want to do something new with your Windows 95, Windows 3.*x*, DOS, or Macintosh computer, start your search here in the Computing channel's Download Software department. This section offers freeware, shareware, demonstration software, sound files, and graphics files in popular Windows and Macintosh formats; hundreds and hundreds of TrueType fonts; plus ready-to-use template files for popular commercial programs like Microsoft Publisher, Aldus PageMaker, Sierra Online's PrintShop, and many, many others.

If you need a particular program, sound, graphic, or whatever-it-is, try using the file search system (use keyword **File Search** or click the Find button and select Software from the drop-down menu). That's your quickest solution. If you aren't in a terrible hurry, wander through the Download Software department, because you may find even more stuff that meets your needs.

Help Desk Department (Keywords Help Desk, PC Help)

Did your computer ever go *ping, beep,* or (my personal favorite) *bzzzrp-sproing-wugga-wugga-wugga?* When you're at work, those peculiar sounds usually mean a quick call to your friendly computer support technician (followed by a bit of a wait while the support folks draw straws to decide who gets to answer your question). At home, though, and in many small businesses as well, those same sounds usually precede weeping, wailing, and gnashing of teeth as you try to figure out what on earth just happened to your faithful machine.

Instead of crying yourself a river (or at least a small in-office pond), sign on to America Online (assuming that part of the computer still works) and check out the Help Desk department. This area is chock-full of hardware and software assistance, plus areas that make the online world itself easier to comprehend.

Companies Department (Keyword Companies)

It takes hundreds and hundreds of programs to keep computer people happy. Some people want word processors, other people want database managers, and a third group just wants to have fun (preferably in 3D, with vivid color displays, huge military vehicles, and lots of alien-shattering explosions).

To keep these programs coming (especially the many titles in the just-have-fun category) requires the skill and single-minded effort of a huge number of software companies and their programmers. Although you probably don't regularly use more than a dozen programs, you should still try to stay current on what's new with the company that wrote the program, what new versions of the program are available, and what technical challenges (also known as bugs) your application struggles with at the moment.

AOL's Companies department makes finding almost any software company (as well as some hardware companies) quite a snap. Just get into the channel and scroll through the list of companies until you find the one that makes your software or device. Double-click its name to see the company's online area or Web site. After you know the company's keyword, you can just type it in!

Online Classroom Department (Keyword Online Classroom)

Find out all about computer hardware, object-oriented programming, World Wide Web page design, and more at this Mecca of online education, the Online Classroom department. Regular classes cover the basics of computer hardware, software, programming, graphics, and almost anything else you can imagine. Most classes are free, although some require a small fee.

If you miss a session or just want to find out what an online class is like, check the class transcripts area (click the Class Transcripts button in the Online Classroom department window). Inside the various course areas, look in the Tutorials and Books sections for downloadable tutorials and links to other online lessons.

Newsstand (Keyword Computing Newsstand)

Computing without magazines is, well, a real pain when you get right down to it. You *need* magazines to stay current on changes in hardware and software technology, printers, monitors, and all the other things that keep the crazy computer industry running. The best way to do that is by picking a few computer periodicals and reading them religiously. Read them every week — if not every *day* for the Web-based ones.

To start the process, browse through the Computing channel's Newsstand and explore the publications you find there. Some of the magazines are general, covering the entire computer world, while others aim for specifically targeted audiences, like Macintosh aficionados, C++ programmers, hard-core computer gamers, and so on.

If you love to read about the computer industry itself and get some sneak peeks under the hood to see what really makes it tick, check out `http://www.upside.com`, the Web version of *Upside* magazine. You won't be sorry!

Buyer's Guide (Keyword Buyers Guide)

Owning a computer means many things, among them the freedom to spend every loose piece of money you have on new stuff to keep your machine happy (because, goodness knows, you don't want to upset the computer). To help you find the best deals on hardware, software, and other miscellaneous digital goodies, wander into the Buyer's Guide channel.

The department's layout is pretty straightforward. It offers lots of quick reviews covering current hardware and software. Peripherals, like printers and digital cameras, are in there as well — just look under the Hardware area.

Classifieds (Menu Access Only)

Buy, sell, trade, and (hopefully) walk away with a great deal here in America Online's answer to crossing Radio Shack with the Home Shopping Network — the Buyer's Guide department, your home for researching hardware and software, and buying it, too.

With choices for regional job and product listings, specific topic areas, various PC hardware and operating system platforms, and tons of individual programs themselves, this is a must-visit area if saving money on computer stuff is your goal.

Don't be misled by a price that sounds *too* good. As with any endeavor involving people, sometimes you run across a less-than-scrupulous character who wants to make a fast buck. While most of the people selling things through AOL's classifieds are on the up-and-up, I'm sad to say that others aren't. You shouldn't run into trouble if you just take care.

Chat & Messages Department (Keyword Computing Chat)

If your life is (horrors!) devoid of computer people, or if you just want to swap computer tips with whoever wanders by, check out the various chat and discussion areas in the Chat & Messages department. These are great places to find solid technical help, because you never know *who* you may run into there. One night, I bumped into a couple of consultants having a deep discussion about Windows NT as a network server (don't laugh — it *was* interesting!) and soaked up all kinds of cool things about networking in the process.

The best way to join any technical discussion is to listen first, then contribute later. If you have a question, don't be afraid to ask it, but be sure to ask it in the right place — particularly in the discussion boards. Double-check the discussion board topic before posting your question. Putting the question in the wrong place just delays your answer!

On The Net (Keyword On the Net)

The online world grows by the second (oop! — there it went again . . .) thanks to the worldwide span of the Internet. America Online offers you everything you need to join the fun, from software support, to Web browsing, to space for your own Web pages. To help you make sense of the possibilities, check out the Computing channel's On the Net department.

The On the Net department holds the Computing channel's Internet-related stuff, including tutorials, file libraries, and advanced tricks for the personal-life-challenged. No matter what your level of expertise, you can find something in here.

Search & Explore (Keyword Explore Computing)

Keeping up on the latest information in the fast-moving world of computing is a never-ending (and nearly impossible) job. Things change so quickly that the information you got yesterday may change by tomorrow (heck — by then, it may have changed *twice!*).

To keep as close to current as possible without pulling out all your hair in the process, use the Search & Explore department. This tool scours areas throughout the Computing channel for news, tips, and just about anything else relating to your topic of interest.

For a detailed look at the searching process, see the section called "Finding Places: Tracking Interests and Meeting Informational Needs," in Chapter 11 in the main part of this book (not in this minibook!).

Chapter 4

Entertainment Channel (Keyword Entertainment)

*1*f you take America's top three entertainment capitals (New York City, Hollywood, and Branson, Missouri) and digitally roll them into one place, toss in a computer game or two, season the concoction with a touch of Las Vegas in the summer, and then hang Christmas tree lights on it, you can be *close* to the flavor of the America Online Entertainment channel. Close, mind you, but still not *quite* there.

This area simply *is* entertainment. No matter what you're into, you can find it all here (within the bounds of good taste, of course — no accordion players need apply). Movies, theatre, music, sports, trivia, entertainment news, online games, and even places to mix and mingle with new people — the Entertainment channel is all that and more.

Looking at the Entertainment channel window (if you can pick it out among the photographers and TV camera crews in Figure 4-1), you can see that the Entertainment channel is exciting, engaging, and packed with information, yet carries itself with a certain panache — it's stylish without being over the top (as they say in the entertainment biz).

Figure 4-1: Now presenting the Entertainment channel, home of the stars on America Online.

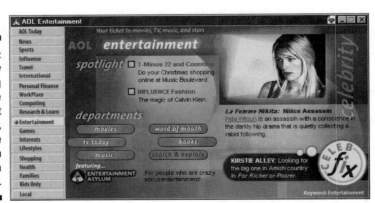

Sitting to the side like a bunch of studio executives are the channel's department buttons. Each of these areas focuses on a different facet of the entertainment industry, from movies (my favorite) to books (my other favorite). Arrayed throughout the rest of the window are the featured areas, the online version of this week's hot entertainment properties. Like the real-life version (stars of the moment, as it were), the featured areas change regularly.

Movies Department (Keyword Movies)

When I think of entertainment, the silver screen immediately pops into mind. Movies *define* Hollywood, and they dominate a big part of the entertainment industry. If you're a movie fan like me, then the Movies department is waiting to thrill you. Turn here for the latest news, reviews, and inside scoop on who's doing what and when the results will show up at a theatre near you.

TV Today Department (Keyword TV)

I've heard it said that television is a vast wasteland, but I'm reasonably sure that the quote wasn't uttered by any current media executive. After all, with direct broadcast satellites, mega-channel cable TV systems, and at least four different editions of HBO, there has to be *something* worth watching out there.

To cut through the tripe and find the shows with the most promise, turn to the TV Today department. Its witty repartee and insightful analysis (tempered with more than a bit of old-fashioned public relations hubris, I might add) promise to fill all your tube-related desires.

Music Department (Keyword Music)

Before reading this section, you simply *must* put your favorite CD, tape, or even one of those big vinyl things on the stereo and crank up the volume. With tunes filling the air, you're ready to find out more about the Music department, America Online's haven for music makers, listeners, and lovers. The areas in here cover all kinds of music, plus the artists, labels, and technologies behind the beat. You can even find online versions of magazines like *Rolling Stone* and *Spin*.

In addition to general features, the department organizes itself into basic areas by musical genre, giving each one its own button on the main Music department window. Each of the genre areas includes its own discussion boards and chat areas, plus tons of links to other online fan areas and Web pages. Keep your eyes peeled for special items in each area, too.

Word of Mouth Department (Keyword Word of Mouth)

They don't call it the entertainment *industry* for nothing — it's a big business, with a *lot* going on at any given moment. To keep up with the latest entertainment news and gossip — and meet other people along the way who love the industry as much as you do — check out the Word of Mouth department. Between the chats, discussion boards, and links to great online areas, you may never want to leave.

Books Department (Keyword Books)

I have to be honest about this: I love books. Sure, I write them (although I don't play an author on television), but *reading* is truly one of my joys. If you love books as much as I do, there may be help for us yet. Turn to the Books department to indulge yourself in the latest tidbits about the newest titles and the hottest authors.

Search & Explore Department (Keyword E Search)

Thank goodness for the Search & Explore department! (Okay, so it's very late and my naturally nerdy side *is* showing a little bit — but can't a guy get excited about something that takes your request, digs through a ton of material, and then delivers your answer in record time, and all without asking anything in return?)

The Entertainment channel's Search & Explore department uses the new Web-based search system like its fellow channels, so you have a set of tweakable tools at your service. It also offers the A-Z Channel Guide, a peppy Best Of area, and the always-popular multimedia slide show designed to sell you on the wonders of the channel. When you simply can't find what you're looking for (at least in entertainment information, that is), turn here for help.

Chapter 5

Families Channel
(Keyword Families)

*T*he kids are in bed (or safely away at college), the house is neat, and you're too tired to leave the house. Maybe you've spent all day matching wits with a 4-year-old, or you need some advice on living day by day with a teenager. Instead of spending the last daylight hours sitting numbly in front of the tube, hop onto America Online and check out the Families channel (proudly appearing in Figure 5-1).

Figure 5-1:
Find all
sorts of
family and
home
information
in America
Online's
space
dedicated
to the
home-
lovers in all
of us.

Featured areas

Department buttons

America Online combined all the home and parenting areas in one handy channel. From the Families channel window you can read up on your child's current phase, research the iguana your daughter wants to bring home, or discover new project ideas that your family can complete together.

Unlike a lot of the channel windows, the Family Channel window contains just a few items (after all, your familial world is complex enough as it is). Most of the window's right side is devoted to the current *featured areas,* which change frequently during the week. The left side offers the *department buttons* — your links to all of the good stuff in the channel.

Family Timesavers (Keyword Family Timesavers)

When couldn't you use a little extra time? Use Family Timesavers when you want to shop, but don't have the extra hour needed to run to the mall; you need to tabulate those recent purchases in a Budget Calculator; or you're dreaming about (or planning) your next family vacation. Whether you want to remind yourself of an upcoming (or recurring) family event, send a greeting card via e-mail, or prepare yourself for a real estate move, Family Timesavers is the place to start.

Family Ties Department (Keyword Family Ties)

Each family, although unique in its own right, shares delightful traits with other families. Explore the ties that hold families together as well as those that link various families one to another — commiserate with other parents, share your newfound adoption joys (or the pain of your search), and find out how to keep track of online friends through the areas and forums available through Family Ties.

On the main Family Ties window, click the Special Chats button for a daily listing of the hottest family chats online. Whether you want to chat with other stay-at-home moms, touch base with single parents, or drop into a scouting chat, you can discuss your family's interests and meet new online friends at the same time.

Parenting Department (Keyword Parenting)

Sometimes I wish children appeared with little parenting manuals tied to one foot with a pink or blue ribbon. The manuals wouldn't have to be exhaustive; simply a few paragraphs under headings like *Extremely Sensitive* or *Active and Energetic* would give parents some helpful hints on dealing with the little person-bundle they bring home from the hospital. In future years, the dog-eared little manuals might offer guidance when the 6-year-old mysteriously breaks into tears or the 10-year-old lives life nonstop for 18 hours a day.

Until that future day of beribboned birth manuals (and like you, I'm not holding my breath), parents need to figure out their offspring with the help of cuddle and reading time, bedtime discussions, and parent-to-parent networking. This is where the Families Channel's Parenting Department comes in. The Parenting Department offers reviews, advice, and tips for low stress family life, whether your kids wear diapers or a traditional cap and gown.

In addition to the department's parenting forums and message boards, you can find a button on the main window called Connect in Family Ties (keyword **Family Ties**). Click it to visit the channel's conversation department. Attend a chat or read and respond to the message boards' postings. You just may meet a new online friend or two.

Babies Department (Keyword Babies)

Baby powder, nursery furniture, and teeny-tiny diapers evoke feelings of "Ah, isn't she cute?" in almost everyone. Join the baby party in the Babies Department. Whether you're expecting a new bundle at your house, your bundle-turned-baby is gnawing on your furniture as you read this, or you want to remember the baby days, this department supplies some excellent information.

Swap information about nursing, calculate the costs of your new little guy, or find a perfect name for your baby-in-waiting. Find answers to your questions about the terrific toddler stage, or attend a chat where you talk about infants. And if you're in the market for baby stuff, look no further than the Baby Picks Stuff section for reviews on strollers, baby carriers, car seats, and lullabies.

Newsstand Department (Keyword Families Newsstand)

Sometimes you want to curl up with a cup of hot cocoa and a good magazine. When those moods strike, turn to the Families Newsstand department. The department contains links to several family-oriented magazines that maintain an area on America Online. From *Consumer Reports* to *Highlights for Children,* and from *Family PC* to *Seventeen,* you can find articles from the magazine's current issue, some "Best of the Best" from past issues, and even some online content that you won't find anywhere else.

If you completely fall in love with a few of these magazines by reading their online versions, most of the forums contain subscription information so that you can receive the magazine via postal mail. Many times you can subscribe to the print version of the magazine while you're online. If you don't find exactly what you're looking for in the item list, try the Magazine Outlet button (keyword **Magazine Outlet**) for subscription information on hundreds of magazines.

Homebase Department (Keyword Homebase)

You sleep there, you eat there — you may even work there. It's big enough to entertain your closest friends, yet small enough to keep clean without inviting the local Army Reserve over to help. You call it home, and it's here that the family meets for pow-wows, you create and treasure holiday traditions, and the new puppy learns the meaning of potty training.

America Online calls it the Homebase Department, and this department devotes its time to the "home subjects" in our lives. Not how to fix, repair, or maintain the building — look for that in the Interests channel. Rather, in Homebase you can find information on pet care, easy recipes to tide you over during those rushed times, and articles and chats designed to help you with home management.

Kids & Teens Department (Keyword Kids and Teens)

You've made it past potty training, the kids walk and talk on their own, and they're beginning to show interest in their own projects. Now often computer literate at an amazingly early age, today's kids and teens can surf the Internet for games, program a computer, and type up a report on their word processors — all in the same evening. Keep up with them, and find a few family projects they may really enjoy, with a little help from the Kids & Teens department.

Also use Kids & Teens to visit America Online's Kids Only channel, the AOL Teens area, an area devoted to books for teens, and activities designed to keep kids' boredom at bay. The main window features links to articles that change frequently, plus a Connect in Family Ties button (keyword **Family Ties**) that takes you to the chat-and-message boards Family Ties department.

Parental Controls Department (Button Access Only)

Find out about America Online's Parental Controls, and how they're designed to keep your kids safe online. From the Safe online access for kids window that opens, you can take a tour that explains the controls in detail. To bypass the tour and set the controls, or to set the controls after you've read about the Parental Controls feature, click the Try it Now button.

Search and Explore Department (Keyword Families Search)

Sometimes things aren't where you think they should be. In the same way that I leave coffee cups all over the house, and then need to go on a roundup mission before the next dishwasher load, America Online periodically drops forums into channels where you wouldn't think of looking for them. If you think you may be missing something in the Families channel, or you simply want to see what's out there, use the Search and Explore department to view the breadth of Families.

Search for articles located somewhere in the Families channel with the engine built right into the Search and Explore window. If you want a few ideas where to start browsing in the Families channel, the Best of AOL Families button leads to a list of some of the coolest forums in the Families channel. For more information about the Search and Explore Department, flip to Chapter 1 of this minibook.

Chapter 6

Games Channel
(Keyword Games)

Many years ago when I was a little nerdlet, I discovered the family
Monopoly set. I immediately fell in love. Those cool little playing
pieces, the crisp feel of the multicolored money, and the tasty little houses
(okay, so I ate one — I was really little) forever hooked me on gaming. If
playing games ranks among your true loves, join me for a jaunt through the
ultimate gamer's candy store: America Online's Games channel.

Whatever your pleasure, this channel covers it. Drop in for a dogfight
between classic World War II fighters, match wits and drinks with a few
dozen ogres in the local inn, race to remember the name of Dudley Do-
Right's horse in a national trivia challenge, engage a new friend in a friendly
game of chance, and then download the Doom patch that turns the mon-
sters into Homer Simpson look-alikes. Hmm — not bad for your first 15
minutes!

The Games channel window, merrily displayed in Figure 6-1, is split into
three distinct areas. Starting on the left, you find the channel highlights,
which keep you up-to date on everything to do with the channel itself
(Games Insider, keyword **Games Insider**), the premium games (Games
Guide, keyword **Games Guide**), and the free game shows (Game Shows,
keyword **Game Shows**).

Figure 6-1:
It's wild,
fun, and
high-tech
— it's the
America
Online
Games
channel!

Right down the middle of the window are the Games channel departments. Here's where the fun really starts, as you link up with other gamers, swap tips, download programs, and generally wreak havoc with your computer. Finally, taking up the right half of the window, are the current featured areas. Usually these are devoted to various premium games, although the game shows and general information areas pop up there from time to time as well.

If online games make your heart flutter like nothing else in the world, pick up a copy of *Internet Games For Dummies* (written by yours truly and published by IDG Books Worldwide, Inc.) and find out more about the incredible world of multiplayer, online gaming.

Games Central Department (Keyword Games Central)

The whole Games channel thing starts here, at the Games Central department. This area brings you links for both games and gamer interest areas all over America Online. Be sure to check out the Cool Links (keyword **GC Cool**) and the Gaming Forums (keyword **OGF**) areas in particular, because they're the real gems of this department.

Video Games Department (Keyword VGS)

If your favorite games live on a Nintendo 64, Sega Saturn, or Sony Playstation, then the Video Games department has your name written all over it (and the maintenance crew wants to discuss that with you, by the way). Console games rule the day here, with areas devoted to news, gossip, tips, and chat about your favorites.

If you love classic arcade games like Asteroids, Centipede, and Tempest, or home video game systems such as the Atari 2600 or the original Nintendo system, relive your glory days with a visit to Dave's Video Game Classics (http://www.davesclassics.com). This site offers emulators — programs to make your computer behave like the brains behind the video games of days gone by — and the actual programs for your favorite arcade and video game classics. It's all free (well, some of the emulators are shareware, so you should pay for one if you fall in love with it), so give it a try!

PC Games Department (Keyword PC Games)

Why buy a computer in the '90s? I can only think of one reason (other than to use America Online, that is) — so that you can play games! Indulge your love of things that go bang, crash, and rooooooar in the night by visiting the Games channel's PC Games department. Whether you want to download a demo of the new game you just read about, join in a lively discussion about weapon selection in Quake II, or try your hand at an online game of skill against a few hundred of your fellow gamers, everything you want is here in PC Games.

Games Store Department (Keyword Games Store)

What good is reading about the hot new games if you can't go buy a few to add to your collection? With that marketing-driven thought in mind, check out the Games Store, America Online's answer to catalog shopping for the hard-core computer gamer. The store carries games in just about every genre, including action, strategy, sports, and role playing. It even includes a special section for joysticks and game classifieds, just to make sure that nobody walks away empty-handed.

Newsstand Department (Keyword AOL Games Newsstand)

Although I hate to say it, I'm very disappointed with the Games channel's Newsstand department (at least in its current incarnation). As of this writing, the links in here are a spaghetti bowl of pointers to other places in the Games channel — almost none of them actually lead to game magazines or information at all. I hope that the content folks at America Online fix this little problem by the time you actually read these words.

Because I hate to see anyone go away empty-handed, Table 6-1 offers some great Web-based places to look for game news and reviews. Browse through the sites, see which one (or ones) you like, then make it a point to check back regularly. You never know what you may find out on the Web!

Table 6-1	Web-Based Game Information Sites
Site Name	*Address*
Game Alert	http://www.gamealert.com
Game Briefs	http://www.gamebriefs.com
Gamecenter	http://www.gamecenter.com
GameSpot	http://www.gamespot.com
Happy Puppy	http://www.happypuppy.com
Multiplayer Dot Com	http://www.multiplayer.com

Search & Explore Department (Keyword Games Search)

Gamers don't have a lot time on their hands (if they did, they could play more games). To make the most of your online (non-game-playing) time, use the Games channel's Search & Explore system to help you find information right now. This channel uses the new and improved search system, including the flexible I'm-thinking-of-a-word search window, the A-Z Games Channel Guide, the Best of AOL Games area, and the channel's slide show, dedicated to how wonderful life is in the Games channel.

Chapter 7

Health Channel
(Keyword Health)

Everyone wants to be healthy. Millions of Americans lower their fat intake, partially eliminate meat from their diets, and begin an exercise program in an effort to maintain or regain health. America Online's Health channel helps you along the way, with departments devoted to illnesses, living healthfully, support groups, and the various stages of life (shown in Figure 7-1).

Figure 7-1: Research an illness, join a support group, or celebrate life in the Health channel.

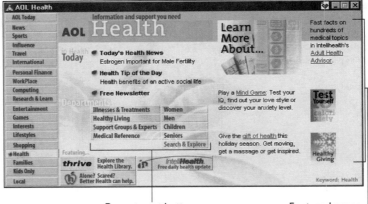

Department buttons   Featured areas

The window also features several department buttons containing links that whisk you to current health news articles, health-related areas, and seasonal information. Find a button that looks interesting and see where it takes you. Perhaps you want to visit an online health area, read an article about virus protection (the germ kind, not the computer version) or have the chance to post your opinions in a health poll. The other areas on the window are featured areas, special spots within the Health channel that are worth an extra look. These areas change quite frequently, so the ones on your screen may not look exactly like the ones in Figure 7-1.

For a little healthy fun in your day, visit the Health Interactive area (keyword **Health Interactive**). This area is full of tests and quizzes: You can find out whether you live a healthy lifestyle, take an IQ test, determine whether you're an optimist or a pessimist, and find out how much you know about nutrition. Each item takes you to a specific quiz. Take one or two and see how you fare.

Illnesses & Treatments Department (Keyword Illness)

When you or a loved one suffer from an illness of some kind, you long to find more about it, discover ways to cope, and meet other people who can relate. In the Illnesses & Treatments department you can meet all three goals at once. The department contains folders on many different illnesses, from allergies to cancer and all the way down to skin illnesses. Select one of the areas and find out about it; in most cases, the specific illness window contains information about online support groups, where you can connect with members who understand.

Healthy Living Department (Keyword Healthy Living)

Join the ranks of the healthy with Healthy Living — a department completely devoted to prevention and right living. Find out about eating healthfully, fitness, and wellness. On those occasions when you do need a helping hand, the alternative medicine section proposes alternatives to traditional medicine. If you'd like to shed a few pounds before terming yourself completely healthy, you can find weight-loss information and support here as well.

Support Groups & Experts Department (Keyword Health Support)

You (or someone you love) struggles with a health problem, and you'd like to talk about it? The Support Groups & Experts department is here to help. Select the support group that interests you, and open its folder to find out more about it. Some support groups meet in scheduled chats several times a week to discuss various topics; others meet only once a week. To view the scheduled chats listed by day of the week rather than category, click the View by day tab at the top of the item list box. Then open any daily folder to see the support groups that meet on that day of the week. For most purposes, finding the chat by topic is much easier than browsing for it through the daily listings.

Medical Reference Department (Keyword Medical Reference)

Find the answers to your health questions in the Medical Reference department. Divided into two sections, Medical Reference provides medical databases as well as health organizations.

The Medical Reference databases provide information on first aid; finding a doctor; drugs and alcohol; and general health issues. For terms and definitions, try the Merriam Webster Medical Dictionary (keyword **Medical Dictionary**).

Women Department (Keyword Women's Health)

Women's health demands specific information. Find what you need to know in the Women department. From information on cancers that only affect women to eating disorders and pregnancy, Women successfully delivers information unique to the female body's health.

Men Department (Keyword Men's Health)

Men have special health needs, too. That's why the Health channel created the Men department — to discuss men's health issues apart from the general illness or healthy living departments. Look here for information specific to men and the bodies they inhabit: male baldness and hair loss, cancers that only affect the male body, and other illnesses and problems that men may incur.

Children Department (Keyword Children's Health)

Nothing is quite as joyful as a healthy child. Healthy children run, leap, jump, and ask millions of questions. Use the Children department for information to enhance the health of the children in your life. Look here for information on topics that range from the snuffly-nosed cold and otitis media (ear infection) all the way to extremely serious illnesses such as leukemia. You also find info on school-related health issues, such as attention deficit disorder and other learning disorders. Pick a folder and dive in.

Seniors Department (Keyword Seniors' Health)

Just as children sometimes suffer with specific age-related illnesses, the senior set faces its own unique challenges at the other end of the age spectrum. Look in the Seniors department for information about arthritis, glaucoma, osteoporosis, and a range of other concerns. You can also find a folder entitled Parenting & Caregiving, which contains links to support groups and Web sites designed to help the elder caregiver.

Search & Explore Department (Keyword Health Search)

When I checked the Search & Explore department, nothing much was going on. Use this department to sign up for the free Health channel newsletter, which America Online drops into your e-mail box each week. By the time you read this, however, the Health channel Search & Explore department will probably let you search for articles by topic in the Health channel. See the Search section in Chapter 1 of this minibook, *AOL Channels For Dummies,* for more information on how to use the system.

Chapter 8

Influence Channel (Keyword Influence)

*W*hat is *influence?* It has many things, depending on the situation. It's a seen or unseen force that indirectly affects or alters events. It's the power to change opinions based on a person's wealth, prestige, or business or social position. And it's the America Online channel that wins my personal award for least comprehensibly named. The first time I heard about the Influence channel, I thought it had something to do with organized crime or political corruption — and, based on the content in it, I may be right yet!

If you love New York and Los Angeles because they're the hubs of prestige and power in the United States, then the Influence channel is for you. This channel is a collection of stylish, expensive, well-dressed, correctly invested, and media-savvy areas both within America Online and out on the World Wide Web (but only the *right* part of the Web, mind you). The Influence Channel is an eclectic mix, which makes it worth a stop.

Looking at the channel window itself in Figure 8-1, you see the departments centered in the screen, surrounded by various featured areas. Given its focus on power, I'm not surprised that the Influence Channel wants to guide you directly into the departments if at all possible (although I'm not sure that I like an online area that's so pushy).

The department windows in the Influence Channel work a bit differently from departments in other channels, but don't let that worry you. Instead of sporting a bunch of big buttons leading to the various department areas, the departments section here includes a couple of spotlight areas and a single box, labeled Departments, with a pull-down menu. That pull-down menu is your key to the department areas — just yank on it by clicking the down arrow button, then select your favorite area from the list.

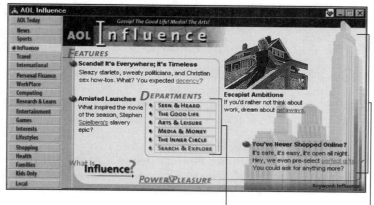

Figure 8-1:
The
Influence
Channel,
America
Online's
home for all
that's
socially
powerful
and media-
savvy.

Department buttons⏋　　　　Featured areas⏋

Seen & Heard Department (Keyword Seen & Heard)

Psst — hey buddy. Yeah, you. Ya wanna know a secret? Well, then you should head into Influence Channel's Seen & Heard Department right away! Whether you're looking for insightful political commentary, hot society news, or unconfirmed inside information (what people used to call gossip), you can find it all waiting for you in here.

Top picks in here include the Drudge Report (keyword **Drudge**), George Online (keyword **George**), and one of America Online's best destinations for a good laugh, Buzzsaw (keyword **Buzzsaw**).

The Good Life Department (Keyword Good Life)

Living the good life is what most of us fantasize about — but just what the heck *is* this thing in our dreams anyhow? What does it look like? Can I visit this nirvana without moving in lock, stock, and modem line? The Good Life department (despite the fact that it sounds like the area next to Automotive at the Twilight Zone Sears) seeks to answer all those questions and more with its wide variety of informational links.

The links themselves are stored in the requisite pull-down menu. On the menu, everything is organized around facets of the good life, including fashion, food, travel, and home decorating (little concrete geese need *not* apply).

Arts & Leisure Department (Keyword Arts & Leisure)

Keeping up with movies, theatre, and books is a full-time occupation for some people (although I want to know how they got those jobs), but it's a part-time obsession for many others. To stay on top of the newest things in the arts and entertainment business, drop by the Arts & Leisure department regularly.

The areas inside the department are split into two groups on the pull-down list. The Arts section includes film, theatre, and dance, with the whole Smithsonian Institution thrown in at no extra charge. Down a little farther on the list are the book links, featuring The Book Report (keyword **Book Report**) and Book Central (keyword **BC**).

Media & Money Department (Keyword Media & Money)

Media is big business, so I'm not surprised that the Influence channel devotes a whole section to following and analyzing the media. Considering how much the media like to observe and comment on the lifestyles of the rich and well-connected, it's mildly amusing that this same channel *also* looks squarely at the society side of business and investing as well. (It makes you wonder whether the various menu items glare suspiciously at each other when nobody else is around.)

As you expect by its name, the list of services inside the Media & Money Department are organized into two groups: Media and Money. The Media entries focus primarily on the marvelous online publication Slate (keyword **Slate**), although they also include nods to the New York Observer (keyword **NYObserver**) and Salon Magazine (keyword **Salon Magazine**). In the Money end of the menu, look for Business Week (keyword **Business Week**) and the Motley Fool (keyword **Fool**) among others.

The Inner Circle Department (Keyword Inner Circle)

Being part of a group's *inner circle* means taking your place as a member of the ruling elite. Your words carry weight; people seek out your opinions. And so it goes in the Inner Circle department, where you can comment on the Influence channel, meet your fellow channel hoppers, and trade opinions in the channel discussion board.

Like its namesake in the social strata of life, it's not as easy as it looks to move completely into the Inner Circle department. Sure, the window is friendly and inviting, and includes a wide variety of chat areas and discussion boards, but here's a trick to breaking into the much-coveted core: Get into the drop-down menu that contains the department's areas, then select either the Featured Message Boards or Featured Chats entries. These two innocent-looking items are secret doors leading to an incredible number of influential chat and discussion areas.

Search & Explore Department (Keyword Influence Search)

Like its brethren in the channels list, the Influence Channel offers its own dedicated Search & Explore department. It includes the standard go-find-it controls, as well as the A-Z Channel Guide and Best of AOL Influence areas. The Influence slide show also sits in here, looking just a little lost and forlorn.

For help using the search system, see the Search & Explore information in Chapter 1 of this book-within-a-book.

Chapter 9

Interests Channel
(Keyword Interests)

. . . .

*S*everal years ago, a research study appeared stating that people who regularly engage in hobbies or follow special interests outside of work concerns live longer, happier lives. And if my memory's a bit faulty, and this "study" actually appeared in the form of a textbook writer's opinions, please forgive me. The adage is one we follow religiously; my photos and computer games proudly take their places beside my wife's textile studio and the kids' chess sets.

Once in a while, though, lacemaking loses its charm and you'd like to research a new hobby or meet a fellow hobbyist. On those days, visit the Interests channel (shown in Figure 9-1) where interests and hobbies await you. Select from the channel's eight departments to explore your favorite interest.

Figure 9-1: Widen your horizons through the myriad pastimes awaiting you in the Interests channel.

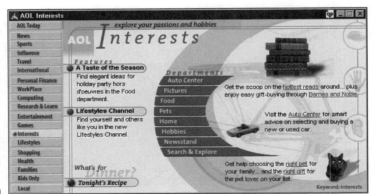

If you find yourself in a cooking rut, you may find a welcome lift in Interests. A button labeled Tonight's Recipe takes you to the Food department, where you can find a suggestion for this evening's dinner or browse through the recipe folders until you find a dish you like.

Auto Center Department (Keyword Autocenter)

Whether you're thinking about a new car purchase this season or you find all cars fascinating, you can find a wealth of information in the AutoCenter department. Read about new cars, browse classified ads for used vehicles, and share your love of automobiles (or motorcycles) in Car and Driver or Wheels.

Pictures Department (Keyword Pictures)

Explore traditional photography, digital photos, and video in the Pictures department. Pictures contains information for beginners as well as serious amateurs. Even professionals may be interested in the Photography Forum's Buy & Sell section. After all, you can never own too many camera bodies or interchangeable lenses!

If you're just beginning your photography journey, start with Popular Photography or the Photography Forum. Both areas contain hints and tips for beginners as well as more advanced topics. These areas also contain information on digital photography, in case your new digital camera and your computer long to know each other a little better.

Food Department (Keyword Food)

Humans don't survive long without food, but some of us have taken culinary interest to an art in itself. The Food department is your destination for those times when you don't know what to fix from the leftovers in the 'fridge, you have friends coming for dinner tomorrow night and you're at a loss, or you'd like to explore different ways of eating.

The Food department gives you recipes, informational articles, and tips on a whole host of food-related topics. For that special dinner, try the Electronic Gourmet Guide's vast collection of recipes from around the world. For general, everyday types of dishes, look in either the Cooking Club or Woman's Day Cooking. Both forums do a great job assembling meals from easy-to-find ingredients.

Pets Department (Keyword Pets)

Sharing your home with a furry roommate brings its own set of challenges and joys. Whether your friend is a dog, cat, gerbil, mongoose, or tarantula, concerns abound. Is your pet getting the right food? What signs of sickness do you look for? How do you redirect those less-than-desirable behaviors?

Find answers to these questions and more in the Pets department. In addition, you may meet and fall in love with a whole new section of the animal kingdom. Use the links on the main Pets window to read the latest Pet Connection article, browse the Pet Web site of the Week, or locate useful supplies or that perfect gift for Fido.

Home Department (Keyword Home)

More than its life as a structure, *home* evokes feelings of warmth, security, and brightness. America Online's Home department gives you the tools you need to create your own haven. Take a peek at how to transform your house for each season and enhance your home's coziness with decorating tips, home improvement instructions, and craft and gardening projects.

If you enjoy traditional home hobbies, such as woodworking, sewing, quilting, or gardening, you can find these areas in Home. Whip up a new drapery treatment, create furnishings and decorations in your workshop, or design new landscaping.

Hobbies Department (Keyword Hobbies)

Read reviews of new books on the market, find out who located that antique whatzit you've been looking for everywhere, or meet fellow star gazers in Astronomy. No matter whether you enjoy creating items from scratch, rebuilding cars for fun, or collecting yesterday's toys, the Hobbies department leads to pastimes online. Check out this department to brush up on an old hobby, maintain your skill level in an interest you currently enjoy, or research a new hobby or two for the winter.

Newsstand Department (Keyword Newsstand)

Does your favorite hobby or interest magazine have an area on America Online? Use the Newsstand department to find out. Newsstand links you to the forums maintained by publications like *Boating Online, Cycle World,* and *Stereo Review.*

Search & Explore Department (Keyword Interests Search)

Use the Search & Explore department to locate some of the best portions of the Interests channel. Search for specific articles online that pertain to your interest or look at the channel's contents in alphabetical order. The Best of AOL Interests button gives you a list of some of the Interests channel's favorite spots — to find your own favorites, however, you may want to cruise through the other departments and see what you find. For more information on using the Search & Explore department, see the Search section at the beginning of this *AOL Channels For Dummies* minibook.

Chapter 10

International Channel
(Keyword International)

Despite what I learned during my southern Indiana childhood, the world is made up of more than the United States — why, there's a whole world more! Africa, Asia, Australia, Europe, North America, and South America all await you. Of course, all that travel either takes big bucks or lots of frequent flier miles. If you're a little low on both but still want to find out how the rest of the world lives, the International channel is for you.

And this chapter is your native guide to the wild and woolly international world. It starts off with a quick look at the International channel and then points you toward some of the coolest content online. Whether you want a photograph of an Uzbekistan market or feel like perusing the British version of America Online, you won't find a better spot to start the quest.

When you're ready to join the International channel's jet set, sign on to the system and select the International channel as your destination. Shortly after boarding, the in-flight menu in Figure 10-1 pops up, offering you a variety of pleasant destinations.

Featured areas   HotMap

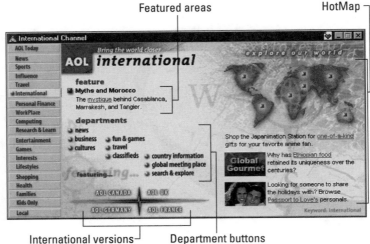

Figure 10-1: The International channel is your online window to the world.

International versions   Department buttons

Prominently displayed on the right side of the window is the *HotMap*, a term I made up myself. The HotMap's six pulsating buttons (one for each continent on the map) are your main links into the International area. They lead to windows filled with Web links, discussion boards, chat areas, and other information about the continent you clicked. Both to the left and beneath the HotMap are featured areas of the International channel. These change frequently, so don't fret if your areas look different from the ones in the figure.

Opposite the HotMap are the channel's department buttons. Beneath them are the most distinctive offerings in the entire channel: links to America Online's various International versions for Canada, France, Germany, and the United Kingdom.

To truly experience the world of America Online, try using the special international AOL client software. Download it for free from the AOL Germany or AOL France area (alas, you won't find a direct keyword to get you there), install it on your computer, and sign on as our international members do. The software cohabits just fine with your United States America Online program.

News Department (Keyword Intl News)

Nothing keeps you up-to-date on another country like reading its news. A country's culture, concerns, biases, and beauty all emerge from the pages of its news articles. Whether you want to improve your knowledge of a specific country, maintain your knowledge of a nation you miss desperately, or find out about the world in general, the International channel's News department provides the means. Use the sections listed here for business travel, international newspapers (many in languages other than English), and weather around the world.

Drop into the International News chat room to discuss late-breaking stories from distant shores. You'll find it under the Chat button in the News department window. Or post your views in the International News message boards, located under the Message Boards button.

Business Department (Keyword Intl Business)

Before you pack your bags for an international business trip, take a peek at the International channel's Business department. Find essential business etiquette for your destination country; taking the time to know what's proper may save your business transaction. Check current currency exchange rates; a poor rate may change the amount of cash you plan to carry.

If you invest internationally, you want to know the status of the economy in particular countries. Find information in the Business department that discusses global investments as well as international business news.

Cultures Department (Keyword Intl Cultures)

Foods and traditions beloved in one country are often taboo in another. Pastimes and sports that delight one nation bore or astonish another. Differences such as these carve a country's niche in the world and help to develop each country's uniqueness — that special something that we call culture.

America Online devotes an entire department to cultures around the world. Here you can delve into a culture different from your own, or research your family's cultural heritage. Use this department to find a place where you fit, whether the country you research shows up in your ancestral line or you recognize a new spiritual and ideological home.

Fun & Games Department (Keyword Intl Fun)

Quick! Think of your favorite online games. Name That Flag? Foreign Language Trivia? No? How about international trivia games like Trivia Info in French or Tiger Trivia in German? If none of these come to mind, you're missing some of the most unusual games on America Online. In these games, along with the other sections listed in the Fun & Games department, you can practice a foreign language, find out about leisure time events worldwide — such as films and music — or meet an international pen pal.

The next time you find yourself online with a few unscheduled moments to spare, give the International channel's Fun & Games department a try. You may discover a whole new way to play.

Travel Department (Keyword Intl Travel)

Ready to pack your passport and board the plane for exciting destinations? Before you pack your laptop — maybe even before you book your flight — sign on to America Online and check out the International channel's Travel department. You can find information on possible travel destinations, tips to help you plan (and pack) wisely, and ideas on what to see while you're there.

If your budget dictates vicarious travel, look in Tales from Road Warriors for some interesting travel stories. In addition, Your Travel Memories holds downloadable travel photos of exotic places.

Classifieds Department (Menu Access Only)

Looking for an international bed & breakfast, an opportunity to study abroad, or a job somewhere outside the United States? Does your company need workers from outside the United States or Canada? You may find what you're looking for in the Classifieds department. Here AOL members post ads for business, travel, study, employment, real estate, and collectibles. Oh — you also may find some international personal ads in this area.

Country Information Department (Menu Access Only)

Research countries of the world continent-by-continent. The Country Information department provides the same information as the International channel's HotMap; if you'd rather open folders than click dots, this is the department to use. Select any continent from the item list (the Middle East has been lifted out of Asia and given its own folder). The only exception is Antarctica. Because you find neither people nor culture in Antarctica, the America Online International folks left it out of the continent listing. I hope you don't mind.

Global Meeting Place (Keyword Global Meeting Place)

Where do you go online for a rousing international chat session? How do you locate an international pen pal? If you're studying a particular culture, such as British or German, how do you meet people from those countries?

America Online provides the answer to those questions in the form of the Global Meeting Place. This department links you to chats in languages other than English, members' family immigration stories, and international lifestyle and people areas. Don't be shy — drop into an international chat and say hello . . . or bonjour . . . or Guten Tag.

Search & Explore Department (Keyword Intl Explore)

Find out what gems await you in the International channel by taking a trip to the Search and Explore department. Use the A-Z International Channel Guide for an alphabetical overview of the channel's contents; although it looks exhaustive when you scroll through it, the guide doesn't contain each country by name or individual small areas under the larger keywords. You may be better off, in the International channel, to use the extensive departments list rather than the A-Z directory.

If you want an article on a specific international topic, use the search system located in the Search & Explore window. For particulars on how to use the system, as well as more Search & Explore information, see the Search section in Chapter 1 of this *AOL Channels For Dummies* minibook.

Chapter 11

Kids Only Channel (Keyword Kids Only)

"*W*hen I was a kid . . ." Do any words put as much fear and trepidation into a child as the threat of yet another parental tale of the good ol' days? (How about "We're disconnecting the cable TV"? That may come close.) Well, kids, here's something for you to lob back when Mom and Dad get into reminiscence mode: "Yeah, but you didn't have your own online hangout. We're talkin' *digital tree house* here."

America Online has set aside a channel just for kids and has marked it pretty plainly, too. Kids Only (shown in Figure 11-1) offers activities, forums, discussion areas, research sources, and interactive hangouts specially designed for kids ages 5 to 14. You can even find homework help. This chapter goes through all the Kids Only channel choices and buttons, giving you a pretty good overview of what's waiting for you.

Figure 11-1:
Full of fun and great information, the Kids Only channel is America Online's special spot for the 14- and-under crowd.

Most of the people who hang out in Kids Only are there to have a good time and learn stuff. Unfortunately, it seems like a few bad apples are always trying to spoil things for the rest of us. If you run into a person in a chat room who's being obnoxious, if someone sends you an Instant Message that makes you feel weird, or if *anyone* asks for your password, get help from a Kids Only guide. To do that, choose Go To⇨Keyword from the Channels window, type keyword **KO Help**, and press Enter. Follow the instructions on-screen, and help will arrive shortly!

Central Department (Keyword KO Central)

At the heart of the Kids Only channel, you find the Central department — a potpourri of great places to go. Think of Kids Only Central as a sampler of the best of the best that Kids Only has to offer. Whether you want to share your opinions about something or share your life with a pen pal, check the Weather or check your favorite comics, Central is the place to do it.

Chat Department (Keyword KO Chat)

Kids, like adults, *do* love to chat. Even though the topics may focus on some slightly different subjects than the other online chat areas, the Kids Only chat rooms make great places to meet and be met among other online kids. The Chat department houses the channel's special chat and discussion rooms, plus offers links to several other kid-centric chat areas.

When you first hop into the Chat department, you're accosted by the official first Kids Only Safety Tips screen. If you're new to online chatting (or if you never stopped to read the tips before), take a moment to look through these. They offer good ideas to stay safe online. (In fact, you may even want your parents to review them, too, so they won't worry about the time you spend chatting with your friends.)

In addition to the chats listed below, the Kids Only channel sponsors six regular chat rooms organized by topic. During the school year, these special chat rooms open up after school hours and close in the evening (so if you're home sick from school, no chatting for you — but you should be in bed anyway!). During the summertime, the rooms run most of the day, so when it rains, you may want to drop in for some online talking time. Specially trained Kids Only staff members hang out in the rooms to keep the chats moving and on-topic.

You can easily pick out Kids Only staff members, because their screen names always begin with KO, for Kids Only. If you have a question or problem, always feel free to ask a Kids Only staffer — they want to hear from you!

Clubs Department (Keyword KO Clubs)

Come one, come all! Join a club and have a ball! (Sorry, no more poetry. I promise.) Taking its place as one of the best places to have fun and meet new people in the whole Kids Only channel, the Clubs department gives you a place to follow your interests and find cool friends in the process. Just pick your favorite hobbies (or a hobby you always wanted to try), find the club that matches them, and join in the fun!

Create Department (Keyword KO Create)

Expand your creativity in the Create department, the Kids Only channel's answer to arts, crafts, theatre, and writing all rolled into one. Try your hand at drawing in the Big 'Fridge, check out some cool comics in Wanna Be in Comics?, or show off your wordsmithing talents in Blackberry Creek. Wherever you go, the best and brightest minds in all of Kids Only are waiting to meet you.

Games Department (Keyword KO Games)

Games, I firmly believe, are the only reason computers exist. Well, games and America Online access — but that's strictly it. Everything else is just icing on the digital cake. The Kids Only Games department takes this idea and runs with it, proving beyond any doubt that the best things in life explode, fly, drive fast, or make peculiar *boinging* sounds.

The Games department offers so many diversions that you may find it hard to stay focused long enough to write this paragraph. (Whoops, sorry — it's now tomorrow. I got a bit sidetracked, but I promise to finish this section without getting lost again. Really.) Take your brain for an entertaining and even *educational* (remind mom and dad about that one frequently) spin through some of the most entertaining games, puzzles, and contests anywhere in the online world.

Homework Help Department (Keyword KO HH)

Stuck on that geometry assignment? Need a little push to get through an English paper? When homework closes in around you, leaving you more than a bit frustrated and forlorn, turn to the Kids Only Homework Help department for the energy and tips that help you over the hump (and, more importantly, open up time to spend in the Chat and Clubs departments with your friends).

The folks you find waiting in Ask a Teacher *won't* do your assignments for you, no matter how much you beg and whine. They *do* offer all the help they can, and go to great lengths to make sure you find the resources you need. Putting the pieces together, though, is still your job.

Shows & Stars Department (Keyword KO SS)

Whether you love cartoons or comics, the Shows & Stars department brings everything you want to know about your favorite, well, shows and stars right to your screen. Take the time to dig beneath the surface of areas like Kids WB and Nickelodeon because lots of cool stuff hides away in there. You never know exactly what (or who) you may find!

Sports Department (Keyword KO Sports)

Play ball — or whatever other sport activity you enjoy — in the Kids Only channel's nod to the action-packed world of sports. In addition to all its regular sports coverage, the Sports department profiles well-known athletes, giving you some insight into what they like, how they started out, and what they do to stay on top of their sport. Uncover new tidbits about your favorite sports stars and swap notes about the sports you love right here, in the Sports department.

Web Department (Keyword KO Web)

The Web (even apart from its fairly eerie name) sometimes sends stout adults into fright-filled spasms. Of course, kids aren't the least bit fazed by little things like new technology, so the Kids Only Web department focuses on getting around the Web and finding new places to visit instead of spending a lot of time explaining how the whole thing works.

If, despite being a member of the techno-literate younger set, you need some information on how the Web actually works, don't worry — I won't tell a soul. Find out everything you need to know about the Web in Chapter 14 of the main book (not of this minibook!).

Chapter 12

Lifestyles Channel (Keyword Lifestyles)

● ●

*H*ow do you show the world who you really are? What parts come together to make you unique? Your beliefs, ethnic background, and stage of life all play a part. Celebrate your uniqueness in the Lifestyles channel, and find other members who believe, live, and dream in much the same way as you.

Divided into nine departments (including the mandatory Search & Explore department), Lifestyles helps you connect with people who share your background, your dreams, and your views of the world. And if you've found something about yourself that you'd like to change, the channel also includes a Self Improvement department to support you along the way. Don't be shy — select an interesting-looking department, hop right in, and explore a facet of Lifestyles.

Wandering through the Lifestyles channel window (Figure 12-1) doesn't take much out of you at all. In fact, the Lifestyles window is pretty straightforward. Centered in the window are the aforementioned department buttons, leading you straight to the content you seek. Surrounding the department buttons on either side are the featured areas for this particular moment in life. Because they change often, don't stress if your window isn't emblazoned with the same pictures as the figure.

Figure 12-1: Find out, observe, explore, and connect in the Lifestyles channel.

Self Improvement Department (Keyword Self Improvement)

An important anniversary rolls around, you pass one of life's milestones, and you wake up one morning deciding that you, or something about you, could be better. The Self Improvement department helps you in your quest for change, whether you want to drop a few pounds, tone your voluntary muscle groups, or connect with somebody who understands.

If you need to find a support group or support information *right now,* click Having a Crisis or use keyword PEN to see the list of support groups and chats available through the Personal Empowerment Network. You also may check under Online Psych's Community lists at keyword **Online Psych**. Online Psych lists forums on topics like sleep disorders, suicide prevention, depression, and anxiety.

Ages & Stages Department (Keyword Ages&Stages)

Drop into Ages & Stages for age-appropriate fun, whether you're 13, 23, 43, or 63 and beyond. Select a forum to find people like you — check the Knot for wedding advice, the Hub for 20-something humor, or Baby Boomers to find other adults who remember when. You can find a community or two that meets your needs, no matter which stage you currently occupy.

Beliefs Department (Keyword Religion)

Your belief system dictates your lifestyle. Dip into the Beliefs department when you could use a little encouragement, or you want to know a bit more about others' belief systems. Beliefs lists all the major world religions, plus a few extras like Numerology. If you don't see your particular belief brand listed, try the World Religions or Spiritual Mosaic buttons along the side of the window.

To access several of the beliefs areas quickly, including some topical Web sites, use the buttons along the right side of the window. The Christianity, Judaism, World Beliefs, Spiritual Mosaic, and Ethics & Values buttons take you to their featured areas in a flash.

Ethnicity Department (Keyword Ethnicity)

Where does your family originate? Did they journey across the seas to come to North America at some point, or did they begin already planted on North American soil? Which country's traditions have you adopted as your own, either through your family or because of interest? Connect with others who share your traditions and your background when you visit the Ethnicity department.

The department lists ethnic groups from practically all over the world, with the possible exception of Antarctica. Despite all their good intentions, however, America Online missed including at least one important international ethnic community in the listing: the Irish. Use keyword **Irish Heritage** to dig up information about the Irish in America and the country of Ireland (and be sure to point out the inequities of being forgotten by the Ethnicity department).

Women's Network Department (Keyword Womens Network)

Discuss women's issues and loves in the Women's Network department. Here you can relax, drop into the Talk Women chat room, and meet other women who think like you do. Or explore how women feel about relationships and family in two of the department's sections. Whichever section you decide to explore first, you can find plenty to engage your mind and emotions in the Women's Network.

Romance Department (Keyword Romance)

A little wine, a gourmet meal for two, and a glowing fire in the fireplace — with soft music wafting through the air. Who wouldn't be in heaven? Indulge your romantic fantasies (and maybe find someone to share them with) in the Romance department.

Before you jump in with both feet in a search for Mr. or Ms. Wonderful, be sure to read the Dos and Don'ts Online article, along with Safety Tips. Both are designed to keep you and your friends safe while online. Then use any of the buttons labeled Personals, Chat, or Shop to go right to the action. Or, if you're the cautious type, find an interesting forum in the list and explore.

Gay & Lesbian Department (Keyword Gay)

Find lots of information and many kindred spirits in the Gay & Lesbian department. Visit France's New Attitudes area, read about the AIDS Quilt Names Project, or check out the cities most open to gay travelers. You can also find a couple of well-developed areas in OnQ and PlanetOut.

Communities Department (Keyword Communities)

Jump right into the community spirit with the Communities department. Although each of these windows is available from the other department windows, you can skip the departments and visit the community topic of your choice. From Ages & Stages to Self Improvement, they're all here.

Search & Explore Department (Keyword Lifestyles Search)

Looking for something in Lifestyles, and you can't quite put your finger on it? Search & Explore helps you find what you need. Either search by topic for articles anywhere in Lifestyles or check the A - Z Channel Guide to be sure you haven't missed anything. To see an overview of the Lifestyles channel, try the Lifestyles slide show.

For more information on using the Search & Explore features, see the Search section in Chapter 1 of this minibook.

Chapter 13

Local Channel
(Keyword Digital City)

*A*ccording to the wise old sage (who probably moonlights at the automobile club), "Getting there is half the fun." Thanks to the cool stuff in America Online's Local channel, though, you may think that *not* getting there is almost *all* the fun.

Local is Digital City in disguise (shown in Figure 13-1). Digital City, in turn, is an area that chaperons you through a slew of cities all over the United States. Big cities, small towns, and quaint burgs await your virtual visit. Each town offers the best in tourist information, city maps, travel tips, and hot sightseeing spots, all available without leaving the comfort of your home. Who could want more?

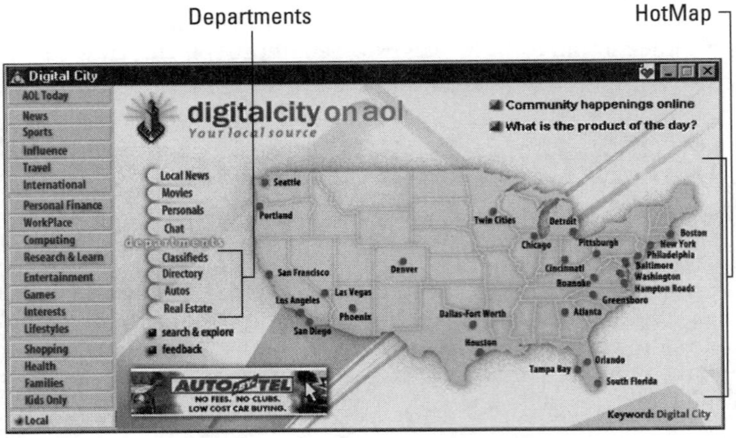

Departments   HotMap

Figure 13-1: Take an online vacation with Digital City, the Local channel's star attraction.

Occupying most of the window is the *HotMap,* my own highly technical term for the clickable U.S. map image. To the left of that are the Digital City departments, with their links to local news, movies, the search area, and still more.

To visit one of the cities on the HotMap, click its red button. A window opens, inviting you to explore that city's news, entertainment, people, sports, travel, and communities. You can read current news articles, find out which movies are playing in your city, read personal ads, or drop into a city's chat room by clicking any of the items above the departments list.

None of the departments in the Local Channel includes its own keywords, so you must use the on-screen buttons. Sorry — such is life in the Local lane.

Classifieds Department

Trying to find a pedal car from the '50s, a job halfway across the country, or an apartment to rent? You may just find what you want in the Classifieds department. Select a city and see what its classifieds contain. Some of the cities offer general classifieds entries, while others give information under headings like Suburban Shopping.

Directory Department

Looking for someone? The Digital City Directory may just have who you're looking for. Click the HotMap button that corresponds to the person's (or business') city, click Continue if the computer returns the correct city and state, and then select either Find a Business or Find a Person. Enter the name or names, click Find, and you're on your way.

Autos Department

If you live near one of the nation's larger cities, such as Atlanta or Washington D.C., and you're in the market for a new car, the Digital City AutoGuide could save you a lot of work. Access car dealerships' Web sites, read about the new cars from manufacturers' Web sites, and get a quote from Auto-by-Tel, all in one place. Digital City's AutoGuide makes that new car purchase almost a pleasant experience.

Real Estate Department

Before you pull up stakes and travel halfway across the country for a new job, use Digital City's Real Estate department to help you locate that perfect house or rental. The Real Estate department contains listings for many cities; choose your destination and then search the database to find a home listing, look up possible rentals, or determine your purchasing power.

Chapter 14

News Channel
(Keyword News)

Keeping up with the news gets harder all the time — so much to think about, so many things vying for your attention, and so little time to pursue mundane trivialities like staying informed. What's a hoping-to-be-informed person of the '90s to do? Check out the America Online News channel — that's what.

The News channel (displayed in Figure 14-1) promises quick and timely stories, delivered right to your screen. This area covers everything from headlines on the Middle East to late-breaking scores in the world of cricket. You can even use a search function to pick and choose from the news of the day and keep up on the stories important to you.

Headlines

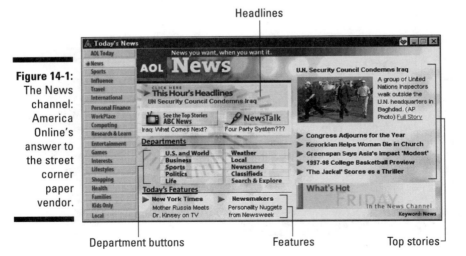

Figure 14-1:
The News channel:
America
Online's
answer to
the street
corner
paper
vendor.

Department buttons   Features   Top stories

For its size, the News channel window packs quite an informational wallop. Scrolling through the upper left side of the window are the hour's News Headlines. Click a particular headline or anywhere in the Headline area for a window with capsule versions of the moment's top stories. Just below that are the current ABC News slide show story and a link to the news chat area (also known as The Land Where Arguments Happen). Further down you find the Department buttons, which lead to the various news detail areas. For more about each department, flip through the listings below. Rounding out the window are the Features (along the very bottom) and the top stories (along the right side). To dive into any of these, click the little button next to the story that interests you.

U.S. and World Department (Keyword Usworld)

U.S. and world headlines are the first thing you see in Today's News. This news is the top of the top — the best national and world news from the Reuters wire. The stories in here are, for the most part, what's known as *hard news* — violent storms, political maneuverings, international incidents, and the discovery of letters predating the birth of Christ stashed in a van behind some Chicago post office. In short, it's front page stuff. New stories are added every hour or so, depending on how the news day is going. If you're a serious newshound, checking this area every couple of hours should keep you on top of all major world developments.

Business Department (Keyword Business News)

If holding a thumb to the pulse of business sounds like your kind of fun, then the Business department is definitely the place for you. (Of course, you *may* need to get out a little more, but that's something to think about later.)

The Business department tackles business from all angles, offering a high-level summary of current goings-on, plus detailed stories covering the economy, technology, international business, the financial markets, industry notes, and consumer briefs. To truly inundate you with information, you can even find a business newsstand option that unleashes the online versions of your favorite business magazines (like *Inc.* and *BusinessWeek*).

Sports News Department (Keyword Sportnews)

Track your favorite games, teams, and players with stories from around the world in America Online's Sports News department.

Is news of the sporting scene important? Take a look at the Sports News department and then tell me what you think. With a slew of main categories, plus the wonderful More Sports option, you find more news here than any three fanatics could want. All the major sports (professional baseball and basketball, college basketball and football, and so on) have their own categories, but my favorite has to be More Sports. Where else can you follow badminton (yes, it *is* spelled correctly), cricket, handball, and luge from the same news window?

Politics Department (Keyword Politics)

Nothing makes headlines quite like the political process. Between new legislation, research announcements, and old-fashioned dirty laundry, the political news machine never stops running. To plug into this constant stream of Beltway tidbits, march over here. You can find the latest scoop on the White House, Congress, the judiciary, and almost anyone (and sometimes *anything*) else that draws a government paycheck and lives in Washington, D.C.

Life Department (Keyword Lifenews)

Fulfill your wildest desire to know more about everything that's *almost* news (including Tinseltown, which thinks that this stuff is news but doesn't always make the grade) with the Life department. One click on the Life department button and you're knee-deep in the top movie, music, and theatre stories, many straight from the industry's primary source of truth and public relations, *Variety,* plus a selection of the best people-oriented tales rolling through the news wire.

Topics in here include the entertainment industry, online world, art, culture, film, theatre, music, television — well, the list goes on and on, as you can tell by now. When you need to take a break from the stressful stories pouncing on you elsewhere in the News channel, take a break here. It really does help — I promise.

Weather Department (Keyword Weather)

You won't find a better way to track the weather than with the Weather News area. Whether you're trying to figure out what to pack for your trip, or wondering if it will rain on your way to work, Weather News has you covered.

The department offers a variety of forecasts, reports, and satellite images. Travelers can use the U.S. Cities Forecast to make doubly sure that they take the wrong clothes. You can even find a Weather Classroom area dedicated to the study of weather and weather forecasters. Finally, for you hard-core weather aficionados, this department contains a Weather Mall area to, well, buy weather-related stuff at (every time I see that entry, all I can think of is *dehydrated boxed rain* and *lightning-in-a-can*).

Local Department (Keyword Local News)

Right now, the Local News department falls under the category of *tries hard but still fails*. The concept is good — an area that lets you zero in on the latest happenings in your little corner of the world — but the execution and content still leave a bit to be desired. As time goes on, I expect this area to get significantly better, but for now, keep your expectations low and you won't be disappointed.

Newsstand Department (Button Access Only)

Welcome to the world of magazines with windows instead of covers, with e-mail addresses instead of phone numbers, and with interactive chat areas instead of letters to the editor. This world is the Newsstand department, one of the News channel's most interesting areas.

When I wrote this, the list of publications here seemed, well, short. The new channels were just going into effect, though, so the odds are high that more magazines will populate the digital racks by the time you read this. For now, though, be sure to check out Slate (keyword **Slate**), one of the best examples of what an online publication can be. Of course, the other publications, like Newsweek (keyword **Newsweek**) and the New York Times (keyword **Times**) aren't anything to shake a mouse at, either.

Classifieds Department (Keyword Classifieds)

What would a news section be without the classified ads? (Hmm . . . is this a trick question? Will this be on the final exam?) Well, for one thing, it wouldn't be America Online's News channel, because the Classifieds department is a proud member of the news team.

Whether your interests encompass antiques, business, electronics, home and garden, music, tickets, or travel, you can find something in the Classifieds department. Advertise your goods for free or just browse around and see what other people want to unload. Either way, the Classifieds department offers fun and good deals for all.

News Search & Explore (Menu Access Only)

If you're not a browser (and with the volume of stuff in America Online's news area, I can hardly blame you), try the News Search feature. News Search thumbs through stories from the other Today's News sections, helping you zero in on stories *you* find interesting, not the ones that the helpful wire service editors chose for you.

To use the service, click the Search & Explore button on the News channel window, then, when the News Search & Explore window appears, click the Search button. (Of course, you can short-circuit the whole process by just using keyword **Newssearch**.) This brings up the News Search dialog box. Type a few words that describe the kind of stories you're looking for and then press Enter or click List Articles to see what's out there. After a few moments, the window fills with story headlines that contain the word or phrase you're looking for.

- ✔ If the system can't find any stories that match your search, try searching for something more general (*music* instead of *new rock groups,* for example).

- ✔ Likewise, if you're suddenly the proud owner of hundreds of matches, narrow your search terms (*small business* instead of *business*) to cull the reports that you really don't want. Also, try limiting your options with the special search commands (see Table 14-1 for more details).

- ✔ To make a more detailed search, try using the tools AND, OR, and NOT. Table 14-1 shows you how.

Table 14-1	Special News Search Commands	
Command	*Example*	*Description*
AND	government *and* waste	Links two words or phrases together; finds only articles that contain *both* examples.
NOT	software *not* buggy	Finds only articles that contain the first word or phrase and do not contain the second. Prevents unwanted matches (and occasionally provides moments of humor).
OR	Windows *or* Macintosh	Finds articles that contain either example *or* both of them.

Chapter 15

Personal Finance Channel (Keyword Personal Finance)

M oney makes the world go around. (Well, I think some laws of physics are involved, too, but you get the idea.) It also keeps you up at night, makes you work 50 hours a week, and leaves you feeling vaguely defeated after paying the month's bills.

Suppose — just suppose for a moment — that you had control over your money. Pretty neat thought, eh? That's what the Personal Finance channel is all about. It covers saving, investing, dealing with credit, owning a home, and lots of other stuff. You can find help for tuning your portfolio and for finding out what exactly a portfolio is and whether or not you can take it out in the rain.

The channel window, displayed in Figure 15-1, is your doorway to the online world of personal finance. The prominently displayed *stock market indexes* welcome you to the channel. In addition to displaying the current value of these popular investment barometers, the index names are also links to high-low-close performance charts covering the last 30 days. The area also includes buttons for America Online's popular Quotes and Portfolios systems.

Below the stock area, you find the department buttons, which lead to Personal Finance's 10 focus areas. Right under the departments are buttons for the four financial centers. Look there for online banking, brokerage, insurance, and mutual fund information. Finally, on the right side of the channel window are the featured areas. These change daily, so don't worry if your screen shows buttons different from the ones in the figure.

Stock market indexes

Featured areas

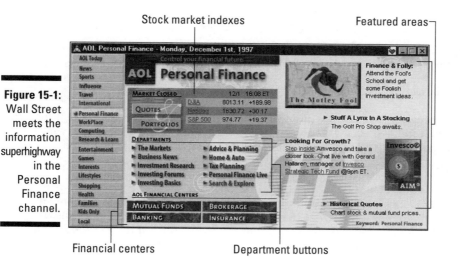

Figure 15-1:
Wall Street
meets the
information
superhighway
in the
Personal
Finance
channel.

Financial centers

Department buttons

Opinions and Information Are Different

Before wading too deeply into the Personal Finance channel, I want to reinforce something that you probably already know: Opinions are not information, and vice versa. You may not think that this is a groundbreaking statement, but it's important to keep in mind in the Personal Finance channel.

The forums and services in the Personal Finance channel contain a lot of cold, hard data: financial calculations, sales reports, stock price fluctuations, and company histories. They also harbor many warm, soft opinions floating around in the discussion areas. To get the most out of the Personal Finance areas (and not lose a bunch of money on wacky investments), you need to carefully discern the difference between the two. Suppose someone posts a message saying, "You're an idiot if you don't buy SciPhone Video and Tanning because it's going through the roof." That is an *opinion.* If you read a news story that says SciPhone Video and Tanning just won a huge contract to put hundreds of their patented combination satellite TV/video conferencing/pay phone/tanning booths into the Pentagon, that's *information.*

My advice to you is simple: Don't let someone else decide on your investments for you. Everyone has a right to an opinion — just don't blindly adopt someone else's as your own.

If You Meet Buddha in the Discussion Board, Look for a Shark Fin under His Suit

A long time ago, a wise and learned person taught you an important lesson: Don't believe everything you read. Before you get too carried away in the Personal Finance channel, please write down that lesson in big letters and tape it across the top of your monitor.

Don't get me wrong — Personal Finance contains some wonderful places. Areas like Vanguard Online (keyword **Vanguard**) and Fidelity Online Investments Center (keyword **Fidelity**) clearly lay out the facts and perils of investing. Remember, however, that not everything in the Personal Finance channel is like that.

Keep a particularly tight grip on your wallet while perusing the investment discussion boards throughout the Personal Finance channel. Most of the messages in there are from small investors like yourself — but some sharks lurk in those waters, too. It's your money, so rely on *your* research and intuition.

If you're new to investing, do the smart thing: Remember the disclaimers in the Personal Finance areas. Nearly all the services have them. They say things like *don't take this as professional advice* and *watch who you give your private information to* and *please oh please oh please don't send money to* **anyone** *without reading the full prospectus.*

If you're really, really new to investing, do your money a favor and buy copies of *Personal Finance For Dummies* and *Mutual Funds For Dummies,* both published by IDG Books Worldwide, Inc. The author, Eric Tyson, did such a good job on both of them that they even made sense to me (and that's saying a lot).

Quotes (Keyword Quotes)

Many years ago, having a brass-and-glass ticker-tape machine busily spewing forth a constant stream of letters and numbers in your office was a tangible sign of success. Today, society measures success differently (and it's a darn good thing, too, because those ticker-tape machines were noisy). Late-breaking stock market news isn't the sole domain of the rich and powerful any more. Instead, this information is freely available to everyone on America Online through the Quotes system.

To check the current price (well, actually the *mostly* current price, because data in the Quote system is delayed about 20 minutes) of a particular stock, just put the stock's symbol into the Enter Symbol box, then click Get Quote. In just a moment, America Online coughs up the information on your favorite stock, just like Figure 15-2.

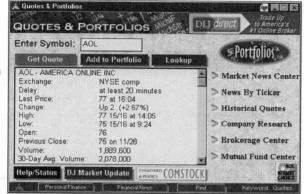

Figure 15-2: Let's take a peek at America Online and see how it's doing.

 If you don't know the stock's ticker symbol, click the Lookup button. When the Search Symbols window appears, put in the first part of the company's name, then click Search By Company. America Online responds with a list of matching companies and their stock ticker symbols. If you have a ticker symbol and want to know what company it belongs to, repeat the same process, but enter the ticker symbol instead of the company name, and then click Search By Symbol.

Portfolios (Keyword Portfolios)

Good investors don't leave all their financial eggs in one basket (and even if they do, you can bet the basket lives in a bomb-proof refrigerator). Because most investments are a mix of stocks from several different companies, keeping up with your holdings on a symbol-by-symbol basis would take forever. You need a tool that monitors your whole stock portfolio at once — and, as luck would have it, America Online provides one in its Portfolios system.

This system helps you manage your stocks by grouping them into one or more portfolios and displaying a single window that gives you an at-a-glance summary of how everything is performing. Because you are building the portfolios, everything about them is up to you. Create them according to industry, investment risk, or whatever other way you want.

For details of building and managing your stock portfolio with the Portfolios tool, flip to Chapter 12 of the main book (not of this minibook).

The Markets Department (Keyword MNC)

Look into The Markets department when you need either current numbers or trend graphs for stocks, bonds, currencies, or futures. Data for the major United States economic indicators, like the Gross Domestic Product (GDP) and the Consumer Price Index (CPI) live in here too, along with current information and daily trend lines for international stock indexes such as the Japanese Nikkei, German DAX, and the British TFSE.

For information on stock performance on a country-by-country basis around the world, check the list box in the lower right corner of The Markets department. If you're new and need help with some financial terms, try the Look Up Market Terms option. It leads you to the Wall Street Words area (keyword **WSW**), which is guaranteed to make your store of investment terms take off overnight. (I don't suppose I could buy a few shares in your vocabulary before you try out that area, could I? No, I guess that would be insider trading.)

Business News Department (Keyword Business News)

Put your finger to the pulse of the world's business headlines with the Personal Finance channel's Business News department. This links you directly to the News channel's Business News area, offering up the latest tidbits in technology, the economy, the markets, and the international scene.

To focus on stories from a particular segment of industry, check out the Industry news area. The Newsstand deserves a special mention as well, thanks to its plentiful links to online versions of everything from *BusinessWeek* to the *New York Times*.

Investment Research (Keyword Company Research)

Many people think that making money with investments is a matter of luck, a case of being in the right place at the right time with the right type of zebra on the right color leash during the right phase of the moon. Even though the Fates do play a role in stock market success, the people who consistently win at the money game do it through careful research.

The tools in the Investment Research department put a whole library of financial information at your fingertips (or at least at the tip of your mouse pointer). All the important corporate filings and financial statements, including the always-popular 10K and 10Q reports required by the Securities and Exchange Commission, live in here, as do historical quotes, company profiles, and detailed stock reports.

Investing Forums (Keyword Investing Forums)

Heard a hot tip about your favorite company? Want to argue the merits of one stock over another? Feel like venting about the performance of your mutual fund? For these and other communicative moments, turn to the Investing Forums, the community discussion areas of the Personal Finance channel.

The stock discussion boards are organized alphabetically by stock ticker symbol. Just browse through the board list, dive into the right letter, and find the folks talking about your favorite stock. Further down the list from the stock boards, you find the general investment discussion boards, plus areas for futures, mutual funds, stock index options, and trading strategies.

Remember that what you read in these areas are *opinions* that could be posted by *anyone*. Before pinning your life savings to some hot advice you discovered in here, be sure to read the sections "Opinions and Information Are Different" and "If You Meet Buddha in the Discussion Board, Look for a Shark Fin under His Suit" a few pages earlier in the Personal Finance section.

Investing Basics (Keyword Investing Basics)

Attention new investors: Your informational ship just came in! For a good introduction to the basics of making money with stocks, bonds, mutual funds, and other investments, carefully work through the eight Becoming an Investor steps in the Investing Basics department. They're free, they are insightful, and they won't try to sell you anything — which is more than you can say for many so-called investment managers out there.

Even though I mentioned it before, I'm going to say it again: Be *very* wary of whom you accept investment advice from, particularly if you find the tips in the discussion boards or broker areas. You worked hard for your investment dollars, so treat them with the care they deserve.

Advice & Planning (Keyword Advice & Planning)

Every stage in life comes with its own unique physical, emotional, and monetary challenges. Even though you just have to buck up and endure some of them (such as the teenage years), the right planning and advice promises to smooth the way during others. That's why the Advice & Planning department is here — to offer sage advice and an understanding shoulder just when you need it most.

Starting with the wooly world of being single, and carrying you on past retirement, the areas in the Advice & Planning department offer sound suggestions for managing your money at every step along life's way. Take a look at the tips for where you are right now, as well as the ones covering where you're headed in the coming years. You won't find a substitute for good planning — and a few ways to catch up if you discover that you started planning too late. Don't let money slip through your fingers!

Home & Auto (Keyword PF Home)

Measured by total dollars spent at one time, the two largest purchases most people make in their lives are their home and their car. (For the nerds of the world, of course, it's usually home and *computer,* but I digress.) The multithousand-dollar outlays demand special care and attention, but their complexity often leaves us utterly bewildered and at the mercy of a sharp-tongued sales rep.

To overcome the bewilderment and arm yourself for battle with the sales-people, turn to the Home & Auto department. Unlike your local retailer, Home & Auto doesn't stock tires, batteries, or tree-shaped pine-scented air fresheners (although, with America Online's move toward putting advertising everywhere, I'm sure it's only a matter of time), but it does offer the best in consumer information for the big buys of your life.

Apartments and home-buying both earn spots here, as do a variety of sources for solid automobile information. Because loans and insurance are usually must-have items as well, the department offers links for them too.

If you're in the market for a car, check out Edmund's Automotive (`http://www.edmunds.com`, or click its entry in the services list on the right side of the department window). Their information is free and correct — best of all, if you follow their instructions, you'll send waves of abject terror through your automobile salesman. (I used their service when I bought my last car, and, thanks solely to their information and suggestions, got an extra $2000 for my trade-in _and_ shaved several thousand dollars off the sticker price. It was almost a religious experience!)

Tax Planning (Keyword Tax)

Although some people would disagree with me, the word _tax_ really contains three letters and not four. That knowledge doesn't make its monetary bite any less painful, though. The only remedy for that is the advice awaiting you in the Personal Finance channel's Tax Planning department.

Rustle through the areas in the Tax Planning department for the latest tax news, forms, and planning tips, plus the best in tax-focused forums. Tax software is enshrined in its own special section, with support and discussion forums, as well as file libraries covering all of the major packages.

Personal Finance Live (Keyword PF Live)

Hear top experts in financial matters from all over the country in the privacy of your own computer in the Personal Finance Live department. These presentations bring you the latest tips in saving, investing, retirement, and tax planning. And, best of all, AOL doesn't charge you any extra for hearing these titans of the money world — it's a regular part of America Online!

Some events, like the Sage and Motley Fool chats, take place on a regular daily or weekly schedule, while others are special this-night-only happenings. Keep an eye on upcoming events by checking the schedules here and in your favorite chat areas. If you miss an event, dig around in the Transcripts area to see what transpired without you.

Search & Explore (Keyword PF Search)

The Personal Finance channel has so much stuff that you can't possibly look through all of it by hand. Your computer, though, makes short work of whatever searches you require, thanks to the Search & Explore department.

The Search & Explore window offers two different approaches to the department's information. On the left is the typical enter-something-to-look-for-it system, including controls that adjust how wide or narrow the search is. Use this part of the system when you want to search a broad cross-section of the areas in the Personal Finance channel.

Opposite the search area are the subject buttons. These offer to show you a thorough A-to-Z list of the areas in the Personal Finance channel, along with a Best of Personal Finance area, with selections of the neatest and most useful spots the channel offers.

Chapter 16

Research & Learn Channel (Keyword Research & Learn)

• •

*H*ere's a wild statistic for you from one of my favorite authors and information architects, Richard Saul Wurman: A single weekday edition of the *New York Times* contains more information in its pages than the average person in 17th-century England was exposed to during his or her *entire life* — and they didn't even have direct broadcast TV! Is it any wonder that people sometimes feel overwhelmed when trying to look up even the simplest informational ditty?

America Online created the Research & Learn channel as a tool to rescue you from the anxiety of not knowing where or how to uncover the information that you need. Its links include sites inside America Online and treasure troves of goodies on the Web. The channel covers all kinds of subjects, from business to health, and still finds room on its shelves to tackle the day-to-day needs for dictionaries, encyclopedias, and other standard reference books.

Looking relaxed and helpful, the Research & Learn channel window (shown in Figure 16-1) offers up its subject areas and references on the left side of the window. These choices sit atop the main content in the channel: the research areas you long to see. Opposite the window from the subject area buttons are the current featured areas, which change with Swiss watch–like regularity.

Subject areas   Featured areas

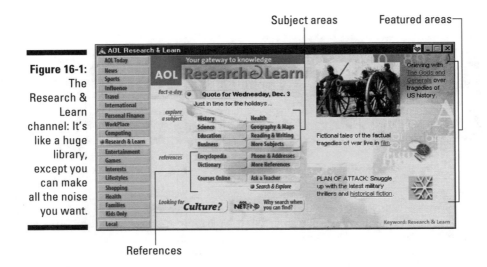

Figure 16-1:
The
Research &
Learn
channel: It's
like a huge
library,
except you
can make
all the noise
you want.

References

Looking at the Subjects

The subject area is the real heart of the Research & Learn channel. Beneath these areas are a horde of searchable databases, fact-filled Web sites, and unique information providers. Because they're free to use — they're included as part of your normal America Online access — then the sky (or at least your attention span, which in my case is the shorter measure) is the only limit to your research success.

Encyclopedia (Keyword Encyclopedias) and Dictionary (Keyword Collegiate)

Sometimes, you just need the basic facts — and you need them right *now*. If your research question isn't large, or if you're just starting out and need some general information to launch your quest in the right direction, turn to the Research & Learn channel's Encyclopedia area. Among the three online encyclopedias available to you through America Online, the odds are good of finding the information you need.

The channel also includes a link to the Merriam Webster online dictionary, a handy tool for resolving those online Scrabble squabbles in record time. Don't forget about the online thesaurus at keyword **Thesaurus**, either. I spend more time with that reference than with anything else on my bookshelf.

Phone & Addresses (Keyword Phonebook)

Keeping your personal address list and phone book current is a challenge for almost anyone. Unless your circle of friends is particularly limited, the odds are good that, thanks to moves, job changes, and the other vagaries of life, your stock of jotted-down addresses and phone numbers goes stale in short order. Of course, you often don't find out about the problem until it's absolutely vital for you to find that person, which helpfully throws a little more stress into your world.

Before giving up on the friend thing entirely and committing yourself to a life of solitary noncommunication, seek refuge in the Phone & Addresses section of the Research & Learn channel. This area provides links to online white and yellow pages, search pages that cover e-mail addresses and toll-free phone numbers, plus all kinds of other clever goodies like area code and zip code lookups.

More References (Keyword More References)

As if the rest of this channel weren't enough, the America Online research folks just couldn't resist the temptation to toss in a few more reference resources. They jammed all the stuff they could think of into the More References area, then sat back with pleased grins all around at a job well done.

Some of the items in here, like the dictionary and the encyclopedias, already appear elsewhere in the channel (they're repeated here to make them easier to find — or perhaps because somebody messed up and forgot to take them out). Others, like the online thesaurus (keyword **Thesaurus**) and the Web-based Robert's Rules of Order, are new to the Research & Learn channel.

Courses Online (Keyword Courses)

Want to expand your knowledge without leaving the house? Thinking about picking up a new skill or adding another college course? If that sounds like you, then check out the Courses Online area in the Research & Learn channel. This area links you to several online-based education options, including both enrichment courses and classes for college credit.

If you want computer classes, check out the Computing channel's Online Classroom department. It offers all kinds of great courses, many of which are *free* — yes, you heard it right — they're free.

Ask a Teacher (Keyword Ask-a-Teacher)

For lots of kids, getting help with a tough homework problem ranks right up there with finishing a collection of digital pets or earning a week of chocolate ice cream for dinner. You remember the feeling: It's late at night, the problem makes no sense at all, and your teacher wants it tomorrow (funny, but that's how I feel about this book).

America Online's homework help areas may be some of the system's best kept secrets. Regardless of the age level, your favorite students (or you, for that matter) can get a gentle push in the right direction toward solving those awful homework problems. The helpers in here don't just blurt out answers. Instead, they're careful to help students find the answers themselves.

Search & Explore Department (Keyword Research & Learn)

The Research & Learn channel sports the system's new super-search area in its Search & Explore department. In addition to the fill-in-the-blank search window, the department also offers an A-Z Channel Guide (which, like several other channel guides, seems a little short compared to the number of items listed in the channel's areas) and an online slide-show that sings (well, *speaks*) the praises of the channel for all to hear.

Chapter 17

Shopping Channel (Keyword Shopping)

*S*hopping is a drag. You leave your comfortable home, brave the wilds of modern transportation, and then walk around some glitzed-up store, following carefully marked paths just the right size for a thin 11-year-old. After bumping into innumerable displays and more than a few other shoppers, you clutch the prizes of your quest and head for the recycled cattle queues — pardon me, checkout lanes. After a certain amount of mooing time, you make your purchase and begin the trek homeward.

Online shopping is *nothing* like that. You don't have to mess around with crowded stores, pushy clerks, long lines, or wailing children (yours or anyone else's). Your goods arrive at the door of the comfortable home you didn't ever have to leave.

If this kind of stress-free shopping experience sounds interesting to you, America Online's Shopping channel is the place to go. This area has a variety of stores for your browsing and purchasing pleasure. Better still, many of the items for sale include online pictures to show you exactly what you're buying. You can even use a special classified advertisement section to help you clear out the old stuff and make room for the new. (Can life get better than this?)

Like an unusually good mall, the Shopping channel is laid out in an easy-to-navigate format, as Figure 17-1 shows. On the left side of the window are specialty areas — helpful destinations featuring shopping tips, ideas, and suggestions, all designed to make your shopping experience easier and more fun. Below these are the departments, where everything from apparel to zydeco CDs await you and your credit card. Finally, on the opposite side of the window, you find the Shopping channel's featured areas. These change often, much like the seasonal goody aisles at your favorite department store.

Figure 17-1:
The
Shopping
channel —
America
Online's
digital
shopping
experience.

Hot Savings (Keyword Hot Savings)

Everybody loves a bargain (particularly my wife, in whose heart the cheap bird merrily sings his "Cheap, cheap, buy it cheap" song). Apparently, the folks at America Online adore good deals as well, because they built the Hot Savings area specifically to highlight special prices. Drop in regularly to check the Deal of the Day, then browse through a bargain hunter's paradise of stores with the buttons on the Hot Savings window.

Shopping Services (Keyword Shopping Services)

Sometimes, finding the right gift isn't hard at all. Instead, the challenging parts of the process are finding the right store (especially for the more esoteric gift recipients on your shopping list) or, as in my case, simply remembering that you're supposed to buy something at all.

Whether your problem is the where or the when of shopping, the Shopping Services area is here to help. Among other things, the services contained in here help you track down shoppable malls, order gifts to be delivered on an emergency basis, and send you e-mail reminders of dates that are too important to risk missing (again).

The Mall (Keyword Shop Talk)

Even though this area is formally called the Mall, its keyword, **Shop Talk**, really says more about what goes on in here. The Mall is home to the Shopping channel's chat rooms and community bulletin boards — places for you to meet and be met, swap shopping tips, and rediscover stores and companies long forgotten.

If you're a serious shop-a-holic, sign up for one or both of the Shopping channel's newsletters. The Weekly Goods brings you an overview of what's happening in the channel's stores, while the Real Deal focuses on great bargains and cool sales. They're free, so why not sign up for both?

Shopping the Departments and the Stores

There's nothing like starting big — and in the Shopping channel, that means hitting the departments. With more than 100 stores out there, the departments contain such a diversity of product lines that you're likely to find just about anything you want or need to purchase. Table 17-1 lists the channel's departments, along with the keywords for each one (in case you don't feel like slogging through the Shopping channel window to get there).

Table 17-1	Shopping by the Departments
Department	**Keyword**
Apparel & Accessories	**Apparel Shop**
Auto & Travel	**Auto Shop**
Book, Music & Video	**Book & Music Shop**
Classifieds	**Classifieds**
Computer Hardware	**HW Shop**
Computer Software	**SW Shop**
Department Stores	**Department Stores**
Electronics & Photo	**Electronics Shop**
Flowers, Cards & Candy	**Flowers & Cards**
Gifts	**Gifts**
Gourmet Gifts	**Gourmet Gifts**
Home, Kitchen & Garden	**Home & Kitchen Shop**

(continued)

Table 17-1 (continued)	
Department	**Keyword**
Home Office	**Office Shop**
Sports & Fitness	**Sports Shop**
Toys & Collectibles	**Toy Shop**

Each department contains a number of stores that either cater to the department's focus area or offer a selection of related products that's part of a bigger mix. Don't be surprised to find some of the larger stores, such as J.C. Penney (keyword **Jcpenney**) or Hammacher Schlemmer (keyword **Hammacher Schlemmer**), listed in several departments. Most of the stores at these keywords are open to everyone, although some, like Shopper's Advantage (keyword **SA**), reserve the best deals for paying members.

For lack of a better place to put them, I included the America Online Classifieds in the shopping department list as well. Even though they're not technically one of the shopping departments, they are the home of some really great deals, provided you take the time to look. Shop carefully, though, and remember the old saying that if a deal looks too good to be true, it probably is!

Search & Explore Department (Button Access Only)

As of this writing, the Shopping channel still used the old Marketplace channel index for its search system. By the time you actually read this book, though, the programmers should have that little issue fixed. Assuming they make the search system work like it does in the other channels, flip to Chapter 1 of this minibook — *AOL Channels For Dummies* — and check out the search information there.

Chapter 18

Sports Channel (Keyword Sports)

*T*he smell of the engines, the roar of the crowds (or do I have that backwards?), that little *schussing* sound the skis make right before the announcer says "Oh, that had to hurt!" — the world of sports brings to life all kinds of sights, sounds, and medical opportunities. It also fills the news wires and magazines with scores, stories, gossip, and colorful photographs. In fact, the sports world generates so much information that, out of sheer self-defense, America Online has dedicated an entire channel to it: the aptly named Sports channel.

Unlike many of its department-filled brethren, the Sports channel (shown in Figure 18-1) includes only three main areas: Scoreboard, Top Stories, and Grandstand. Each of these departments, of course, merits its own special coverage below. In addition to the three departments, the main channel window also provides quick access to focus areas for football, basketball, baseball, and many other popular sports and sports-related pursuits (Table 18-1 offers a rundown of the focus areas and their keywords). The window also includes a never-ending ticker tape of sports headlines that appear right below the big Sports channel logo.

Headlines   Spotlight areas

Figure 18-1: The Sports channel looks sharp, runs fast, and even does its own color commentary.

Featured areas   Focus areas

Along the right side of the Sports channel window, you see the day's spot-light areas. These links take you to interesting and timely online areas throughout the system. Along the bottom of the window are the Sports channel's featured areas, offering still more sports goodies, in case you aren't already blowing mental fuses and gaskets all over the place from sports information overload.

Table 18-1	Special Areas for Almost Every Sport in the Book
Area	*Keyword*
Pro Football	Pro Football
College Football	College Football
Pro Basketball	Pro Basketball
College Basketball	College Basketball
Hockey	Hockey
Baseball	Baseball
Fitness	Fitness
Outdoors	Outdoors
Extreme	Extreme Sports
More Sports	More Sports
Search & Explore	Sports Search

Scoreboard Department (Keyword Scoreboard)

When you want the scores and nothing but the scores, turn to the Scoreboard department. As the name suggests, this is *the* place to get fresh statistics on your favorite NFL, NCAA football, NBA, and NHL contests. In addition to quick scores, the Scoreboard department also serves up a sampling of the day's best individual performances. As an added bonus, the department also includes links to the top sports stories, and a couple of often-changing feature areas.

The real gold in the area lives beneath the four league buttons. Each of these buttons leads you to a sports fan's dream scoreboard, filled with statistics for current games, previews of coming games, and enough raw box scores to put your calculator in a coma for weeks. In a really neat touch, the football preview and summary windows even provide a weather button so you can find out what kind of climate your favorite team has to endure in the game.

Top Stories (Keyword Sportnews)

For all its statistical wonderment, sports is more than mere numbers. Behind every average and total are the athletes themselves, their teams, and the cadres of coaches, trainers, owners, and other personalities who make sports the wild place that it is.

When you need the freshest stories about the sporting scene and its people, turn to the Top Stories department. This link sends you directly to the News channel's Sports window, the true pulse of online sporting information. From there, you make just a short hop to the news wire stories and scoreboard coverage of everything from football to soccer (which, depending on where you live, may or may not be a long trip), racing to rowing, and far too many other sports to think about here.

Grandstand (Keyword Grandstand)

Apart from their adoration of the games and teams, sports fans love nothing better than talking (sometimes loudly and with great emphasis) about their pastime. Because communities of all kinds are an integral part of life on America Online, it's no surprise that the system boasts a thriving digital sports center like the Grandstand.

You can easily find a place to hang your online hat in the Grandstand, because hooks of every type abound. Professional sports, amateur sports, team sports, individual sports, fun sports, beautiful sports — they're all here, complete with discussion boards, chat rooms, and software libraries. Look up your favorite activity, drop into its Grandstand area, and enjoy yourself!

Chapter 19

Travel Channel (Keyword Travel)

Suppose you're trying to plan this year's vacation. So, where and when will it be? Perhaps Carnivale on the French Riviera . . . Oktoberfest in Munich . . . or does your budget have something a little closer to home in mind, like the annual Pork Belly Push in beautiful, metropolitan Floyds Knobs?

Whatever your plans (or budgetary constraints), make the most of your vacation with the help and forums available in the America Online Travel channel. You can find all kinds of information in here, in addition to lots of discussion boards and travel tips of the trade (which help you find those marvelous out-of-the-way restaurants that make trips worth taking). You may even find out a thing or two about your hometown.

Like an old hand at globetrotting the days away, the AOL Travel window (see Figure 19-1) uses every bit of space to pack lots of goodies. The left side of the Travel window holds the *departments list.* Opposite the department buttons — excuse me, the travel resource buttons — are a group of *featured services.* A single click on any of them sends you careening off into one of these popular areas. Along the bottom of the window are links to the channel's *sponsor areas,* all of whom would all cherish your continued patronage.

Departments   Featured services

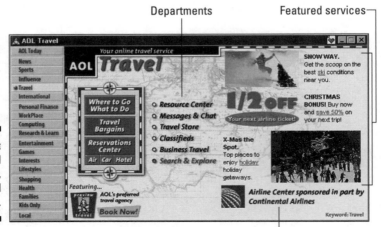

Figure 19-1:
The Travel channel, your digital port o' call.

Sponsor area

Resource Center Department (Keyword Travel Resource)

You have so much to do before leaving on a trip that remembering every little detail is hard. Stop the mail, pack the dog, feed your clothes — oh, did I mention you *still* need to keep all the other confusing details of life straight at the same time? And I haven't even mentioned figuring out your destination. I'm amazed that anyone travels anymore.

The collection of forums and services in the Resource Center department makes the all-important planning stage of your trip a smashing success. Find restaurants, flight information, currency conversion tips, unusual sights to see, and more. (Okay — who put the dog in my suitcase?)

Messages & Chat Department (Keyword Travel Messages & Chat)

Particularly in the world of travel, nothing beats first-hand experience. Sure, the guidebooks paint swell pictures with broad brushstrokes, but that's nothing compared to the photographic detail provided by someone who walked the streets, ate in the cafes, and got lost in the subway system. To help you soak up information from the experience of others, the Travel channel includes the Messages & Chat department.

The message boards and chat rooms in this friendly haunt are great for swapping real-world answers to tricky travel questions. No matter what kind of information you need, the advice of a friendly, seasoned traveler is usually mere steps away. This is also the home of the Travel channel's newsletter, a must-have item for any traveler's kit.

Travel Store Department (Keyword Travel Store)

Traveling and shopping have a strange, symbiotic relationship. A trip away from home requires all kinds of things, ranging from power converters to see-through plastic cases that protect your luggage from scuffs (don't laugh — not only do these cases exist, but I actually witnessed someone using them in a major airport; scary, isn't it?).

To simplify your pretravel shopping experience, check out the Travel Store department. It quickly puts you in the travel section of several online stores, including Avon, Barnes and Noble, Eddie Bauer, Sharper Image, and others. Whether you need luggage, books, or a travel-size bottle of Skin So Soft (the cosmetic industry's version of the Swiss Army Knife), it's all here in the Travel Store.

Classifieds Department (Button Access Only)

Few things are more American than buying and selling things through classified advertisements. Although the classifieds made their name in newspapers, the online world brought new searching and notification capabilities that the old hard-copy ads just couldn't match. That's why you should turn to the Travel channel's Classifieds department when you want to buy or sell tickets, accommodations, or any other travel-oriented things.

Before you marvel at how much America Online obviously values the Travel channel because the programmers set up a classified ad section just for it, I should mention that the Classifieds department is a subset of the much larger America Online Classifieds area, at keyword **Classifieds**. The Travel department just gives you a quick way to see most of the travel-related ads.

"Wait a minute — what do you mean *most* of the ads?" I hear you cry. You heard me right. You must tread carefully in the classifieds, because if you rush, you may miss a *huge* number of ads. How? Because the America Online Classifieds contain two advertising sections.

The first section consists of the *premium* classified ads — the ones that cost money to place. Granted, the ads don't carry a huge fee, but you're still sending bucks out the door. These premium ads appear in both the Travel channel's Classifieds department and in the main windows of the America Online Classifieds.

The other ads in the Classifieds are free — that's right, *free*. Does the Classifieds department in the Travel channel show *these* ads? Noooooooooo. So what's the trick to seeing (and creating, for that matter) the free ads? Just go to keyword **Travel Classifieds** and click the area that interests you, then look for a link to the bulletin board ads (that's what America Online calls the free ad section).

Business Travel Department (Keyword Business Travel Center)

"Attention business travelers: For the latest information on your flight, don't bother picking up the white courtesy telephone. Instead, please report to the Travel channel's Business Travel department. You don't have to wait, and numerous digital agents are there to make the inevitable inconveniences more bearable. Thank you."

Even though you won't ever hear that message echoing through the halls of your favorite metropolitan airport, that doesn't change the fact that the Business Travel department is a true miracle for busy corporate fliers. This department is the kind of place travelers love — one-stop shopping for America Online access numbers, airport information, flight details, frequent flier programs, weather forecasts, and much, much more.

The Business Travel department is also a great place for a traveler's significant other to find out about delays (and think of ways to spend all those frequent flier miles).

Search and Explore Department (Keyword Travel Search)

You can find so much in the Travel channel that you almost need a book to find it all. (Hmm . . . come to think of it, you _do_ have a book, but I digress.) To ensure that you find everything you could possibly want in the Travel channel, the programmers assembled the Search and Explore department.

The window offers two different approaches to the department's information. On the left is a classic enter-something-to-look-for system, complete with controls to govern how wide or narrow you wish the search to be. Use this when you want to interrogate a broad cross-section of the areas in the Travel channel.

Opposite the search area are the subject buttons. These offer to show you an A-Z listing of the areas in the Travel channel (although I found the list to be _very_ short and missing many areas — hopefully that's something that the channel staff members have fixed by the time you read this). You can also fiddle with the Best of Travel area, with a selection of the best and brightest areas the channel offers.

Answering the Fateful Questions: Where? When? and How Much?

Now that the various areas in the Travel channel whetted your appetite to see the world, you actually have to do something about it. When the moment strikes, turn to the bright red buttons on the left side of the channel window. These three buttons take care of the biggest issues in travel: the questions of where to go, when to go, and how much it costs to get there.

Here's a quick look at what they offer:

- Where to go, What to do button (keyword **Destinations**): You know you need to go, but where will you head? Another city, another state, or maybe even another country? Are you a plan-it-yourself person or do you long for the organized approach of group travel? The Where to go, What to do button focuses resources for picking the right destination to mollify your wanderlust. The Know Before You Go area is particularly helpful, with its currency converter, insider opinions, and other cool spots.

- Travel Bargains button (keyword **Travel Bargains**): Once your destination is firmly in place, you have to consider your pocketbook. Can you get there within your budget? Sure — if you put the Travel Bargains area to work for you. Dig through the Bargain Box, prowl Frommer's Secret Bargains, and discover the intricacies of inexpensive air fares here in this penny-pincher's nirvana.

- Reservations Center button (keyword **Travel Reservations**): With the dust nearly settled, the Reservations Center awaits to actually take your order and send you on the road. It's all-inclusive, offering airplane, bus, and even train reservations, plus hotels and rental cars.

Chapter 20

WorkPlace Channel (Keyword Workplace)

• •

*W*ork makes the world go round. At least, it makes the economy go round. If you're like most of us, you spend most of your waking hours at some sort of job. You wake up, putter off to work, make a difference in the world through what you do, and wander back home to collapse in front of the computer at night. Perhaps you own the business — in that case, you only relax when someone whisks you out of the country for a couple of weeks!

Filled with its ups and downs, its unique hassles, and the camaraderie that comes only from spending long hours together, the workplace takes its place as a fixture in American culture. America Online recognizes that, and presents the WorkPlace channel (shown in Figure 20-1). WorkPlace gives you business help, career guidance, and job finding tips. You can network with others in your field, find out about a completely different career before you take the plunge, or discover how viable a home business may be.

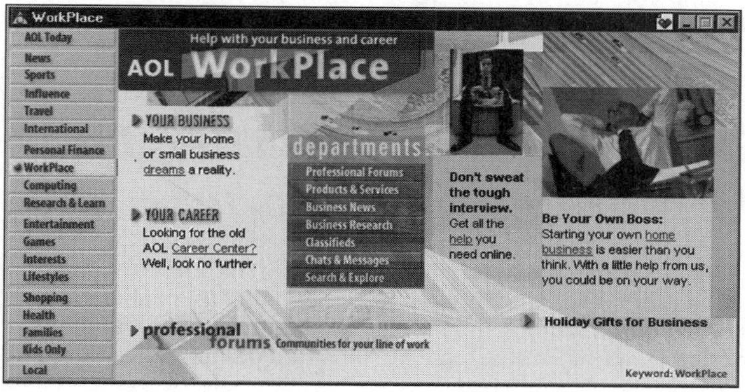

Figure 20-1: The WorkPlace channel centers around business life.

Your Business (Keyword Your Business)

When you own your own business, whether it employs only you or a thousand people, you can use all the help you can get. Especially when you're a one-person business — and you need to fulfill federal requirements, keep up with inventory, take care of your phone and mail needs, and still get something done during the day — you may think the 24-hour day provides only half the necessary hours for you to get everything done.

Take a deep breath, fix yourself a soda (ice cream or not), and drop into Your Business. Not exactly a department, this featured area remains constant and provides you with all kinds of business help. From information on starting your own business to regional government resources you may be able to tap, Your Business is one-stop shopping for the business owner.

Your Career (Button Access Only)

What do you want to be when you're grown? Some of you knew when you were 12, while others (me included) still wonder when you'll grow up and have to make that final decision. No matter where you fit in the flow, Your Career provides welcome tips and guidance.

Your Career gives you professional forums where you can meet and network with others in your field, tips for advancing your career in the direction you want it to go, and some much needed help with finding that first job — or changing your career path. Delve in and discover the priceless career assistance that awaits you.

Professional Forums Department (Keyword Professional Forums)

How do you advance in your chosen career? Where do you find information on jobs related to yours? When you're looking for real-life information on a career different from yours, where do you turn? Begin your search in America Online's Professional Forums department — and maybe end it there, too.

Professional Forums provides more than message boards. Look in the forums for scheduled chats that discuss your profession, recent news articles specifically related to what you do, and links to work-specific Web sites. So whether you're currently working in a particular profession or you're thinking of taking the plunge, check the Professional Forums department first.

Products & Services Department (Keyword Products & Services)

As a business owner or swamped professional, you don't always have the time to run to the store for office supplies. Sometimes researching a new purchase costs more in time than the item is worth. If these statements describe you and how you think, you'll love the Products & Services department.

From one window you can order office supplies, check into building a business Web site, find out about the newest modems for your computer, and subscribe to a magazine you've had your eye on for months. Or book your next business trip's travel arrangements, order a book for your spouse's birthday, or register for online continuing education classes. Endless possibilities? Not quite — but you can find enough here to save you loads of time. You may also use one area America Online didn't add to this list. Use keyword **Reminder** to set up a Reminder Service profile that gives you advance notice of those special days in your life.

Business News Department (Keyword Business News)

What happened today in your corner of the world? Keep current on business happenings, company news, the economy and investment markets, and technology through the Business News department. Instead of wading through the general news window for specific business news, come directly to Business News and read all the news you want to know. Then click the Business Talk button and discuss what you read with other members in the Business News Chat room.

Business Research Department (Keyword Business Research)

A particular company catches your eye. Maybe you'd like to work for them. Or perhaps you want to invest in the product or service they provide. No matter what your reason (even if you need a subject for your latest term paper), the Business Research department offers several different online sources to speed your search. Within the forums listed in Business Research, you can look up abstracts from articles published in major medical journals, search for news related to a specific company, read past business articles written about your subject, or read about trends in home businesses.

Classifieds Department (Menu Access Only)

You'd like a change of scenery, so you're looking for a job halfway across the country. Or perhaps your company needs a business vehicle of some kind, and you'd like to save money by purchasing a used one. In either case, dip into the WorkPlace Classifieds to find employment and business-related ads. You could find some real bargains or the perfect coastal job.

Chats & Messages Department (Keyword Business Talk)

On those days when you feel like connecting with someone, drop into the Chats & Messages department for a rousing chat room conversation or to browse the business message boards. Two weekday standards, Your Business Lunch and Your Business Dinner, invite different special guests each day. Topics range from public relations to starting your home business, and from Internet marketing to effective management.

Search & Explore (Keyword Workplace Search)

Can't find what you need in WorkPlace? Give Search & Explore a try. Here you can search for specific work-related articles by topic, take a look at the channel's contents from A to Z, and find some of the best destinations in WorkPlace. For more information on using Search & Explore, read the Search section in Chapter 1 of this minibook, *AOL Channels For Dummies*.

Index

YOUR ONLINE RESOURCE

WWW.DUMMIES.COM

Discover Dummies Online!

The Dummies Web Site is your fun and friendly online resource for the latest information about ...*For Dummies*® books and your favorite topics. The Web site is the place to communicate with us, exchange ideas with other ...*For Dummies* readers, chat with authors, and have fun!

Ten Fun and Useful Things You Can Do at www.dummies.com

1. Win free ...*For Dummies* books and more!
2. Register your book and be entered in a prize drawing.
3. Meet your favorite authors through the IDG Books Author Chat Series.
4. Exchange helpful information with other ...*For Dummies* readers.
5. Discover other great ...*For Dummies* books you must have!
6. Purchase Dummieswear™ exclusively from our Web site.
7. Buy ...*For Dummies* books online.
8. Talk to us. Make comments, ask questions, get answers!
9. Download free software.
10. Find additional useful resources from authors.

Link directly to these ten fun and useful things at
http://www.dummies.com/10useful

WWW.DUMMIES.COM

For other technology titles from IDG Books Worldwide, go to
www.idgbooks.com

Not on the Web yet? It's easy to get started with *Dummies 101*®: *The Internet For Windows*®*95* or *The Internet For Dummies*®, 4th Edition, at local retailers everywhere.

IDG BOOKS WORLDWIDE

Find other ...*For Dummies* books on these topics:
Business • Career • Databases • Food & Beverage • Games • Gardening • Graphics • Hardware
Health & Fitness • Internet and the World Wide Web • Networking • Office Suites
Operating Systems • Personal Finance • Pets • Programming • Recreation • Sports
Spreadsheets • Teacher Resources • Test Prep • Word Processing

The IDG Books Worldwide logo and Dummieswear are trademarks, and Dummies Man and ...For Dummies are registered trademarks under exclusive license to IDG Books Worldwide, Inc., from International Data Group, Inc.

IDG BOOKS WORLDWIDE
BOOK REGISTRATION

We want to hear from you!

Register This Book and Win!

Visit **http://my2cents.dummies.com** to register this book and tell us how you liked it!

- ✔ Get entered in our monthly prize giveaway.
- ✔ Give us feedback about this book — tell us what you like best, what you like least, or maybe what you'd like to ask the author and us to change!
- ✔ Let us know any other *...For Dummies*® topics that interest you.

Your feedback helps us determine what books to publish, tells us what coverage to add as we revise our books, and lets us know whether we're meeting your needs as a *...For Dummies* reader. You're our most valuable resource, and what you have to say is important to us!

Not on the Web yet? It's easy to get started with *Dummies 101*®*: The Internet For Windows*® *95* or *The Internet For Dummies*,® 4th Edition, at local retailers everywhere.

Or let us know what you think by sending us a letter at the following address:

...For Dummies Book Registration
Dummies Press
7260 Shadeland Station, Suite 100
Indianapolis, IN 46256-3945
Fax 317-596-5498

BUSINESS AND
GENERAL
REFERENCE
BOOK SERIES
FROM IDG

COMPUTER
BOOK SERIES
FROM IDG